T0313802

Tokyo Boogie-Woogie

Tokyo
Boogie-Woogie

Japan's Pop Era and
Its Discontents

HIROMU NAGAHARA

Harvard University Press
Cambridge, Massachusetts
London, England
2017

First printing

Library of Congress Cataloging-in-Publication Data

Names: Nagahara, Hiromu, author.

Title: Tokyo boogie-woogie : Japan's pop era and its discontents /
Hiromu Nagahara.

Description: Cambridge, Massachusetts : Harvard University Press, 2017. |
Includes bibliographical references and index.

Identifiers: LCCN 2016044092 | ISBN 9780674971691

Subjects: LCSH: Popular music—Japan—History and criticism. |
Popular music—Social aspects—Japan—History—20th century.

Classification: LCC ML3501 .N18 2017 | DDC 781.630952—dc23

LC record available at https://lccn.loc.gov/2016044092

Contents

Tokyo Boogie-Woogie

Introduction:
The Popular Song Era

"Tokyo March," "Tokyo Dance," "Tokyo Rhapsody," and "Tokyo Boogie-Woogie"—all of these are titles of songs produced by Japan's recording industry between the late 1920s and the late 1940s. On a first hearing, these songs seemingly have little in common with each other, aside from the obvious reference to Japan's capital city. "Tokyo Dance" ("Tokyo ondo," 1933) sits on one end of the musical spectrum as a song in the mold of traditional dance music for the summer Bon festival, while "Tokyo Boogie-Woogie" ("Tokyo bugiugi," 1947), as the title suggests, sits on the other end as a powerful symbol of Americanization after World War II. The other two songs, "Tokyo March" ("Tokyo kōshinkyoku," 1929) and "Tokyo Rhapsody" ("Tokyo rapusodī," 1936), further muddy the water by being so thoroughly syncretic, containing musical elements that could be easily identified as either "Western," as in the instrumentation for both songs, or "Japanese." Taken together, they not only defy attempts at drawing a simplistic narrative of a clear, linear transformation of Japanese popular music into a something more "Western," they also seem to resist any categorization that would place them within a common musical culture, even though they were produced by the same industry.

It is this industry, however, that presents some of the most convincing evidence that these diverse songs about Tokyo should in fact be considered as belonging to the same musical genre. In the middle decades of the twentieth century, Japan's recording companies produced these and other songs that they simply called "popular songs." *Ryūkōka,* the Japanese term for this genre, was a neologism that was created by combining the Chinese ideograms for *ryūkō* (popular, fashionable) with *uta* (song). Quite literally, the recording companies meant for their products to be recognized as songs that were popular, just as soon as the phonograph records rolled off of the production lines in their factories. The name of the genre did not connote any particular musical style but instead came to be a catch-all term that encompassed a diverse range of songs, including those that were produced in the style of American jazz as well as those that self-consciously incorporated native musical idioms.

At first glance, it may seem obvious to associate these popular songs with our own, present-day understandings of similar-sounding terms like "pop music" or "popular music." After all, these terms have also come to refer to a broad range of musical cultures that have been produced around the world since the middle decades of the twentieth century. Those familiar with contemporary East Asian culture might also suspect that what is being discussed here is simply an early iteration of a musical genre known as "J-Pop" (short for Japan Pop), which has come to gain not only national but global popularity since its emergence in the late 1980s, along with its regional cousins like K-Pop (Korea Pop) and C-Pop (China Pop). Despite such contemporary and global resonances, however, this book looks at modern Japanese popular songs as a historically bounded phenomenon—that is, as something that really only existed in Japan in the middle decades of the twentieth century.

Such specificity is due, in part, to the fact this particular historical period corresponds to the years during which the term *ryūkōka* was used in common Japanese parlance. While the same combination of Chinese characters was already in use earlier in the Meiji and Taishō periods, it had a different pronunciation (*hayariuta*) which in turn implied a subtle but important difference in meaning. In particular, *hayariuta* was not associated with any particular industry but simply referred to songs of whatever origin that were perceived to be in vogue at a given moment. Strikingly, *ryūkōka* had fallen almost completely out of use as a catch-all term that referred to contemporary hit songs by 1970, replaced as it was by another term, *kayōkyoku* (ballad songs).[1] As a result, *ryūkōka* took on an increasingly antiquated, nostalgic connotation during the subsequent decades, effectively fixing its association to songs that were produced in Japan primarily between the 1920s and the 1950s.

The historically bounded life span of *ryūkōka* helps to highlight the specific ways in which the contemporary listeners associated these songs with the dramatic historical forces that were seen to be transforming not just Japan's musical culture but society as a whole. From the outset, most Japanese seemed to take it for granted that the popular songs somehow authentically represented the realities of their own society, or, as many simply called it, "the times" (*sesō*), despite—or, more often than not precisely because of—the fact that the entire genre was the invention of the recording companies through and through. This assumption was best captured by the adage that was repeated during this period: "As the world goes, so go the songs; as the songs go, so goes the world" (*Uta wa yo ni tsure, yo wa uta ni tsure*). As banal as this sentiment may be, almost no Japanese interested in popular songs seemed to be immune from it.

Between the late 1920s and 1960s, an impressive array of musicians, intellectuals, government officials and other members of Japan's cultural elite not only debated the merits, or lack thereof, of popular songs, but also made attempts at managing and countering the broader set of societal problems that were associated with the songs. This was true from the very outset of the genre's emergence in the late 1920s. Produced by record companies that were largely funded by Western capital and disseminated through channels such as cinema, radio, and cafés, popular songs quickly came to be recognized as the audible symbols of what contemporaries called *modan* (modern)—a term that gained currency in the late 1920s as an adjective to denote all that was seen to be part of Japan's mass-oriented, speed-driven urban modernity. As such, the popular song genre was immediately associated with contemporary trends such as the perceived Americanization and eroticization of Japanese culture—trends that found critics across the political spectrum and were captured by another, more sensational, contemporary phrase, *ero guro nansensu* (erotic, grotesque, nonsense).[2] In this way, numerous songs came to be identified, with varying degrees of plausibility, with countless contemporary cultural, social, and political phenomena, be it mass consumption, wartime nationalism, occupation-era poverty, or—as is perhaps true even today—the allegedly ever-degenerating juvenile mores.

What ultimately proved to be far more revealing about the historical realities of mid-twentieth-century Japan, however, were the ways in which the debates over popular songs were carried out—that is, the language and rhetoric that were employed, the attitudes and affects exhibited by the critics in discussing music, as well as the political and intellectual alliances that were formed against the songs. In particular, both the language of popular song critique and the underlying attitudes it revealed remained remarkably consistent from the emergence of the genre in the late 1920s to the time of its ultimate demise in the 1960s. The most common accusations leveled against these songs were that they were decidedly "vulgar" (*teizoku*) and "lowbrow" (*teikyū*). Just as it was assumed that popular songs naturally reflected "the times," it was also taken for granted by the Japanese elites who debated these songs that they were inherently and, for some of them, irredeemably déclassé. Nor was this assumption limited to the shrillest critics of the genre; even those who personally enjoyed some of these songs more often than not spoke of the need to "elevate" not only the quality of the entire genre but also the tastes of the broader, listening public as well.

The consistent and overwhelmingly elitist nature of popular song critique initially seems to run against the grain of what we have come to understand as Japan's first mass media revolution, which took place precisely in the decades this book considers to be Japan's "Popular Song Era." Popular songs emerged simultaneously with other equally new forms of media, such as mass circulation magazines, radio, and sound film, all of which connected a vastly expanded proportion of Japan's population to the widening web of media products as readers, listeners, and viewers. This new media-consuming public in turn came to play a key role in Japan's ultimate transformation from what was a society deeply cognizant of the social and cultural divisions within itself during the chaotic decades preceding World War II to one whose inhabitants were beginning to believe that it was, in fact, made up of nothing but the "middle class" by the 1970s. In this transformation, those whom observers identified as Japan's masses (*taishū*) emerged not only as the chief consumers of mass media and mass culture but also as the protagonists of the broader social change that was seemingly upending existing cultural norms and hierarchies.

The history of the popular song genre has tended to emphasize the genre's emergence as part of this process of massification and the growth of shared lifeways among the Japanese—it is a story of the inevitable, if gradual, diffusion of common musical culture among an increasing audience.[3] The story of modern Japanese popular songs is, at least in part, that of a mass consumer culture that not only survived but thrived throughout what some historians have come to identify as Japan's "transwar" era.[4] And yet, at the same time, the history of popular song critique reveals that these songs emerged not simply in the context of the rise of mass media and mass society but, more accurately, at the intersection of forces that encouraged the standardization of culture and everyday life in modern Japan *and* those that persistently reinscribed hierarchy and difference on the newly emerging mass society.

The ongoing contention between these two sets of forces is precisely what this book seeks to highlight as one of the most enduring and consequential dynamics that shaped twentieth-century Japanese culture. Considering modern Japan's cultural politics in terms of the Popular Song Era not only enables us to examine it across some of the most tumultuous decades of the twentieth century, but also brings some of the most important historical dynamics that have shaped it into view. In particular, it highlights the ways in which the assumption of hierarchies, the desire for a democratized culture, and the interplay between these two competing inclinations among Japan's elites consistently undergirded many of the most consequential sets of ideas and forces that guided the ways in which people produced, consumed, and critiqued culture throughout the century.

Such dynamics include the ongoing tension between Western aesthetic notions and conventions that had been adopted since the Meiji period and the ongoing attempt at creating authentically *Japanese* culture in response. They also include the process by which Japan's empire and the long period of war that led to its destruction were deeply influential in shaping the popular culture of those periods, and, in the post-World War II period, the centrality of Japan's relationship with America, not only as an external military presence but also, as was increasingly the case after Japan regained its independence in 1952, as something that was experienced "within" as the object of consumption and desire.[5] Even as contestations over developments like Westernization, wartime mobilization, and Americanization made their influences felt across various cultural expressions, the story of the popular song genre points to the importance of the ongoing preoccupation with hierarchy among Japan's cultural elites in the same phenomena. Many of these developments revolved around the tension between the sense, starting in the 1920s, that Japan was being transformed into mass society and an equally strong perception that the same society was still deeply divided by social and cultural hierarchies.

Establishing *Music* in Modern Japan

However, it would be a mistake to assume that these phenomena were simply a matter of class-based divisions or that the cultural politics surrounding this tension was limited to the Shōwa era (1926–1989). On the contrary, the history of musical culture in modern Japan is especially instructive in revealing how many of the foundations for the politics that was provoked by the emergence of popular songs in the late 1920s had in fact been laid at the outset of Japan's experience of modernity in the late nineteenth century. In his masterful essay on the domestic origins of the Meiji Restoration of 1868 and Japan's subsequent transformation into a modern, industrial society, the historian Thomas C. Smith points to the cultural flattening that was brought about by the Meiji Restoration: "Success in [post-Restoration Japan] had very little to do with traditional skills and tastes and much to do with double-entry bookkeeping, commercial law, English conversation, *German music,* French painting, and Scotch whiskey. . . . In respect to such things all classes of Japanese, *during the first generation or two after 1868,* were born cultural equals. One could not learn of these things at home any more than one could learn there a foreign language or the calculus. Such subjects were taught only in the schools, and the schools were open to everyone."[6] As first glance, this is a striking image of cultural democratization, coming as it does at the end of an essay in which Smith emphasizes the *aristocratic* nature of Japan's transformation under the Meiji state by pointing out that the dramatic overthrow of the Tokugawa regime, along with its centuries-old status system, was primarily driven by none other than the members of the ruling samurai class, who ultimately chose to abolish their own legally privileged status in order to forge a modern nation-state.

And yet Smith's caveat regarding the chronologically limited nature of the flattening proves to be of particular importance, as various hierarchies did in fact (re)emerge in Japan's cultural landscape precisely in the decades after the emergence of "the first generation or two after 1868." The most striking example of this was the rise of a plethora of professionalized artistic and intellectual circles that came to be recognized as the elite practitioners and gatekeepers in various fields. Recognized by the common suffix *-dan* (dais or platform), these circles related to music (*gakudan*), visual arts (*gadan*), literature (*bundan*), and, even more generally, critique (*rondan*). Schooled in the Western canons and associated with the key cultural institutions of the post-Restoration state such as the university, members of these establishments constituted the self-appointed guardians of aesthetic and intellectual hierarchy in modern Japan.

What characteristics, then, defined the nature of the newly emerging cultural hierarchies? The case of the creation of Japan's music establishment reveals two particularly important types of hierarchy that were already at play in the immediate wake of the Meiji Restoration. The first, and perhaps the more obvious, was the gradually accelerating drive toward adopting Western standards not only in areas such as military organization, economy, and politics, but also more broadly in the realms of culture and everyday life—a drive that would eventually be encapsulated by the term *bunmei kaika* (civilization and enlightenment), which was attributed to Fukuzawa Yukichi (1835–1901), the pioneering introducer of Western intellectual tradition to the Japanese audience. The notion that music formed a significant part of a Western-centric civilization was apparently impressed on the minds of some members of the Meiji state's governing elite within a few years of the Restoration. A noteworthy example of this was the famous Iwakura Embassy in 1871, which took half of the leadership of the post-Restoration government along with fifty students on a multiyear, globe-circumnavigating journey through the United States and Europe. In particular, the records compiled by Kume Kunitake (1839–1931), the embassy's official historian, contain a sustained discussion on music based on the embassy's visit to Boston, Massachusetts, in June 1872. There Kume and others attended a multiday musical event entitled "The World's Peace Jubilee and International Music Festival," which was held in celebration of the conclusion of both the American Civil War as well as the more recent Franco-Prussian War.[7] The event itself took place in a temporary "Coliseum" built for the occasion in the Back Bay district of Boston. On its first day, the event was devoted to American-themed music, including the singing of "The Star-Spangled Banner" by a twenty-thousand-strong choir. Each of the other days was devoted to a specific European nation, including Great Britain, Germany, France, and Austria.[8]

While Kume was apparently struck by the beauty of much of what he heard, he was far more impressed by the power that the music seemingly had on his fellow audience in inspiring their patriotism: "A piece was played which was about an American, captured in the War of Independence, whose patriotism hardened and who never yielded. The American audience, upon hearing this, could not stop applauding. They clapped and stamped their feet, demanding encore after encore, and it was some time before the hall settled down."[9] This led him to turn his attention to the broader implications of such an effect: "Although the countries of the world differ in size, each is dedicated to its way of life, and if a nation achieves independence, a spirit of patriotism inevitably wells up [in their hearts]. It is rather like loving oneself and one's home [above other places]. . . . Therefore, the patriotic mind naturally gives rise to humane feelings and becomes a source of loyalty. When the people of Europe and America talk about civilization, it is based on patriotism. Any person who forgets himself, abandons his house, turns his back on his home village and despises his own country is not only ignorant of Confucian principles but has also failed to grasp Western civilization." Here Kume not only points to music's efficacy in inspiring patriotic sentiment among the audience, but does so in relation to civilizational hierarchy that key members of the embassy were becoming keenly aware of as their journey progressed—a hierarchy within which, in Fukuzawa Yukichi's formulation, the Western nations set the standards of "civilization and enlightenment" and Japan occupied the status of a "semideveloped country" (hankai).[10]

The sense that music was somehow necessarily part of a civilized society was apparently already shared by other members of the Meiji state, as seen in the fact that a government decree made in 1872 not only created mass compulsory education for the first time in Japanese history but also included music as part of the national curriculum. At the same time, the fact that no formal action was taken in regard to music education for another seven years, until Izawa Shūji (1851–1917), the head of Tokyo Higher Normal School, was appointed as the head of the Music Investigation Committee by the Education Ministry in 1879, also suggests that there was not an inconsiderable amount of confusion as to precisely what kind of music ought to be promoted by the state.[11]

In fact, for others among the Meiji elite music was in itself an apparently deeply problematic phenomenon. This is especially evident

View of the Great Coliseum built for the World's Peace Jubilee and International Musical Festival (courtesy of the Library of Congress, Prints and Photographs Division, Washington, D.C., LC-DIG-pga-02283).

in the English-language autobiography of Kikkawa Chōkichi (1860–1915), who was one of the first Japanese graduates of Harvard College. Born as the second son of the daimyo of Iwakuni domain, Kikkawa joined the Iwakura Embassy and, like many other students on the journey, he stayed in the United States to pursue further education, attending Rice Grammar School and Chauncy Hall School before graduating from Harvard in 1883. As Kikkawa recalled, he and his Japanese colleagues actively pursued their studies on a wide range of topics while in the United States, with one exception: "There was also singing at the school, but I, with others of my countrymen who attend the school, obtained excuse on the ground that we had all we could do in pursuing other studies. But in reality, we had in those days the old Japanese notion that singing was vulgar. It might be said en passant that I never learnt dancing, for I had the same sort of feeling on that subject."[12]

Part of Kikkawa's aversion to music may have simply stemmed from the foreignness of Western musical culture. In fact, the Western elites' seeming penchant for dancing endlessly at stately balls drew particularly barbed reactions from the earliest Japanese visitors to the West, including from none other than Fukuzawa Yukichi, who noted that "early on [in my visits], I found it exceedingly difficult to suppress my laughter at the site of men and women jumping around the room in a strange manner."[13] In the case of dancing, many objections seemingly stemmed from the visitors' discomfort with what they perceived to be the casual and indecorous intermingling of the sexes in West. Kikkawa's reference to "the old Japanese notion," however, hints at another cultural hierarchy that was at play in the creation of Japan's music establishment, namely the existing elite bias against music, in general, as a form of vulgar entertainment. This was in part the product of the strong association of a variety of entertainment forms and aesthetic pursuits with specific status groups under the Tokugawa regime.[14] Within this context, all forms of music, with the exception of those sponsored either by the imperial court (*gagaku*) or the shogunate (*nohgaku*), were more or less associated with commoner culture as forms of "entertainment" (*yūgei*).[15] While it is important not to overstate the samurai aversion to commoner culture, it is nonetheless worth noting that such bias clearly emerged in the experience of high-ranking samurai like Kikkawa, even in contexts where he was presumably eager to learn as much as he could as an officially sponsored student abroad.

The contrasting experiences of Kume and Kikkawa point to the fact that the Meiji elites' encounters with Western music were mediated by considerations for hierarchies both old and new. Per-haps not surprisingly, both types of hierarchy were brought to bear in the development of the Meiji state's official policies regarding music, especially in the realm of education. Shortly after Iwakura Embassy's visit to the United States, Izawa Shūji, who would even-tually lead the Education Ministry's investigation into implementing music education, was also sent to Massachusetts, where he encoun-tered the latest American methods in music education. In 1884 Izawa and his Education Ministry colleagues published the first songbook designed to be used in elementary schools, moving grad-ually toward the implementation of music within the national edu-cational curriculum.

Within this process, one can see how both the samurai disdain of "commoner music" (*zokkyoku*) and the growing identification of Western cultural practices as part of the civilizational norm clearly shaped the contours of the kind of music that was going to be pro-moted by the state. Izawa himself described such music in a letter to his American collaborator, Luther Whiting Mason (1818–1896), in this way: "our aim is not the total adoption of European or Amer-ican music but the making of a new Japanese music. . . . Those pieces imported from foreign lands must more or less [be] natural-ized. The songs must be of necessity of the Native Words. I know not of any case where the songs were sung from a foreign tongue except in some bigoted mission schools."[16] While Izawa couches his policy in terms of the protection of Japanese culture, what this meant in effect was that the heart of state music education would be based on Western music, which would be "naturalized" by Japanese textual overlay.

For Izawa, there was no question that native Japanese musical culture, as it existed, was unsuitable to serve as the basis for the creation of what he called "national music" (*kokugaku*). In particular, the music that was actually popular among the vast majority of

Japanese—commoner music—was, as far as Izawa was concerned, hopelessly morally debauched and an affront to "national prestige."[17] By contrast, the courtly *gagaku* and samurai *noh* music were considered to be overly refined. Consequently, the only clear choice, from Izawa and his colleagues' perspective, was to adopt Western art music as the standard for Japan's new, "national music," even as they sought to "naturalize" it through text. In other words, the Meiji state's decision to adopt Western music into the national educational curriculum was not simply because it was the music of the more "civilized" world but because it satisfied existing elite bias regarding music.

However, Izawa and his colleagues' work reveals that they also couched their adoption of such hierarchies in terms of bringing about the kind of cultural flattening that Smith alluded to earlier. For example, Megata Tanetarō (1853–1926), one of Izawa's collaborators at the Education Ministry and himself one of the first Japanese graduates of Harvard Law School, described the state of musical culture in the Tokugawa era in this way to an audience he addressed at the New England Conservatory of Music in Boston in 1877: "A strong feudal system of government prevailed from the thirteenth century to 1868, with its mighty rigors and prejudice [that] divided the people to classes. Manner and custom of the people were equally divided and strong isolation prevailed among them."[18] According to Megata, such divisions were no longer acceptable, for they flew in the face of the emerging priority of the Meiji state to break down the status-based social divisions of the Tokugawa era and thereby unify Japan's inhabitants into national subjects.

Megata's reductionist emphasis on the strictness of Tokugawa social divisions was ultimately the product of post-Restoration drive to reinvent the memory of the Edo period as Meiji Japan's "feudal" past.[19] Status-based divisions eroded significantly during the course of the Tokugawa era and many members of the samurai class were not above indulging in commoner entertainment, including music. Nonetheless, as was the case for Kikkawa Chōkichi, a cultural hierarchy that relegated music to the realm of "vulgar entertainment" persisted into the early Meiji era among the elite strata of the samurai. For Megata and Izawa then, the chief goal of music education was none other than the creation of what they repeatedly identified as "national music" that could overcome the hierarchy that led Kikkawa and others to seemingly dismiss music as a whole. In other words, even as the Meiji state's policies regarding music were clearly informed by hierarchies old and new, their ultimate purpose was simultaneously articulated as a form of cultural democratization by the bureaucrats who were crafting them.

Institutions, Enthusiasts, and Critics

The Meiji background to the Japanese state's adoption of Western music serves as a key prehistory to the subsequent transformation of Japan's musical culture. In the course of the twentieth century, these and similar policies laid the groundwork for the creation of cultural establishments not only in the case of music but also in the field of visual art. In both cases, the initial efforts by the state led to the creation not only of curricula for the national compulsory education system but also of key institutions that would come to produce the leaders of both Japan's artistic establishments.[20] In the case of music, Izawa himself was involved in the creation of the Tokyo Music School, the national conservatory, in 1887, while the Education Ministry also established the Tokyo School of Fine Arts in the same year, under the leadership of individuals like Okakura Tenshin (1863–1913) and Ernest Fenollosa (1853–1908). While the initial focus of the former was centered on the creation of music teachers for the compulsory education system, the latter was designed from the outset to train new generations of visual artists.[21]

In subsequent years, however, the institutional mandate of the Tokyo Music School also gradually transformed into a more art-centric focus on the training of Japan's top performers, conductors, and composers. While the school was by no means the only possible training ground for the practitioners of Western music, it did become the primary producer of the most celebrated and powerful members of what emerged as Japan's music establishment, including Kōda Nobu (1870–1946), Taki Rentarō (1879–1903), and Yamada Kōsaku (1886–1965).[22] These two institutions were united after World War II to form the Tokyo University of the Arts, which remains the preeminent institute of art education in Japan to this day.

At the same time, it is also important to note that the broader educational framework created by the Meiji state also produced two other closely related subgroups within the music establishment, namely the amateur "enthusiasts" (*aikōka*) and the professional "critics" (*hyōronka*). The first subgroup primarily emerged in the context of elite institutions of secondary and higher education, where students largely pursued Western music as a form of extracurricular activity within the context of a broader liberal arts curriculum.[23] These student enthusiasts tended to come from wealthy urban families of both the "old" and "new" middle classes, as well as the aristocracy (*kazoku*), many of whom attended the Peers School.[24] While most of these students "graduated" from music fandom after completing their education, a smaller subgroup went on to become prominent members of the music establishment as critics, translators, publishers, etc., including Ōtaguro Moto'o (1893–1979), Tanabe Hisao (1883–1984), and Horiuchi Keizō (1897–1983).[25] In fact, while a growing majority of elite performers and composers graduated from the national conservatory, the majority of the music critics in the prewar era graduated from secondary schools and universities where they formally pursued subjects unrelated to music.

Together, the conservatory-trained musicians and these highly educated enthusiast-critics formed the core of the Japanese music establishment for much of the twentieth century. The combination of their education and, not coincidentally, their economic and social prominence, gave the group an inescapably elitist cast. It should not be surprising, then, that these subgroups were also heirs to sensibilities that, on the whole, took the cultural hierarchies that were derived from the Tokugawa past as well as the standard of "civilization and enlightenment" for granted. As was the case for Izawa and his colleagues in the Education Ministry, however, many of these elite members of the music establishment were also genuinely committed to the ideal of promoting mass adoption of Western art music as a form of musical culture that could cross class boundaries—an ideal that was as much a legacy of the Meiji state's interaction with music as were the twin hierarchies that shaped the nature of "national music." In other words, the same contradiction between hierarchical and democratizing impulses that informed the Meiji state's music policies persisted within the individuals that formed Japan's music establishment. Changing economic as well as technological contexts in the middle decades of the century, however, would increasingly threaten to bring this contradiction to a head, signaling the beginning of Japan's Popular Song Era.

1

The Invention of Popular Song

In May 1929 the Victor Talking Machine Company of Japan, a subsidiary of RCA Victor, released a record featuring a song entitled "Tokyo March." Within a few months, an unprecedented 150,000 copies of this record were sold, making "Tokyo March" one of the first modern Japanese popular songs in the eyes of contemporaries as well as historians.[1] Satō Chiyako (1897–1968), the soprano who recorded the song, became Japan's first female popular song star (*sutā*). The song also launched the careers of Nakayama Shimpei (1887–1952), the composer, and Saijō Yaso (1892–1970), the lyricist, both of whom ultimately became giants in the popular song scene. During the next decade, Japan's recording industry grew so rapidly that by 1937, the prewar height of record production, there were reports of popular song records that sold as many as five hundred thousand copies—no small feat in a period when the price of phonographs and records remained squarely within the realm of luxury goods.[2] With such growth, popular song records came to be the most popular, and therefore most lucrative, product for the recording companies.

As important as the popular song genre's explosive growth, however, was the fact that it had emerged as the product of a network of media industries, including not just music but also film, radio, and publishing, all of which combined to create a media product that came to boast unprecedented reach among a rapidly expanding audience. While such impressive technological and industrial developments clearly worked to commercialize and standardize what was being consumed by the audience, a close analysis of the making of "Tokyo March" and the controversies that followed its release also reveals the ways the song was recognized by its critics and advocates alike as part of the broader social climate that was rife with the tensions surrounding the apparent contradictions of modernity, including the specter of an impending class-based conflict that threatened to tear Japanese society apart. In particular, critics in Japan's music establishment and their allies argued that popular songs, as déclassé as they were understood to be, actually condemned Japan's masses to a perpetual state of cultural degradation, thus perpetuating class-based cultural divisions.[3] As such, the popular song genre as a whole came to be simultaneously associated with the commercialization and homogenization of culture as well as its destruction by social divisions.

As already noted in the Introduction, the concern over the social impact of music was not, in itself, new at all. When the Meiji state sought to promote Western music as part of establishing "civilization and enlightenment" in Japan, it was driven as much by the concern about music's ability to divide the still-fragile nation as it was by its ability to promote patriotism. In fact, the state's concern about the social and political effects of music can be traced back to the decades immediately following the establishment of the Tokugawa shogunate in 1603. Neither was it the case that what we would now commonly refer to as "popular music"—as in a musical culture shared by a wide cross-section of a given society—simply did not exist before the modern era. What was critically different, however, was the ways in which the definition of what counted as

music, as articulated by the cultural elites in each of these historical periods, interacted with the realities on the ground. What ultimately made the emergence of both the modern Japanese popular
songs and their critique in the 1920s so consequential was the fact
that they signaled a fundamental redefinition of both the intellectual terms and the material conditions within which music was made
popular.

Popular Music before Popular Song

How then was music defined and practiced before the emergence
of popular songs? As the musicologist Hosokawa Shūhei notes, premodern Japan did not, in fact, have an "all-embracing term referring to any humanly organized sound"—that is, the notion of music
as a universal, cultural phenomenon simply did not exist before
Japan's encounter with the West.[4] Instead, a broad range of practices
that we would now instinctively understand as inherently musical
were conceptually divided not only by the hierarchical status of
those who pursued them but also by their gender and locale (as
in the difference between urban centers and the provinces), not to
mention the differences in uses as well as technical features, such
as instruments and methods of notation. In this world, the chants
sung in temples and the sound of *shakuhachi* (bamboo flutes) blown
by a group of officially licensed blind street performers were not
conceived as belonging to the same overarching cultural category,
nor did people seek to place even the highly refined interplays of
instruments and chants in the *noh* theatre, which was typically
sponsored by the samurai elite, on the same conceptual plane as the
ceremonial strains of *gagaku* (court music) performed in the imperial
palace in Kyoto. While the term *ongaku,* used today as the Japanese
equivalent to "music" in English, can be traced as far back as the late
Heian period (794–1185), it was originally used almost exclusively

to refer to specific types of religious and courtly practices that originated in China and Korea (as opposed to those that were deemed to be native) and this significantly limited use of the term largely continued throughout the premodern era.[5]

This is not to say, however, that Japan in the premodern era, especially under the Tokugawa shogunate, was completely bereft of what could reasonably be understood as an increasingly shared musical culture among those within its realm. Scholars have noted that in actual practice the same historical developments that rendered the segregation of the different status groups increasingly untenable during the Tokugawa era also worked to undermine the divisions between various forms of aesthetic and cultural pursuits that were considered to be appropriate by the ruling elite.[6] While the Tokugawa state idealized and mandated the separation of different status groups—in particular the division between members of the ruling samurai class and those who were deemed to be "commoners"—as the cornerstone of social and political order, developments like rapid urbanization and commercialization steadily eroded such distinctions on the ground, as an increasing number of commoner elites rose to economic and social prominence. Under such circumstances, members of the commoner status gradually gained access to cultural forms that were deemed to be "above" them, including *noh* and *gagaku,* whose elite practitioners were increasingly open to taking on commoner students for fee.[7] Perhaps more disturbingly for the Tokugawa rulers, members of the samurai class were equally attracted to decidedly commoner pursuits, such as *kabuki* theater and genres that featured instruments like *shakuhachi* and *shamisen* (three-stringed lute).[8]

The existence of numerous edicts forbidding such cultural intermixing issued not only by the officials of the Tokugawa shogunate in Edo (present-day Tokyo) but also by various provincial authorities throughout the Tokugawa period attest to both the governing elites' enduring insistence on the need for the separation of status groups and the equally consistent futility of their efforts. However, they also reflect the fact that throughout this period the increasingly broadening chasm between the official ideal of separate cultures and the emergence of shared practices on the ground was never bridged by the development of an overarching notion of music that could have been used to privilege certain forms of musical practices over and against others. The Tokugawa officials' edicts were aimed not at mandating, or for that matter banning, any particular pursuit for those they ruled; instead the goal, as the ethnomusicologist Gerald Groemer puts it, was "for all individuals to engage in morally sound cultural pursuits 'proper' to their officially acknowledged rank and station in society."[9] To pursue such an end, it was never deemed necessary to envision the entirety of the disparate cultural practices as a collective.

It is perhaps telling that one of the few premodern exceptions to the limited use of the term *ongaku* originated from the Europeans who visited Japan in the course of the sixteenth and seventeenth centuries and who listed the term as the equivalent to their word for music in their dictionaries.[10] Ultimately, however, it was only in the aftermath of the Meiji state's introduction of Western music into the national educational curricula that the term *ongaku* gained wider currency within Japanese society. In other words, when Izawa Shūji and Megata Tanetarō called for the creation of a "national music" (*kokugaku*), what they had in mind was functionally equivalent to the notion of music as a universal cultural phenomenon; in fact, it did not take long for education officials and others to stop using *kokugaku* altogether, defaulting instead to *ongaku*. Either way, for the first time in history, Japan's governing elite possessed a single cultural category that could, theoretically, bring together the disparate sound-making practices that had existed in Japan—an intellectual tool that suggested to possibility of bridging the Tokugawa-era

contradiction between the reality of a shared musical culture and
its official denial.

The soundscape that confronted the Meiji state, however, was
far from simple. It included the various forms of Edo-period
"commoner songs" (*zokkyoku*) that had continued to maintain their
popularity into the new era, including *kouta* (ditty), *hauta* (short
song), and *nagauta* (long song), all of which were accompanied
by traditional instruments like *shamisen* and drums. They were, of
course, what Izawa and his colleagues had in mind when they referred to parts Japan's musical culture that were, for them at least,
beyond the pale. During the first and highly contentious session
of the Imperial Diet that met in December 1890, Tsuji Shinji, the
deputy education minister, was forced to defend the funding for
music education, along with other government priorities that came
under the fierce attack of opposition legislators. Echoing Izawa,
Tsuji argued that the state's involvement in music education was
necessary in order to elevate "national dignity" as well as "public
mores," since "much of traditional Japanese music needs to be reformed."[11] Outside of the Diet, Yatabe Ryōkichi (1851–1899), the
former head of the Tokyo Music School, repeated this refrain by
lamenting the detrimental effect that commoner songs allegedly had
on society and argued that "music is essential for the education of
public mores."[12]

However, Edo-era ditties were not the only ones to test the limits
of the modern Japanese state's definition of acceptable music. Nurse-
maids in rural villages and young women working in factories, for
example, also used traditional song styles to make their own songs—
some lewd, others plaintive—that protested against the various
forms of oppression they faced, to the chagrin of their teachers and
employers.[13] Even more disturbingly for the Meiji state, the antigovernment Freedom and People's Rights Movement of the 1880s
helped to popularize a musical genre known as *enka,* which saw

street singers gain fame by singing songs that satirized the alleged
excesses of the authoritarian state and called for the establishment
of democratic institutions such as a written constitution and a representative assembly.[14] Following the opening of the Diet and the
simultaneous demise of the antigovernment movement, *enka* began
to widen its thematic scope to include love and humor, while continuing to produce some barbs aimed at the foibles of corrupt party
politicians and bureaucrats. At the same time, the scope of these
songs' circulation widened considerably as *enka-shi* (*enka* singer-
songwriters) progressed beyond their humble beginnings as street
performers and utilized the emerging networks of modern journalism and publication, enabling them to reach a greater number
of audience. Some, like Soeda Azembō (1872–1944), gained both
fame and wealth, enabling them to pursue the lifestyles of celebri-
ties before the advent of more highly capitalized mass entertainment
like film and record.[15]

Simultaneously, entirely new musical practices also emerged,
many of which drew in one way or another from the Meiji-era
encounter with Western music. Along with the national education
curriculum, Western music initially entered Japan through largely
noncommercial avenues such as military bands, some of which were
formed as early as the years preceding the fall of Tokugawa shogunate, and through the religious music introduced by Christian
churches following their legalization in 1873. As a new urban landscape dotted with Western-style department stores, suburban
"garden cities," and railroad networks began to emerge in the first
decades of the twentieth century, however, Western and Western-
inspired music was deployed for decidedly commercial ends.[16] In
1909, the Mitsukoshi Department Store in Tokyo organized the
Mitsukoshi Boys' Band, made up of young boys aged eleven through
fifteen who were trained by former members of the Imperial Navy
Band.[17] Other department stores quickly followed suit and created

similar bands as well as choirs, mostly made up of young boys and girls. By far the most successful and enduring of these was the Takarazuka Girls' Opera, which still exists today as the Takarazuka Revue. Kobayashi Ichizō (1873–1957), who eventually developed his railroad business in the Osaka area into a massive conglomerate that included a department store chain, a baseball team, and a film company, initially created the Takarazuka Girls' Opera in 1914 to entertain visitors at a spa that he developed at the suburban Takarazuka terminal of the Mino'o-Arima Railway. However, the opera quickly grew in popularity and eclipsed the spa as a highly successful attraction in its own right. The content of the performances also evolved from simple shows featuring choral singing and plays based on fairy tales to full-fledged Western-style musical revues that included the latest Western songs and theatrical techniques.[18]

During the same period, yet another highly popular "opera" emerged in Asakusa, prewar Tokyo's preeminent entertainment district. The Asakusa Opera, as it ultimately came to be known, featured a creative mixture of Western operettas with comedy and romance. Its first successful production was *The Women's Army Goes to War* (*Jogun shussei*) performed in 1917, written and directed by Iba Takashi (1887–1937) and starring the actress Takagi Tokuko (1891–1919), who had returned from a stint in vaudeville theaters in America. *Women's Army* was a musical comedy satirizing the Western Front in World War I, in which an all-female troop is formed due to a shortage of men. The show featured dances and Western songs, including "Tipperary," and its popularity among its audience, which was reportedly made up mostly of young male students, set the tone for what followed, with an emphasis on humor and eroticism. Subsequent productions included several other original Japanese works, like *Exploring the Women-Island* (*Onagojima tanken*), as well as Western works like Gilbert and Sullivan's *H.M.S. Pinafore*, Rossini's *Barber of Seville*, and

Verdi's *Aida*.[19] While the Asakusa Opera did not survive the Great Kanto Earthquake of 1923 or the fickleness of changing consumer taste, it nonetheless presented some of the pioneer performances of Western classical music and, in particular, opera in Japan. It also launched the careers of Iba Takashi, who went on to gain prominence as a critic, and Fujiwara Yoshie (1898–1976), one of Japan's first opera singers to gain international fame. Despite the eclectic and limited nature of these productions, the Asakusa Opera continues to be remembered as one of the first, if short-lived, attempts outside of the official music establishment to popularize Western art music among a broader audience.

Others, however, sought to challenge the content, if not the entire premise, of the music that had been established by the Meiji state more directly during a period which roughly corresponded to the reign of Emperor Taishō (1912–1926). These included some members of the elite literary circles of Tokyo. In 1918, Suzuki Miekichi (1882–1936), a novelist and a former student of the literary giant Natsume Sōseki, published a children's literary journal entitled the *Red Bird* (*Akai tori*). Featuring prominent literary figures of the period such as Akutagawa Ryūnosuke (1892–1927) and Kitahara Hakushū (1885–1942), the journal heralded the emergence of a movement that aimed to counter what Suzuki saw as the overtly utilitarian and moralistic nature of the kinds of literature that children were exposed to in schools. Suzuki also called on well-known poets like Kitahara and Saijō Yaso to produce alternatives to the lyrics of the Meiji-era school songs that would reflect the natural emotions, experiences, and imaginations of children in what was deemed to be a more authentic manner.[20] While their works did not replace the existing music curriculum in schools, the songs written by these poets gained popularity and recognition to the extent that they were recognized as a significant cultural movement of the Taishō era. Their Children's Song Movement struck a chord with an increasing number of people, especially among the members of the highly educated "new middle-class," many of whom were dissatisfied with what was seen as the state-centric nature of existing songs for children. Despite starting primarily as a literary rather than a musical movement, some of its most prominent poems, such as Saijō's "Canary" ("Kanariya"), were accompanied by music created by notable composers like Yamada Kōsaku (1886–1965) and Motoori Nagayo (1885–1945). Some of these were even recorded by the nascent record industry, oftentimes featuring young girls who gained some amount of celebrity as singers.[21]

The Birth of an Industry

In the aftermath of the Meiji state's cultural and educational reforms, all of these diverse forms of sound culture fit technically, if not entirely comfortably, within the universalized category of "music." None of them, however, ultimately gained the scale of popularity that would have realized, or for that matter threatened, Izawa and his colleagues' dream of "national music." Among the advocates of Western art music, there was a growing anxiety not only that their music was failing to penetrate the hearts and minds of the majority of their compatriots, but also that it was simply falling behind the times as the Japanese social landscape experienced a dramatic transformation. In particular, the nation's urban landscape was undergoing a stunning demographic shift, as urban populations grew rapidly with an influx of rural laborers seeking factory jobs and the growth of the new middle class. Amidst such change there was a growing sense of crisis among some members of the musical establishment that their music was failing to reach many of these new urbanites.

One such musician was the avant-garde composer Ishikawa Yoshikazu (1887–1962) who focused on the issue of "mass music" in a series of articles published in 1925.[22] In these articles, Ishikawa called for a movement aimed at two interconnected goals: what he called the "massification of music" and the "musicalization of the masses." With regard to the former, Ishikawa lamented that the kinds of Western music that were available in Japan at that time, as evinced in concert programs and discussions within music journals, were elitist, catering as it were to the preferences of what he called the "intellectual class, bourgeoisies, and the aristocracy."[23] Should such a state of affairs be allowed to persist, Ishikawa warned, Western music would become something completely beyond the comprehension and interest of the majority of the masses. With respect to the second goal of "musicalizing" the masses, Ishikawa argued that it was far more important to increase the quantity of music available to people, rather than to focus on its quality in order to please elite tastes.[24] To that end, he praised Tokyo City's Social Bureau for creating a concert band that circulated throughout various locations in the city, and he called on other municipalities to emulate their efforts. He also suggested that the existing institutions of music education should be overhauled to increase the number of music specialists. Ishikawa bemoaned the fragmentation of the music establishment in Japan, in which musicians were divided into small fiefdoms organized around affiliations with specific teachers or aesthetic commitments.[25] Each musical genre, from classical music to "children's songs" (dōyō), worked on its own instead of cooperating to produce a more unified musical culture.[26]

Notably, Ishikawa published these articles in a relatively new journal entitled *Music and Phonograph* (*Ongaku to chikuonki*), dedicated to promoting the new technology that was still unknown in most Japanese homes. While he acknowledged that both phonographs and radio would likely play prominent roles in "mass-ifying" music, he lamented that these technologies had yet to prove their efficacy. Within only a few years, however, this situation changed

dramatically as Japan's recording industry not only expanded rapidly but also successfully established an entirely new category of
music that, arguably for the first time in Japanese history, made an
increasingly convincing case for its own near-universal popularity.
Whether Ishikawa and his colleagues in the music establishment
would have approved of what ultimately emerged as "popular
songs," however, is an entirely different matter.

Phonographs first arrived in Japan not long after their development in the United States by Thomas Edison and Emile Berliner
during the last decades of the nineteenth century.[27] In 1896, Fred-
erick Whitney Horn, an American merchant based in Yokohama,
began importing phonographs and records produced by Columbia
Records. Soon other traders followed suit, importing players and
records from Edison's National Phonograph Company, the British
Gramophone Company, and Eldridge Johnson's Victor Talking
Machine Company. Sensing that imported music was hardly adequate to create a new market, Horn established the Japan-America
Phonograph Manufacturing Company in 1907. The company was
renamed Japan Phonograph Company (Nicchiku) in 1910 and
was soon joined by several other companies that produced phonographs and records locally.

During this nascent stage of the industry, record companies relied heavily on existing musical forms to attract customers to their
expensive and unfamiliar machines. In the case of Nicchiku, these
included performance of traditionally Japanese instruments like
shamisen, shakuhachi, koto (harp), and *biwa* (lute), as well as various
forms of singing and speech-based arts, like *gidayū, naniwabushi,*
and *nagauta*. Records of *gidayū* and *naniwabushi*—both of which
were highly popular forms of storytelling that involved something
more akin to chanting rather than singing in the Western sense—
were especially successful, reflecting the enduring popularity of entertainment forms that traced their origins to the Edo and earlier

periods.[28] The popularity of these records also spawned a growing industry of record piracy that operated in a legal gray zone, since Japan's copyright laws did not explicitly include sound recordings as objects of protection. In a notable case that came before the Japanese Supreme Court in 1914, the court ruled against Richard Werderman, a German trader who had sued several Japanese for producing copies of records featuring the *naniwabushi* star Tōchūken Kumoemon (1873–1916).[29] Despite the lower courts' rulings in favor of Werderman, the Supreme Court ultimately handed a major victory to copy makers by ruling that sound recordings, unlike published scores, fell beyond the realm of copyright protection under the current laws. It was not until 1920 that the Diet passed a revision to the Copyright Law to include sound recordings.

Many historians of Japanese popular music have identified two recordings in particular as hits that heralded the emergence of a musical culture that was dominated by the record industry. The first was "Song of Katyusha" ("Kachūsha no uta"), composed by the Tokyo Music School-trained Nakayama Shimpei and recorded in 1914 by the Tōyō Phonograph Company based in Kyoto. The recording featured Matsui Sumako (1886–1919), who was a prominent actress in the Western-style theatrical genre known as *shingeki* (new drama). *Shingeki* specialized in adaptations of Western realist theater, such as plays by Henrik Ibsen and Anton Chekhov, and was also instrumental in producing performers and playwrights who created the Asakusa Opera, including Iba Takashi.[30] Matsui originally sang the "Song of Katyusha" as part of her performance in an adaptation of Leo Tolstoy's *Resurrection* directed by Shimamura Hōgetsu. Tōyō reportedly sold over twenty thousand copies of the record, which was an usually high number for that time.

A few years later, Noguchi Ujō (1882–1945), the poet who was involved in the Children's Song Movement, collaborated with Nakayama Shimpei to create the "Boatman's Ditty" ("Sendō kouta"), which featured a plaintive tune and nihilistic lyrics that likened the singer's life to dead *susuki* (Japanese pampas grass) that never bloomed. Several companies produced recordings of this song starting in 1922, and its popularity was such that it was later blamed by some critics for "causing" the Great Kantō Earthquake through its moral degeneracy.[31] More importantly, both the "Boatman's Ditty" and the "Song of Katyusha" marked the beginning of a long and successful career for Nakayama as Japan's premier composer of popular songs. Despite their successes, however, neither song signaled a fundamental departure from the recording industry's dependence on existing musical resources. Both songs were originally produced within contexts that were independent of the record companies, which only produced the records after the songs had gained popularity on their own. Even after they were produced, much of the records' popularity was due to the efficacy of existing media outlets rather than the record industry's own efforts. Particularly important were the *enka* singers who took these songs to the streets and to those who could not afford to purchase the records.[32] It was no wonder then that contemporaries like Ishikawa Yoshikazu saw phonographs as hardly living up to their potential to popularize music among the masses.

The 1920s started with a rapid reorganization of the music industry. In 1919, Nicchiku began to acquire many of its competitors, including the Tōyō Phonograph Company of "Katyusha" fame, and established its dominance in the Japanese market. However, Nicchiku's expansion was ultimately overshadowed by the massive insertion of Western capital into the industry from the first year of the Shōwa era (1926–1989). In 1926, Japanese importers of the German Polydor label approached its manufacturer Deutsche Grammophon and won rights to press their records locally in Japan by establishing Japan Polydor. In 1927, the Victor Talking Machine Company established a wholly owned subsidiary in Japan and built

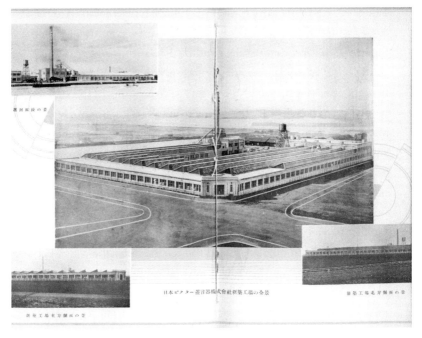

Full view of the new factory of the Japan Victor Talking Machine Company, 1930 (courtesy of the Harvard College Library, Harvard University).

a large factory in Yokohama for local production. In the same year, Nicchiku itself transferred 47.4 percent of its holdings to British and American branches of Columbia Records, merging with one of the largest record conglomerates in the world.[33]

The sudden surge of the Western recording industry's presence in the Japanese market was the result of three developments that made mergers mutually beneficial for both Japanese and Western companies. The first of these occurred in 1924, when the Japanese government established a luxury tax that placed a 100 percent tariff on imported phonographs and records in order to encourage domestic production following the Great Kantō Earthquake. Consequently, there was a greater incentive for Western companies to transfer much of their phonograph and record production to Japan proper.[34] Secondly, technological innovation in record production prompted Japanese manufacturers to seek further cooperation with their Western counterparts. The start of radio broadcasting in the United States in 1920 brought new challenges for the music industry, not least because sound transmitted electronically by radio sounded louder and clearer to the listener in comparison to phonographs. This shortcoming, however, prompted the record companies to develop their own methods of recording and amplifying sound electronically. In the United States, Columbia and Victor licensed the electrical recording process developed by the Western Electric Company, a subsidiary of the American Telephone and Telegraph Company, and began producing electronic phonographs and records by mid-decade.[35] Finally, the entrance of Western record companies into the Japanese market occurred within a broader reorganization and internationalization of the global record industry that was taking place during the last half of the 1920s. American Victor, for example, gained ownership of Victor branches around the world, including Canada, Brazil, and Chile, before it was itself acquired by the Radio Corporation of America (RCA) in 1929, signaling the birth of a conglomerate that cut across the media industries. In the case of Columbia, the American branch was acquired by its British counterpart in 1925, which merged with the Gramophone Company in 1931 to form Electrical and Musical Instruments Ltd. (EMI).[36]

"Tokyo March" and the Birth of Popular Song

Following their establishment in Japan, Columbia and Victor quickly came to dominate the market and the consequences of their emergence ultimately extended well beyond the immediate effects of capital infusion. Within the next decade, these two companies fundamentally transformed the ways in which the record industry as a whole produced music. By doing so, they introduced what was perhaps the most important paradigm shift in Japan's musical culture since the establishment of music education in the Meiji period. At the heart of this change lay what would emerge as the industry's single most valuable commodity: popular songs. The 1929 hit "Tokyo March" is an excellent example of how this new musical genre was created. The song was originally produced for the purpose of advertising a film of the same title directed by Mizoguchi Kenji (1898–1956), one of the foremost Japanese film directors from this period, and produced by the Nikkatsu Film Company. The film was, in turn, based on a popular melodrama written by the celebrated author Kikuchi Kan (1888–1948) which was serialized in the magazine *King* (*Kingu*) from 1928 to 1929.

Kikuchi's story centered on the contrasting lives of two women, Sayuri and Michiyo, who live as next-door neighbors in Tokyo. Sayuri, a daughter of a successful industrialist, is described as a "modern girl" (*modan gāru*) enjoying the life of an upper-class urbanite, all the while attracting numerous suitors with her beauty.[37] Michiyo, despite being more beautiful and clearly more virtuous than her rich neighbor, is an orphan living with poor relatives and working at a nearby factory. As the story progresses, Michiyo is forced to take up her deceased mother's occupation and became a geisha in the fashionable Ginza district in downtown Tokyo in order to save her relatives from financial difficulties. Sayuri's and Michiyo's lives ultimately collide when Sayuri's brother, Yoshiki, falls in love with Michiyo. In the end, however, it is revealed that Sayuri and Yoshiki's father was, in fact, the patron of Michiyo's mother and, even more shockingly, Michiyo's biological father. Throughout the story, Kikuchi fuses the theme of romantic love with various elements that were emblematic of modern urban life

Cover of a theatrical pamphlet for the film *Tokyo March* (courtesy of Matsuda Film Productions).

in the 1920s and 1930s, including department stores, cafés, and cinemas.

Saijō Yaso's lyrics for "Tokyo March" also play on the same themes of romance and modern life:

> Longing for the old willows on the Ginza streets.
> Who knows now of that middle-aged coquette?
> Dancing to jazz and drinking liqueur late into the night.
> In the morning, the dancer sheds her tears.[38]

In the song, Saijō not only mentions the most popular and fashion-able neighborhoods in Tokyo, such as Ginza, Asakusa, and Shinjuku, but also highlights specific landmarks that dotted the urban landscape, including the "Marubiru" (Marunouchi Building), cinema, and a department store. The lyrics also make repeated references to various modes of high-speed transportation that were changing the way in which people physically experienced the city, like the subway, bus, and the Odakyū train. Musically, the song fit into what was emerging as Nakayama Shimpei's signature style, nicknamed "Shimpei songs" (*Shimpei-bushi*), which typically featured a syncretic *yonanuki* minor pentatonic scale, giving the song a distinctly "Japanesey" (*nihon chō*) feel despite its modern theme.[39] This was, in fact, the same style that was used in his earlier hit "Boatman's Ditty," and this became the basis for many of the popular songs that would be produced during the subsequent decades. As such, it is worth noting that even though the word "March" in the song's title refers to Western military music, its actual musical content had nothing to do with it. Instead, "Tokyo March" was only one of the many "marches" that were produced by Japanese record companies during this period, which typically denoted songs that were set in urban spaces like Ginza that were imagined to be the playgrounds of fashionable Tokyoites.[40] Combined with the voice of Satō Chiyako, a classically trained soprano who recorded the song, and Saijō's unabashedly modern-themed lyrics, the music embodied the cultural hybridity of the original story, which would become the hallmark of the popular songs produced by the record industry.

The way in which the "Tokyo March" record was produced, however, reveals even more about how the industry reshaped music making in modern Japan. The first thing to note is the extent to which song production had come under the control of the record companies. Unlike "Boatman's Ditty" or "Song of Katyusha," Victor was involved in the entire process of the production of "Tokyo March," from its composition to distribution. Shortly after Victor established itself in Japan, the company made an exclusive contract with Nakayama, restricting his musical activity to the company in exchange for a regular "exclusivity fee."[41] Satō had also made a similar contract with Victor before the production of "Tokyo March" and had, in fact, already produced several records for the company. While Saijō was not under such a contract at that time, this changed after "Tokyo March" became a hit.[42]

Above these "employees" stood Oka Shōgo, the head of the company's Literary Arts Department, which was charged with developing and recording songs. It was Oka who had the ultimate authority to accept or reject a song and, more importantly, demand changes from the artists in the process of song production. In the case of "Tokyo March," Oka famously instructed Saijō to change the last verse of the song, which originally featured the line "Long-haired Marxist boys, carrying *Red Love* with them." This was a reference based on Saijō seeing "long-haired, serious-looking young men in Tokyo" walking around with a recent translation of a novel by Alexandra Kollontai, the Russian communist author who was known for her critique of traditional love and marriage.[43] Saijō wrote the song in 1928, the same year that the Japanese government had ordered the mass arrest of communists. Oka feared that such a reference would invite official scrutiny and the line was ultimately changed to the more benign "Go to the cinema? Or for some tea? Why don't we run away on the Odakyu train?"[44]

During the subsequent decade, both the practice of making exclusive contracts with artists and the centrality of the Literary Arts Department in the production of popular songs became an industry-wide norm. While Victor took the lead in producing hit songs in the late 1920s by securing the talents of Nakayama, Saijō, and others, Columbia responded by making similar exclusive contracts with other musicians, the most important being Koga Masao (1904–1978), who eventually took over Nakayama's role as the premier composer of popular songs in the industry. In the case of prominent composers like Nakayama and Koga, their roles within their respective companies ultimately exceeded simply writing music, extending to involvement in the broader planning and production of songs.[45] Koga, for example, became involved in running another recording company, Teichiku (Imperial Phonograph Company), in 1934 as an executive.

As the composers, lyricists, and singers increasingly found themselves locked into the corporate structure, the record industry as a whole also found itself enmeshed in a new context during the same period. It is important to note that the original impetus for the production of "Tokyo March" came from the Nikkatsu Film Company.[46] As Saijō recalls it, it was Higuchi Masami, the head of Nikkatsu's Advertising Department, who first recruited him to write a song, telling him, "It doesn't really matter how faithful the song remains to the original story, but just make something that will become a big hit."[47] While the film industry had already made several films based on songs that had gained popularity, "Tokyo March" was one of the first cases in which the song and the film were produced simultaneously as products of cross-industry cooperation. Following the success of the song with record buyers, this form of partnership between film and record companies came to be one of the most common ways in which hit songs were produced— an arrangement that only escalated with the introduction of talkie films in 1931 and lasted well into the postwar period.[48]

The making of "Tokyo March," however, points to the presence of another form of mass entertainment: mass circulation magazines such as *King*, which featured Kikuchi's original story. First published in 1925 by Noma Seiji (1878–1938), the head of the publishing firm Kōdansha, *King* quickly became the most successful mass magazine in early Shōwa Japan, boasting sales of over a million issues per month by 1928. As one of *King*'s editors put it, the magazine aimed at the growing, urban "masses" who were "slightly above the bottom of the [intellectual] pyramid."[49] To that end, *King* focused on providing content that squarely fell in the realm of entertainment in monthly issues that were both voluminous and inexpensive. Notably, its editorial staff also sought to raise the magazine's profile as part of a growing network of mass media and entertainment that included film, radio, and record. Not content with providing materials for films and popular songs, Noma ultimately created the King Record label within Kōdansha in 1931, which began producing its own songs. The label would ultimately survive the *King* and become an independent record company in 1951.

By increasing their control over music production and by establishing strong alliances with other emerging forms of mass media, record companies grew adept at making hits on a seemingly ever-growing scale. Between 1929 and 1936, annual record production nearly tripled, jumping from 10,483,364 to 29,682,590. Phonograph production doubled during the same period from 130,982 to 265,295.[50] In particular, popular songs in the vein of Shimpei songs and Koga's compositions, which were known as

"Koga melodies" (*Koga merodi*), were notable for their rapid emergence as the record companies' chief products. A survey conducted by the Home Ministry toward the end of 1935 indicated that popular songs constituted the largest musical genre being produced by the industry, accounting for a third of all new items that were being recorded. In fact, the share of records featuring popular songs among all of the records that were produced was likely to have been even higher, given that the Home Ministry figures were based on the number of individual songs that were submitted to them for censorship and did not take into account the difference in actual sales figures between each item.[51] Another Home Ministry survey reported in the same year that popular songs had clearly become "the principal source of profit for the record companies" and that the industry devoted their marketing efforts almost exclusively to this genre.[52]

The Politics of "Tokyo March"

"Tokyo March" is today widely remembered as one of the very first hit songs in the history of Japanese popular music, even if most Japanese have forgotten its melody and lyrics. What is less remembered is that "Tokyo March" and other popular songs produced by the record industry attracted almost immediate condemnation from a wide range of critics, including government officials and school teachers. Just as Victor was producing its first hit songs in 1929, newspapers in Tokyo were reporting on various anti-popular song movements that were led by local teachers as well as officials at the Tokyo Music School and Tokyo City's Department of Education.[53] As a November 13, 1929, article in *Asahi shimbun,* a national daily, reported, educators expressed dismay at both the apparent speed with which popular songs spread throughout Japan and their contents, which many of them deemed "plaintive, lewd, and lustful."[54]

Such sentiment was seemingly shared by others beyond the realm of education. Within a few months of Victor's release of "Tokyo March," other voices of critique emerged in *Yomiuri shimbun,* another national daily. The August 3 issue of the newspaper featured an open letter written by a woman named Tanaka Sumiko. The letter noted that Japan lacked "graceful, artistic, and dignified songs that are created for women and mothers" and did not mince words in bemoaning the nature of popular songs that did exist: "As I walk through the streets, I hear students and errand boys singing that indecent song called 'Tokyo March' that is devoid of any rhythm or nuance. I could bear it if that were all, but, when I hear the line 'Longing for the willows of Ginza' come out of the mouths of innocent little children playing in the street, I feel pain more than sadness."[55]

While Tanaka acknowledged that she could not keep film companies and promoters who "have no desire or aim other than making money" from spreading these songs, she expressed shock that the men who were writing the songs were "famous poets and musicians," casting doubt on their "artistic conscience." In fact, even before these critics voiced their concerns, the Japan Broadcasting Corporation (Nippon Hōsō Kyōkai, NHK) banned the song from its airwaves under the instruction of the Tokyo Metropolitan Bureau of Communication.[56] The bureau's chief argued that the radio should have no part in encouraging juvenile delinquency by broadcasting reference to "young men and women having a tryst in Asakusa and running away on the Odakyū [train]."

These critiques, infused as they were with concerns about the effects of popular songs on children's morality, may strike one as being fundamentally similar to complaints that have been leveled against popular music throughout history. But the immediate historical context surrounding "Tokyo March" makes it clear that there was much more at stake. A growing number of Japanese at this time began to see their times as characterized by enormous social change, including the rapid industrialization and urbanization that had taken place since the end of the Meiji period. These developments, as noted earlier, had a particularly profound impact on the demographic patterns in Tokyo and other larger cities in Japan, which saw an influx of industrial as well as white-collar workers. During this period, the number of male industrial workers more than tripled, from 317,388 in 1911 to 968,000 in 1933.[57] Similarly, the members of the white-collar "new" middle class, composed of highly educated, salaried employees of corporations and the government, grew in number, gradually pushing the "old" middle class of small-scale shopkeepers and manufacturers to the margins.

The growing numbers of both industrial laborers and the new middle class led scholars and bureaucrats to envision a new category of urban Japanese that ultimately came to be identified as "the masses" (taishū)—a group that was seen as being simultaneously united by their distinction from the older residents of Tokyo and divided by class. This development had an especially profound effect on an emerging group of scholars dedicated to the study of the everyday life of the urban Japanese and, in particular, their leisure.[58] For these scholars, including Kon Wajirō (1888–1973) and Gonda Yasunosuke (1887–1951), the urban masses were the chief protagonists in the remaking of modern life in Japan—a process in which individuals developed new everyday practices as well as new identities through their interactions with the burgeoning culture of consumption. At the same time, however, the masses were also seen as both potentially at risk of being victimized by the vagaries of modern capitalism and liable to become the source of social and political instability themselves. In particular, the growing domestic tension stemming from economic stagnation and radicalization of politics in the latter half of the 1920s raised the specter of these new urban masses being mobilized in labor strikes and riots, taking over the central role played by the members of the "old" middle class in the disturbances that had rocked Tokyo in earlier decades of the twentieth century.[59] While "Tokyo March" makes no overt reference to those events, both the original novel by Kikuchi Kan and Mizoguchi Kenji's film have the modern Tokyo masses and their diversity as their central theme. As noted earlier, Kikuchi's novel centers on the contrasting lives of Michiyo, the lowly, virtuous factory-girl-turned-geisha, and Sayuri, the headstrong, wealthy modern girl. Both the novel and the film portray Michiyo as a victim twice over. On the one hand, she is a victim of a lecherous capitalist who not only abandoned her mother while Michiyo was still in the womb but also, albeit without knowing her true identity, tries to force himself on his biological daughter after spotting her during one of his regular visits to a geisha house. The coup de grace is, of course, the fact that his paternity ultimately prevents the fulfillment of Michiyo's love for Yoshiki by raising the specter of incest once he was revealed to be her brother. On the other hand, she is also a victim by virtue of her class, an urban proletarian forced into the demimonde by the vagaries of capitalist system. In contrast, Sayuri is depicted as a haughty socialite who not only disdains geisha but also takes pleasure in manipulating the affections of the men who surround her.[60]

While Kikuchi's novel emphasizes the melodramatic aspect of Michiyo's victimhood and the karmic retribution that befalls her and Yoshiki, Mizoguchi's film embraces the story's political implications by valorizing Michiyo as an urban proletarian. In both the novel and the film, Sayuri repeatedly denigrates geisha, declaring, "There is nothing I hate more than a geisha. They are so haughty, even though they are so ignorant and uncultured."[61] Sakuma, Yoshiki's friend and a competitor in the quest for Michiyo's affection, contradicts her by insisting that "even among geisha, there are women with pure soul, no matter how uncultured they may be." In the film, however, Sakuma's rebuttal turns into a pointed social critique: "Who gives birth to the geisha? It is your society that abuses wealth and therefore bears the reasonability for these many, unfortunate women!"[62] It would, of course, be a stretch to characterize the film, let alone the novel, as a serious critique of modern capitalism. Not a few intellectuals who reviewed the film complained of the film's flimsy, clichéd ideological posture that was, in the end, overpowered by the karmic melodrama that dominated the narrative.[63] Moreover, the class affiliations of the main characters are highly ambiguous. The supposedly proletarian Michiyo's identity as a geisha places her directly in the realm of the older residents of Tokyo (even Edo), Sakuma's defense notwithstanding. Sayuri, too, vacillates between her identity as a member of Tokyo's upper crust and her role as a modern girl, itself a media construct that found its real-life counterpart in the growing number of middle class "professional women" (*shokugyō fujin*) or "café waitresses" (*jokyū*).

The ambiguity in Michiyo and Sayuri's class identities, however, allows for a more multifaceted reading that matches the perception of modern Tokyo as an inherently chaotic and contradictory space. This emerges in the novel as well as the film, both of which begin with this statement: "Tokyo—the only truly modern city in the Orient. The center of Japan's culture, academy, cultivation, and art, as well as sin and depravity."[64] Both the novel and the film end happily with all characters, including the lecherous father, being ultimately redeemed. The writers and producers of "Tokyo March" not only to refrained from judging the contradiction found in the city, they also embraced it as the evidence of the city's authentically modern identity. The celebration of Tokyo's modern contradictions is even more apparent in Saijō's lyrics, as they take the listener through the contrasting neighborhoods of Tokyo, including the chic Asakusa, classic Ginza, and energetic Shinjuku.

Nakaya Shimpei's syncretic tune, with its combination of a Japanese scale and Western musical idioms and instruments, further emphasizes this point. In affirming the sociocultural contradictions of Tokyo and its mass inhabitants, the producers of "Tokyo March" defended the value—and values—of mass-produced culture, be it pulp fiction, film, or popular songs. Criticized for the vulgarity and depravity of their products, Japan's newly emerging culture industries responded by laying claim to an authenticity that derived from their purported intimacy with the everyday lives and desires of the consumers.

The Politics of Popular Songs

The debate that was initially provoked by "Tokyo March" and its allegedly deleterious effects on children quickly broadened to one that ultimately centered on how Japan's cultural elites should engage with the popular song genre and, more generally, the broader set of cultural and technological shifts that produced the genre. Perhaps not surprisingly, some of the earliest critiques came from the members of Japan's musical and literary establishments. On August 4, 1929, a day after Tanaka Sumiko's critique was published, *Yomiuri* carried yet another open letter that was critical of "Tokyo March," this one written by Iba Takashi, the actor and playwright who had played a central role in the Asakusa Opera and who had by this time become a prominent music critic with strong connections to NHK. While one might expect that his own work in popular entertainment would make him sympathetic to popular songs, Iba not only defended the broadcaster's decision to ban "Tokyo March" as inappropriate but also went on to characterize the song as "weak, effete, and in bad taste."[65]

Iba's case against "Tokyo March" and similar songs rested, in part, on what he recognized as the unprecedented reach of these

Yomiuri article featuring the Saijō-Iba debate on "Tokyo
March" (courtesy of the National Diet Library).

songs and their perceived power to shape popular tastes. Even those
who might initially object to the songs, argued Iba, would ultimately
become immune to their depravities simply because of their ubiquity. Consequently, the very popularity of "Tokyo March" was
sufficient reason to censor it, insofar as it threatened to degrade the

aesthetic judgment of the masses. His sharpest barbs, however, were directed at the cultural elites who were behind the production of the song, namely Saijō and Nakayama: "First of all, the lyricist and composer are both capable of and experienced in creating works that would elevate the taste of the masses. Given that they deliberately aim at vulgarity, however, they must be blinded to the degradation of masses by their materialistic greed. . . . Secondly, as this type of song becomes more common, publishers, phonograph makers, promoters, and concert managers will force musicians to create similar songs. If that happens, the taste of the citizens of Tokyo will become depraved beyond salvation."[66] Clearly echoing Tanaka's sense of betrayal that "famous poets and musicians" could so easily abandon their "artistic conscience," Iba accused Saijō and Nakayama of not only neglecting their cultural duties but also of setting a dangerous precedent for other artists.

Perhaps assuming that contemporary readers of his article would easily understand what he meant, Iba failed to articulate precisely what he found to be so objectionable about "Tokyo March" aside from the pointed but vague critique of the song's sentimentality. He did however end the article with a discussion of American and European popular music, none of which he found to be anywhere nearly as "vulgar" as their Japanese counterparts. This included "American jazz," whose lyrics, according to Iba, contained none of the coarseness of Japanese songs, even as he opined that it was "avoided by musically inclined households in the West."[67] Iba even suggested that popular music in Western societies was generally transformed into something more "highbrow" in contrast to its degrading effect on Japanese musical culture. Implicit in such a claim was the sense that, both in terms of its lyrical as well as musical content, "Tokyo March" represented a kind of Japaneseness that Iba saw as deeply problematic.

Iba proved to be a persistent critic of Saijō and his popular songs in the following years. In 1932, he published a series of four long articles entitled "Items to be Reformed in the Japanese Music Establishment" in *Music World* (*Ongaku sekai*), a prominent music journal.[68] Iba began this series by citing another Saijō hit, "Love Fulfilled in Heaven" ("Tengoku ni musubu koi," 1932), which was the title song of a film that was produced that year by the Shōchiku Film Company. The film was based on the true story of the recent double suicide of an elite Keiō University student and a woman whose family refused to permit their marriage, which was quickly sensationalized by the newspapers as a tragic love affair. For Iba, however, the song was a "ticket that would take the music world straight to hell."[69] In his opinion, popular songs had ushered in "the darkest of dark ages," not simply because these songs were "vulgar," but because they threatened to undermine the entire musical culture in Japan. Iba pointed to the fact that "Love Fulfilled in Heaven" featured two singers who had been classically trained at none other than the Tokyo Music School, "an official institution that develops musicians using state funds."[70] In other words, these singers, like Saijō and Nakayama, were abandoning their training and duty as cultural elites to elevate the masses by actively seeking to encourage their vulgar tastes, motivated primarily by their greed. In the same article, Iba declared himself the true "champion of the popularization of music" (*ongaku wo minshūka suru tōshi*), citing his experience in the Asakusa Opera as an example of how one could appeal to the masses without degrading them.

Iba's diatribe against popular songs continued in several subsequent articles in *Music World*. He denounced the popularity of record companies' products as a tyranny by the majority that amounted to a form of "bolshevism," and belittled contemporary music critics for their "apathetic" acceptance of the vulgar majority's will.[71] Iba's ire was also directed at Japanese composers, attacking their fundamental lack of progress in quality both as individuals and as a collective. In Iba's opinion, Yamada Kōsaku and Nakayama Shimpei stood out as two of the most important composers of the Taishō period due to their respective works, with the former emerging as an overwhelmingly dominant figure in the more highbrow world of Western art music, and the latter ultimately gaining fame through his eclectic and syncretic tunes that laid the basis for subsequent popular songs.[72] Iba argued that the subsequent generation of composers not only failed to surpass the skill of these two giants, but also focused their creative output to musically simpler genres such as children's songs and popular songs. In other words, Iba saw the rise of the two major attempts at popularizing music during the 1920s as largely the product of a collective failure of musical achievement on the part of Japan's composers, who had satisfied themselves with composing "derivative folk songs" and becoming "composers who can only compose children's songs."[73]

What began with Iba's acerbic critique of "Tokyo March" spiraled within a few years into an indictment of what he saw as the fundamental corruption of Japan's music establishment as a whole. Given how frequently Iba's critiques devolved into ad hominem attacks on a wide range of figures within that circle, it should not come as a surprise that they elicited immediate and equally harsh reactions from his targets in the pages of both *Yomiuri* and *Music World*. What *is* striking, however, is the extent to which even the fiercest critics of Iba's reasoning ultimately conceded key aspects of his understanding of the nature of popular songs, including none other than Saijō Yaso, whose rebuttal to Iba's original critique of "Tokyo March" was featured on the same page of *Yomiuri*. On the one hand, Saijō countered Iba by arguing that the song was merely an authentic reflection of the society they lived in: "Songs become alive when they are sung by the masses. If the popularity of my 'Tokyo March' irritates you, blame those masses. . . . Mr. Iba laments how 'the same Saijō who wrote *dōyō* only ten years ago' wrote the vulgar 'Tokyo March,' but, in my mind, there is absolutely no contradiction between the two types of poetry. . . . 'Tokyo March' is a jazz-like satire of the superficial lives of modern Tokyoites, who dance away as the economy expands with all its contradictions. . . . Art is re-creating life. What's wrong with 'Tokyo March,' which merely depicts what I see?"[74]

Even as Saijō insists that his song was nothing more than an authentic reflection of the realities of modern Tokyo life, however, it is worth noting that he does not actually take issue with Iba's characterization of "Tokyo March" and similar songs. In fact, the understanding of Japanese popular songs as "sentimental and soft" had long been, Saijō asserts, "common sense among those of us who have worked on popular songs."[75] This was not only the consequence of the realities of contemporary Japan but also what he deemed to be the historic, cultural traits of the Japanese: "The problem is the fact that the large proportion of people who have, since medieval times, been immersed in the pessimistic ideology that derived from the Buddhist notion of emptiness will simply not appreciate such vigorous songs [that Iba demands], no matter how many of them you write."[76] Saijō goes on to note that he had also heard Nakayama Shimpei make a similar observation that even when that he produced works in a major key, such as the "Sea Port" ("Defune no minato"), they never gained popularity and were "quickly overwhelmed by works in minor keys like 'Port of Habu' ('Habu no minato')." Saijō, in other words, not only agreed with Iba's association of "Japanese" songs with sentimentality but also made an explicit connection between such songs and a specific musical characteristic—namely that they were typically in minor keys.

While the recording industry did make songs in major keys from the outset and continued to do so throughout the 1930s and beyond, this association between "Japaneseness," sentimentality, and the minor pentatonic scale not only came to dominate the understanding of most observers of the popular song genre but also proved to be something of a self-fulfilling prophecy, as the industry prioritized songs created by the likes of Nakayama and Koga Masao that were deemed to be "Japanesey." This trend was noted by Iba in his 1932 series in *Music World*, when he complained that Japanese composers produced songs based on the blind belief that "the Japanese only love songs in minor key."[77] Notably, Saijō also argues that he considers himself to be "no less insistent than Mr. Iba in demanding the creation of more manly (*danseiteki*) popular songs" and closed his *Yomiuri* article by asserting that Japanese popular songs will follow a linear progression over time: "Even the masses will eventually become bored with the softer (*yawarakai*) songs. When that happens, they will naturally shift toward harder (*katai*) ones without being prompted to do so by anyone."

Following Iba and Saijō's initial exchange, *Yomiuri* invited other figures within Japan's literary and music establishments to weigh in on the debate, noting that it had "generated massive sensation among the readers and prompted many of them to write letters [to the newspaper], since the debate on popular songs relates to the largest segment of the masses."[78] Given the position of the lyricist of "Tokyo March," it should come as no surprise that few, if any, other figures disagreed with many of the fundamental premises expressed in Iba's critique, even when most of them objected to its combative and judgmental tone. For example, the poet Kawaji Ryūkō (1888–1959) argued, on the one hand, that the song could not have gained popularity in the first place had it not contained a "sufficient level of vulgarity within itself to reach the lowest stratum of the masses" and that this characteristic constitutes "the essence of popularity."[79] As such, "It is only natural for Mr. Saijō to assert that the 'contemporary masses embraced the song because they themselves are vulgar.'" At the same time, Kawaji expands on Iba and Saijō's association of such vulgarity with the contemporary social climate, referring to what he deems to be the *traditional* traits of Japanese musical culture: "When one considers the melodies of contemporary popular songs, most of them strangely imitate the folk and commoner songs of the Tokugawa era. They are all in minor keys, soft in tone, and bear a form of melancholy. In other words, the melodies are themselves certainly decadent (*dekadan*). They betray the modest cries of sadness of the social classes oppressed during the feudal era."[80]

Kawaji goes on to argue that this is the characteristic of Asian musical cultures in general and that "the Asian love for music does not go toward the active, cheerful, and bright direction that the Westerners go toward" but toward melancholy. As such, "the greatest problem" for Kawaji was not the songs themselves but the very "emotion of the masses" that created such musical preference—an emotion that "deprives all of our pleasure-seeking of a certain amount of brightness and colors them with decadence instead." Like Iba, Kawaji ultimately prefers the "brightness" of the West to such melancholy: "Americanism contains many illnesses but the simple, innocent cheerfulness of the Americans is one thing that we should emulate ourselves. . . . No matter how unrefined American jazz might be, it has none of the melancholic, ruinous decadence of contemporary Japanese popular songs."[81]

The more optimistic observers suggested that Japanese popular songs were on the right track and that Iba need not fret so much. In two articles published in *Yomiuri* on August 14 and 15, 1929, the music critic Horiuchi Keizō argued that, in general, "[today's] popular songs are shifting from the Japanese to the Western style" and that this constituted "progress."[82] Even if, in his opinion, some of the more jazz-like Japanese songs of his day had yet to attain the "pure jazz style," Horiuchi was convinced that "most would eventually move toward that direction."[83] In another article published in *Yomiuri* in 1933, Horiuchi characterized the popular song genre as a form of "journalism," arguing that the success of these songs came from their proximity to the contemporary social climate and current events.[84] Kanetsune Kiyosuke (1885–1957), another music critic, was even more positive toward both "Tokyo March" and popular songs in general, arguing that the former's depiction of modern life was both convincing and entertaining. For Kanetsune, even the melody of "Tokyo March" contained "significant beauty" that should be celebrated: "It is the fact that both the melody and the lyrics express melancholy that moves my heart. Much of poetry and songs are like that. Why should that be criticized?"[85]

Nonetheless, it was the same Kanetsune that had called for the infusion of "ideology" into popular songs less than two months before this comment in another article published on *Yomiuri*. There Kanetsune encouraged the producers of popular songs to "take the courageous step" of introducing "social consciousness" into their creations, even as he acknowledges that it would be easier to repeat common themes like "fleeing love" the "sadness of a fleeting life."[86] And what might such a song look like? "While I was in Germany," Kanetsune noted, "I saw German labor unions constantly attempting to infuse their ideology into new songs." That the one example he gives comes from his recent visit to Germany is telling. Even for Horiuchi or Kanetsune, neither of whom were anywhere nearly as alarmed by popular songs as Iba was, there was a sense that there was clearly room for improvement in Japanese popular music as they saw it and that such improvement strongly connoted a departure from certain kinds of "Japaneseness" and the embrace of Western-inspired cultural, social, and even political developments.

If Iba, Kawaji, and Horiuchi envisioned such progress largely in terms of a more thorough Westernization of popular songs, others like the leftists Nakano Shigeharu (1902–1979) and Hara Tarō (1904–1988) expressed their hope in more political terms. In an

article published in *Yomiuri* on August 20, 1929, Nakano, the poet
and critic who played a leading role in the prewar Proletarian Literature Movement, criticized Iba's attitude as elitist and went on to
applaud "Tokyo March" as a fitting, if insidious, accompaniment to
Tokyo life as it was in 1929, precisely because of what he characterized as its "cheapness" and "vulgarity."[87] In particular, Nakano
mocked Iba's self-description as a proponent of popular music,
noting that the masses "no longer trust people who claim to labor
on their behalf." At the same time, Nakano chided "the poet Yaso's
disingenuousness" when he pointed to Saijō's claim that "such a
lowbrow song will not, in fact, promote further corruption of public
morals." While Nakano insisted that "songs like the 'Tokyo March'
will continue to be popular, no matter what Mr. Iba says," he con-
cludes with a critique of the song itself: "However, 'Tokyo March' is
a march that does not, in fact, move forward. Marches that do
move forward will emerge from farther below—more joyfully, more
brightly, and more energetically."

In the pages of *Music World,* Hara Tarō, the composer and
member of the Proletarian Music League, further expanded on
Nakano's critique of Iba's misplaced elitism and lack of a more critical sociopolitical perspective on the rise of popular songs.[88] In
particular, Hara pointed to what he saw as a fundamental flaw in
Iba's reasoning: "Mr. Iba simply does not understand the fact that
'Love Fulfilled in Heaven' and other songs were produced as result
of the ways in which the taste of the masses has been shaped, as a
matter of necessity, by the current national crisis and severe economic depression. In other words, it is a society in crisis that, in the
end, determines the taste of the masses and the nature of popular
songs."[89] As such, Hara dismissed Iba's critique as "slander and
abuse" that was "meaningless and worthless," given that, in his
judgment, it was merely the product of Iba's arbitrary and subjective sense of what was culturally "high and low."[90]

What is critical to note here, however, is the fact that this did not lead Hara to embrace contemporary popular songs. To the contrary, he declared that it was his judgment "that this type of music is undesirable," not because of some "high-handed, moralistic, and subjective grounds" but because he found it to be "thoroughly taken over" by reactionary cultural politics. Hara's judgment stemmed from his sense that popular songs were aimed at and embraced by not the entirety of the "masses" but specifically those he identified as the "petit bourgeoisie"—those "who have been closely associated with phonograph records of songs like 'Love Fulfilled in Heaven' and 'Tokyo March,' along with the Asakusa Opera of old." He refused to see it as the music of the "workers and poor peasants" whose travails had forced them "to become politically awakened" and whose everyday lives had come to be dominated by "a serious and intense mood that had been cultivated through their struggles." Such newly emerging segments of the masses, according to Hara, led to the creation of new cultures, including music. Not only did popular songs not qualify as such new culture, they were precisely the kind of culture that was aimed at "serving as a blind-fold" for the members of the "old" middle class by causing them to indulge in nothing more than nostalgic and anemic sentimentality, instead of taking critical perspectives on the social realities that surrounded them. Aided by "the abundance of Japanesey tunes," popular songs ultimately served as "excellent tools for the class that needs and desires such a reactionary nature" to be instilled among the petit bourgeoisie.[91] In short, while recoiling at what he saw as Iba's ill-tempered elitism, Hara nonetheless saw the popular songs of his day as nothing short of being one of the major cultural impediments to revolutionary change within Japanese society as a whole.

In the end, the debates between Iba, Saijō, and other members of Japan's musical and literary establishments were less revealing of the distinctions between the proponents and detractors of popular songs than of what would prove to be a durable set of characteristics associated with the genre. All participants in this debate agreed, for example, that popular songs were produced, in part, by the broader, social realities of their time, in particular the growing economic and demographic complexity of a steadily urbanizing society. They also generally agreed that such social contexts produced a set of primarily negative affects—labeled "soft" and "sentimental" by both Iba and Saijō—among the inhabitants of their society, which were, in turn, embodied by the songs themselves. It was here, however, that the critical consensus surrounding popular songs made a seemingly contradictory turn, with the same affects simultaneously attributed to cultural characteristics that were deemed to be both particularly "Japanese" and ancient. Nevertheless, it was precisely this association of the sentimentality of popular songs with what was deemed to be an undesirable, outdated form of "Japaneseness"— especially as it was musically expressed using the pentatonic minor scale—that not only ended up becoming one of the most enduring characterizations of Japanese popular songs but, in that process, clearly replicated aspects of the Meiji-era tropes associated with the "feudal" musical culture of the Edo period.

The End of Establishments?

If the immediate historical context surrounding "Tokyo March," along with their reflections in the song's multiple incarnations across media, pointed to the factors that contributed to its rapidly gained popularity as well as its notoriety, the critical discourse that emerged among Japan's cultural elites in response to "Tokyo March" proved not only to be far more durable than the immediate controversies but also very revealing in regard to what the fundamental historical transformation that the popular song genre, along with other forms of contemporary media and entertainment, signified for Japan's cultural elites. In a broader sense, the rapid growth of the recording industry and the increasing ubiquity of popular songs pointed to ways in which the paradigm of cultural production had shifted in Japan in the course of the 1920s and 1930s. Popular culture was now produced increasingly within the realm of the highly capitalized, interconnected, and centralized culture industries. This shift also signaled an elevation of the recording industry's status within Japan's musical culture. The recording industry that produced "Tokyo March" and its successors no longer simply reproduced music that existed outside itself, but instead increasingly came to dominate the ways in which music was produced and consumed in Japan.

Gonda Yasunosuke, the previously mentioned scholar of Japan's urban masses, gave perhaps one of the most trenchant descriptions of how this process appeared to himself and many of his contemporaries when he described popular songs in 1936: "Today, popular songs are being created all the time, day and night. Of course, new popular songs emerged in the past as well, but those songs were created out of the collective sentiment of the people. It was the spirit of the times and popular sentiment that made them sing. Nowadays, commercially produced popular songs are created by the record companies and their capital, and machines sing the songs. Dumbfounded, people simply admire this process as it unfolds. As a commodity, all that is expected of each popular song is that it astonish the people momentarily and sell a few hundred thousand records within a short time."[92] Here Gonda not only captures the dramatic rise in both the speed and volume of the music that was being produced but he also attempts to make a distinction between the popular songs of the past and their contemporary counterparts. Popular songs of the present could be distinguished by the fact that the recording industry developed an unprecedented level of control over the entire production process, starting with the writing of the music and the lyrics and ending with the pressing of the records. The recording industry's power was perhaps most dramatically demonstrated by the fact that, as already noted, prominent composers and lyricists like Nakayama and Saijō created their music in the capacity of salaried employees whose works were exclusively made for their employers.

In other words, an entirely new regime was beginning to appear in the cultural politics surrounding music for the first time since the Meiji period, when the state had asserted itself as not only the producer of "national music" but also the definer of what counted as music. The fact that large international corporations like Columbia and Victor had emerged as the chief producers of popular music meant that the critics of popular songs were contending not only with a specific musical genre but with an increasingly powerful network of mass media within which the songs were enmeshed. Put differently, while the scale of the recording industry promised one of the first real possibilities for a national musical culture, it also constituted a significant threat to those who had hitherto considered themselves to be the gatekeepers of the nation's cultural taste. Whereas the Meiji officials never feared that the popular musical culture of their day would somehow gain hegemony over the mainstream culture of the nation, cultural critics of the Shōwa era had many reasons to fear that the forces of commercial mass entertainment would fundamentally alter existing cultural hierarchies in Japan.

It is worth noting that many of the individuals who were part of the initial debate on popular songs had been personally involved in the post-Meiji project of "musicalizing" the Japanese masses. After the Asakusa Opera largely vanished in the wake of Great Kantō Earthquake, Iba produced and directed several opera productions exclusively for radio broadcast. As will be discussed in

Chapter 2, Horiuchi Keizō's entire career was devoted to promoting Western music in general to the Japanese audience, including a stint as a director of programming for Western music at NHK. As the recording industry's popular songs overshadowed these activities and even forced the initially hostile NHK to include some of the songs from this genre in their own programming, Iba and Horiuchi's dreams of building a popular musical culture rooted in Western art music seemed increasingly under threat. As Iba made clear in his *Music World* articles, he blamed this not only on the failure of the elite musical establishment to produce an alternative but also on their compromise with what he considered to be the inherent vulgarity of the masses. Horiuchi lamented in his 1933 *Yomiuri* article, written several months after Japan withdrew from the League of Nations, that Western-style songs, such as the ones he produced, no longer found favor in the eyes of consumers, whose growing "nationalistic sentiments" made them flock to Japanese-style popular songs modeled on Nakayama's and Koga's works.[93]

Underlying these critics' sense that their role as the nation's cultural elite was being fundamentally threatened by popular songs and the industry that produced it, however, was another even more disturbing impression that their very identity was being undermined in this process. The ferocity of Iba's attack was fuelled by the fact that both Saijō and Nakayama belonged to the nation's cultural establishments. Saijō, after all, maintained a parallel career as a professor of French literature at the prestigious Waseda University throughout the 1930s, even as his career as a lyricist specializing in popular songs took off. The revulsion that individuals like Saijō and Nakayama provoked in Iba, in other words, did not merely stem from his fear that their works would degrade the masses but, more importantly, that it would do the same to an entire class of sociocultural elites. In two articles written for *Yomiuri* in 1934, Iba went as far as suggesting that there was no longer any other option than capitulating to the new cultural regime: "The age ruled by the best music has passed long ago. No doubt, even the notion of 'best music' comes from the ethics of the past and there is no need nowadays to judge between good and bad music. . . . The tempo of modernity does not permit any artwork to maintain its supremacy over a long time. The short life spans of popular songs are not due to their inferiority but simply due to the nature of the present times."[94] Within this context, Iba suggested Japan's musical establishment faced a choice between "riding this powerful current or falling behind and dying."[95]

In fact, Iba was far from alone in declaring the "death" of existing cultural hierarchies. In January 1932, the critic Nakai Masakazu (1900–1952) wrote a series of articles entitled "The End of Establishments" ("Dan no kaitai") for the national daily Asahi. Nakai began the first article by identifying several fields in Japan's cultural landscape that possessed clear establishments (dan), including "literature, visual art, music, poetry, haiku, as well as academic and critical circles."[96] Ironically evoking the language of the Meiji Constitution's description of the emperor, Nakai argued that each of these establishments had come to form an "inviolable and sacred" space that was zealously guarded by its members acting as "brokers" of artistic exchange, for the purpose of not only preserving aesthetic integrity but also, more importantly, defending their economic interests. According to Nakai's analysis, however, the very structure of dan faced the imminent threat of dissolution, as shifts in the fundamental economic contexts demanded their transformation into "capitalistic, corporate formations."[97] For Nakai, the film industry best represented this cultural paradigm shift because the "mass-oriented, organizational, and social" characteristics of the medium constituted the most future-oriented, "promising form of art."[98]

Nakai's formulation, in fact, captures the heart of several key developments in mass media that emerged in Japan in the wake of

World War I. The most famous example of this is the explosion of the publishing market, which evolved from one that catered to a very limited and highly educated readership to one that sought out new audiences on a truly mass scale. In 1925, Kōdansha began publishing the previously mentioned *King*, which was among the first magazines to target the growing, urban masses. The established and more intellectually oriented publishers of magazines like *Reconstruction* (*Kaizō*) and *Central Review* (*Chuō kōron*) were forced to respond not only by changing their own contents to broaden their appeal but, in the case of the former, by selling cheaper monographs as parts of series. Starting with *The Collection of Contemporary Japanese Literature* (*Gendai nihon bungakushū*) published by the proprietors of *Kaizō* at the end of 1926, *enbon* (one-yen books), as these inexpensive monographs came to be known, led to an unprecedented decline in the price of monographs, which was accompanied by a dramatic expansion of readership.[99] What resulted was nothing short of a fundamental shift in the economic and technological basis on which cultural critique was possible. The rise of mass media in the 1920s signaled not only the production of new forms of mass culture but also the seeming end of critique as it had existed, typically in tight-knit circles of intellectuals and cultural practitioners with hierarchical, master-apprentice relationships.

Conclusion, by Way of Germany

The rise of the popular song genre in the early years of the Shōwa era signified not only the birth of Japan's first modern pop music industry but a fundamental paradigm shift in the cultural politics that had their origin in Meiji efforts to introduce Western music to Japan. In the face of a highly capitalized, multinational culture industry, Japan's cultural elites feared that the power they had wielded in the past as conduits of Western civilization would be profoundly compromised by the apparent advent of the era of the masses. Not only did the new inhabitants of modern, urban Japan seem less responsive to their guidance, but members of their own rank began to seem equally susceptible to the allures of the new cultural order.

It is important to note, however, that many of the concerns regarding the perceived effects of the commodification and industrialization of music as expressed by the Japanese critics of "Tokyo March" and its successors were also found elsewhere in the world during the same historical period. Perhaps the best known arguments are found in the early works of Theodor Adorno (1903–1969), who is best remembered as one of the key figures based at the Institute for Social Research at Frankfurt's Goethe University, along with Max Horkheimer (1895–1973) and Walter Benjamin (1892–1940), whose foundational works in critical theory have collectively come to be known as the Frankfurt School. In the inaugural 1932 issue of the institute's journal, *Zeitschrift für Sozialforschung* (*Journal for Social Research*), Adorno opened his essay "On the Social Situation of Music" with the following observation: "No matter where music is heard today, it sketches in the clearest possible lines the contradictions and flaws which cut through present-day society; at the same time, music is separated from this same society by the deepest of all flaws produced by this society itself."[100] According to Adorno, that flaw was, as one might anticipate from the Marxist reference to alienation, a society that was dominated by capitalism—a world in which the societal "role of music" has been relegated to "exclusively that of a commodity" and "the techniques of radio and sound film, in the hands of powerful monopolies and in unlimited control over the total capitalistic propaganda machine, have taken possession of even the innermost cell of musical practices of domestic music making." While Adorno conceded the possibility that it may yet be possible for music to "express . . . the exigency of the social condition and to call for change through the coded language of suffering," most forms of music, as they existed, had been fully subsumed under their own commodity character.[101]

In his 1941 essay "On Popular Music," Adorno went further to suggest that, in the end, music was far from the only thing that was changed through this process: "In our present society the masses themselves are kneaded by the same mode of production as the articraft material foisted upon them. The customers of musical entertainment are themselves objects or, indeed, products of the same mechanisms which determine the production of popular music. . . . They want standardized goods and pseudo-individualization, because their leisure is an escape from work and at the same time is molded after those psychological attitudes to which their workaday world exclusively habituates them."[102] In other words, just as music-as-commodity reflects the capitalist domination of music and other forms of art, the consumer demand for such music ultimately arises from the ways in which individual lives have come to be standardized within the same political economy.

Notably, Adorno also saw this process as having the effect of fundamentally undermining the position of would-be critics of such music: "To dislike the song is no longer an expression of subjective taste but rather a rebellion against the wisdom of a public utility and a disagreement with the millions of people who are assumed to support what the agencies are giving them. Resistance is regarded as the mark of bad citizenship, as inability to have fun, as highbrow insincerity, for what normal person can set himself against such normal music?"[103] Adorno went on to argue that, instead of confronting how the music they consume reflects the very ways in which they themselves are "manipulated" and placed in a state of "dependence," consumers "turn their hatred rather on those who point to their dependence than on those who tie their bonds." In such a world, he lamented, "the freedom of taste is hailed as supreme."

However, in "What National Socialism Has Done to the Arts," a 1945 lecture he presented to Columbia University's Sociology Department, Adorno suggested that such dominance of popular music was not merely the result of recent technological advances as seen in the rise of radio or the recording industry but that of a more long-term process that he identified as the "decultivation of the German middle classes," which had been brought on by the gradual transformation of music, and art in general, into "consumer goods." Works of art "are, and were long before the rise of Fascism, in a certain way 'on exhibition,' things to looks at, maybe to admire, maybe to enjoy, perhaps even emotional stimuli, but they became within the general consciousness of the consuming audiences, more or less deprived of any intrinsic and compelling meaning of their own."[104] What resulted was not merely the loss of musical knowledge or the "increasing aloofness of artistic products from the empirical life of society," but "the neutralization of culture in general and of the arts in particular"—a condition that, according to Adorno, amounted to the death of "German humanism" that had served as "the most substantial counter-tendency against violent nationalism."[105] In other words, it was what Adorno saw as the long-term decline of German middle-class culture, rather than works favored by the Nazis such as those of Richard Wagner, that had done most to lay the foundation to transform what was "Beethoven's own people, into Hitler's own people."

Juxtaposing Adorno's discussion of popular music with that of his Japanese contemporaries highlights several important commonalities that bind them together as modernist critics. Adorno's concern about the consequences of what he saw as the relentless commodification of music was clearly shared by many of the Japanese critics, for whom the technological and economic forces behind the rise of popular songs were just as disconcerting. As the literature scholar Michael Bourdaghs points out in regard to Adorno's critique of jazz, many of them also shared Adorno's gendered characterization of mass culture as a "form of castration" of the male "rational ego."[106] Most importantly, all Japanese critics discussed here ultimately took for granted, as Adorno did, the "normative preeminence of one musical tradition over others," namely Western art music.[107] As such, they are susceptible to the same critique that Adorno has rightly faced regarding the fundamental bias and narrowness inherent in his vision of what counts as "good" (i.e., liberating) music. At the same time, it is also important to keep in mind one major distinction between Adorno and the Japanese critics in regard to their stance toward the state. Whereas Adorno's work during this period was increasingly, and understandably, grounded on his concern about the rise of fascism and state power, most of the Japanese critics discussed here exhibited a far more ambiguous stance, even as Japan, starting with the invasion of Manchuria in 1931, entered war-footing years ahead of Germany. In such a context, many of them would in fact prove to be more than happy to engage with the state in the hope of channeling its power toward their priorities. While it was not central to the immediate debates surrounding popular songs, their increasing prominence as a mass culture phenomenon, along with growing political tensions at home and abroad, would ultimately prompt the state to make a direct intervention in Japanese musical culture once again.

2

The State as Critic
and Consumer

On the morning of March 6, 1934, nearly ten thousand people, mostly women, gathered at the Yasukuni Shrine in downtown Tokyo to celebrate the second Women's Patriotic Festival, hosted by the Patriotic Women's Association in honor of the Empress's Birthday (Chikyūsetsu). After conducting group worship and other patriotic rituals at the shrine dedicated to imperial Japan's war dead, the gathered crowd marched onto the Imperial Palace Frontal Plaza, led by the "stirring band" of the military reservist association and a group of women on horseback.[1] Placed under the control of the Imperial Household Ministry during the construction of the palace in the Meiji period, the plaza was gradually transformed during the first decades of the twentieth century into a highly ritualized space that hosted numerous civic rites, including military victory parades and celebrations of imperial birthdays and weddings. On the most important occasions in which the emperor himself appeared, oftentimes on the Double Bridge (Nijūbashi) that connected the plaza to the palace, the plaza became the site in which the gathered crowd recognized themselves not only as members of the Japanese nation but also as a people that were truly "at one with the sovereign" (*kunmin ittai*), to quote a common nationalist slogan.[2] The signifi-

あたら報國行進隊
警官に蹴散さる
『團扇太皷は不敬だ！』と
二重橋前で檢束騷ぎ

受難の報國行進

Yomiuri article describing the confrontation between Nipponzan Myōhōji members and the police at the Imperial Palace Frontal Plaza, March 6, 1934 (courtesy of the National Diet Library).

cance of the plaza only increased with the general rise of patriotic movements since the Japanese invasion of Manchuria starting in 1931, designated by the state as the "Manchurian Incident," making it a natural choice for the organizers of the Women's Patriotic Festival.

Toward the back of the marching crowd, however, was a group of roughly sixty members of the Nipponzan Myōhōji, a group of lay and monastic Buddhists of the Nichiren sect. Moments after they entered the grounds of Palace Plaza, they reportedly clashed with a group of policemen, which led to scuffles and arrests. The March 7 edition of *Yomiuri shimbun* reported on this incident, complete a photograph of the scene of arrest and a sensational headline: "For Shame, Patriotic Marchers Driven Away by Police: Commotion of Arrest in Front of the Double Bridge and Fan Drums Accused of Lèse-majesté." The *Yomiuri* article vividly described the incident with clear sympathy toward the marchers:

> The sixty-odd group of monks, nuns, and lay members, who marched at the end of the great procession, beat their fan drums with the enthusiasm typical of that sect and chanted the Lotus Sutra as an expression of their sincere celebration [of the Empress's Birthday]. Suddenly, policemen repeatedly yelled at them, "Stop the drums! Stop!" . . . However, given that the military reservists' band was loudly beating its own drum in high spirits, [the Myōhōji group] refused to stop [beating theirs], claiming, "Drum beating is our expression of sincerity." Their disobedience angered the policemen who proceeded to charge at them, beating, kicking, and punching the marchers regardless of whether they were women, lay people or nuns. [One policeman] even picked a nun up on his shoulder and threw her down on the concrete pavement. No thanks to such misguided valor [on the part of the police], the sacred feeling of celebration in front of the palace was completely ruined.[3]

The fan drum (*uchiwa daiko*) in question is the signature instrument of the Nichiren sect that has been described by the musicologist William Malm as being so loud that there is "little chance of drowsing during a Nichiren service."[4] The *Yomiuri* article further reported that several members of the sect were arrested and taken to the Marunouchi police station. This led the remaining members to mob the police station and perform another round of drum beating and sutra chanting there, after which all but one of the arrested were released. This was not, in fact, the first time that members of the Myōhōji sect had had a run-in with the law. The group's founder, Fujii Nichidatsu (1885–1985) was arrested in 1924 for approaching an imperial compound where the frequently ill Taishō emperor was resting.[5] While Nichiren Buddhism is a centuries-old indigenous sect that traced its roots to a thirteenth-century Japanese priest, Nipponzan Myōhōji was a modern group that started with Fujii's missionary activities in northern China during the Taishō period. As such, they may well have attracted the attention of the Home Ministry, which kept a watchful eye on various "new religions" that were deemed to be potentially seditious.[6]

Nonetheless, the odd spectacle at the Palace Plaza may well have sunk into obscurity after the commotions of the day died down if not for the fact that the *Yomiuri* article was picked up by Katō Chisei (1873–1947), a member of the Diet, who highlighted the incident in a House of Representatives committee meeting on March 22. Katō, a member of the Friends of the Constitutional Government Party, used the meeting to directly question the home minister, Yamamoto Tatsuo (1856–1947), who was, among other things, responsible for policing. Before the meeting, Katō had submitted a list of questions to the minister in which he criticized the police action not only for its violence but also as a violation of religious freedom. In the actual Diet session, however, Katō spent most of the time criticizing one line in the official response from the home minister, which justified the police by stating that it was a standing policy to prohibit the performance of musical instruments that were deemed to be "vulgar or noisy" (*zokuaku moshiku wa kensō naru*) and allow only ceremonial performances of military bands.[7] Far from being mollified by such a response, Katō demanded the home minister articulate by what standard the most sacred and important instrument in Nichiren Buddhism was deemed to be "vulgar" and "noisy." As the home minister repeatedly attempted to evade this line of questioning, Katō pursued it doggedly, going as far as suggesting that, by such a standard, the bells of the Russian Orthodox cathedral in downtown Tokyo and the drums of the Salvation Army's marching band should also be banned.[8] Coming to the heart of his critique, Katō cornered the hapless minister with the following observation: "The drum beaten by the military reservist association is a Western instrument, which only recently arrived to Japan. The drum of the Nichiren sect represents a uniquely Japanese music that had been passed down since mythical times. Because of this, this drum has been used in Shinto as well as Buddhist ceremonies. Why is such drum deemed to be inappropriate? Why is the drum of the reservist association deemed good and that of the Nichiren sect bad?"[9]

Instead of questioning the accuracy of Katō's musicological assertions, the home minister could only respond by promising to study the matter further with his subordinates. Sensing that "great disturbances might be caused [to the Diet proceedings], depending on the Home Minister's response," the committee chair adjourned the session by inviting the minister to return on a later date.[10] Apparently seeking to avoid another confrontation with Katō, the home minister sent only his representative to the committee when it met again three days later on March 25. While denying that the Home Ministry meant any disrespect to the Nichiren sect or its instrument, the representative argued, nonetheless, that the musical distinction was justified by the fact that "bands (*ongakutai*) are typically understood to perform marches (*kōshinkyoku*), which tend to help maintain the order of a procession."[11] Such reasoning failed to satisfy not only Katō but other, more prominent members of the committee, including Inukai Takeru (1896–1960), the son of the recently assassinated prime minister Inukai Tsuyoshi (1855–1932). Toward the end of the session, Inukai suggested that the Home Ministry's distinction was largely the product of an inflexible status quo that had allowed for performances by Western-style bands at the plaza but failed to account for other forms of music.[12] To this, the Home Ministry representative responded by promising to make efforts to rectify the causes of the "common complaint that the policemen were insufficiently sympathetic to the people."[13]

Within these Diet debates over the Myōhōji incident, the Japanese state was essentially accused of favoring Western music over native music. As the muddled responses from the Home Ministry officials suggested, however, it was unclear in the end if the initial police response was instigated by the official disapproval of a certain form of Japanese music, in this case the fan drum, or whether it was the result of the state's wariness of the Myōhōji as one of the newer religious movements that had a history of activism and confrontations with the authorities.[14] However, far more direct evidence that the state was, in fact, attempting a new intervention in Japan's sound culture could be found in the immediate context within which the debate took place, namely a series of Diet deliberations that was considering a bill to revise the Publication Law. Originally established in 1893, this was one of several laws that formed the basis of censorship conducted by the Japanese state since the Meiji era. As a result of the revisions that were proposed and eventually passed by the Diet in the spring of 1934, phonograph records, including records featuring popular songs, came under the censorship of the Home Ministry, which had long been at the center of the state's censorship apparatus. As we have seen, government officials largely stayed on the sidelines in the early debates surrounding popular songs, even as the state continued to support Japan's music establishment through the sponsorship of the Tokyo Music School and the gradual expansion of music curriculum within the compulsory education system. With the start of phonograph censorship, however, the state gained the power to potentially reshape the entire musical genre, starting with individual songs.

The primary impetus for establishing record censorship was seemingly a technological one, in which officials saw the increasing ubiquity of popular songs and other products of the recording industry as a signal to include audio media within a censorship regime that had hitherto focused on newspapers, journals, and other forms of publications, along with public entertainment like film and theater performances. A technological explanation of the origin of record censorship, however, leaves unaddressed the question of why particular standards—that is, hierarchies of taste and political priorities—were brought to bear in the actual implementation of censorship. To be sure, part of the answer to this question lies in the broader geopolitical context of 1930s Japan, which saw the military increasingly engaged in adventurism abroad. In response, the domestic sphere gradually mobilized and transformed into a home front that was deemed to be in a constant state of "emergency" (*hijōji*), especially after the military embarked on a full-scale invasion of Manchuria in 1931. However, a closer examination of how phonograph censorship, and that of popular songs in particular, was actually conceived and conducted suggests that the demands of wartime mobilization were not the only, or even the primary, reasons why records and songs were placed under the scrutiny of the state. The numerous writings by Ogawa Chikagorō (b. 1896), the Home Ministry official who was primarily in charge of censoring phonograph records during the period stretching from 1934 to 1942, are especially revealing of the competing priorities that were at the heart of the censor's sense of mission. In particular, these documents reveal the significant extent to which Ogawa drew on the existing debates over popular songs among music critics and other members of Japan's cultural elite in shaping his policies, even as the shadow of total war lengthened in the late 1930s. Even more striking, however, was the extent to which Ogawa's preferences and pleasures as an individual consumer seemingly influenced his stance toward popular songs in general, which ultimately proved to be notably more sympathetic toward the genre than that of many of the nonofficial critics. In that process, Ogawa presented himself as an arbiter in the ongoing controversies over popular songs by building working relationships with record company officials as well as leading figures of Japan's music establishment. Presenting himself at times in the guise of the critic and at other times as a consumer, an examination of Ogawa's career not only expands our vision of the scope of the censor's work but also the nature of the Japanese state's engagement with popular songs.

The State of Radio

Before we turn to record censorship, however, it is important to note that it was preceded by another intervention by the state concerning music within the context of the expansion of radio since the 1920s. In 1925, the same year that the mass magazine *King* was published for the first time, the Tokyo Central Broadcasting Bureau (JOAK) began broadcasting, which was, in the following year, merged with two other regional broadcasters to form a national monopoly, the Japan Broadcasting Corporation (Nihon Hōsō Kyōkai, NHK). The newly formed NHK quickly grew and by 1945 over 45 percent of Japanese households owned a radio, a penetration rate that was only surpassed by the United States, Germany, and the United Kingdom.[15] Notably, throughout the pre-1945 period, NHK not only existed as the only radio broadcaster within Japan but also remained under tight state control—a situation that did not change until commercial private broadcasting was legalized in 1951. As such, while radio broadcasting was seen as having as much potential as the recording industry to fundamentally transform how music was consumed, as was the case elsewhere in the world, the nature of NHK as a public broadcaster also created a significant opportunity for the state to intervene in this process.

As political scientist Gregory Kasza notes however, the "state" that was involved with radio broadcasting was hardly a "solitary actor with a unified will."[16] While NHK was primarily under the control of the Communications Ministry, the latter's monopoly was continuously challenged by the Home and Education Ministries, both of which claimed that certain aspects of radio came under their respective purviews. In particular, the Home Ministry attempted to lay claim over radio censorship, given its central role in censorship in general. While the Communications Ministry largely succeeded in fending off such challenges, they nonetheless forced it to be particularly sensitive and thoroughgoing in its own censorship of radio broadcasts, lest it be accused of negligence by the competing authorities. This perhaps explains why the Communications Ministry acted so quickly to ban "Tokyo March" from radio, even as the debate about popular songs was just getting under way. The context of bureaucratic competition, however, should not lead us to assume that radio programming was decided solely by considerations for such dynamics. NHK relied heavily on members of the music establishment such as Iba Takashi and Horiuchi Keizō in creating its music programming, further expanding and complicating the definition of the "state" that was involved in radio.

In fact, Horiuchi's career is especially instructive in how the expansion of the advent of new media like radio, and for that matter phonograph records, in the 1920s also opened up various fields of opportunity for a new generation of cultural critics as well as practitioners who gained new platforms from which they engaged with seemingly endlessly expanding audiences, even as observers like Iba and Nakai Masakazu connected the rise of mass media and the commercialization of culture with the breakdown of the existing cultural order. Born to a wealthy household that made a fortune by developing the popular "Asada-ame" cough drops, Horiuchi spent a comfortable childhood in downtown Tokyo, where he grew up with particular fascination for the early forms of public Western music performances that he encountered, such as the street bands (*jinta*) that roamed through Tokyo streets and the regular concerts held in the fashionable Hibiya Park near the imperial palace.[17] While Horiuchi developed his interest in Western music in a more direct and consistent manner during his primary and secondary education, it was his encounter with Ōtaguro Moto'o in 1915 that drew him into the heart of Japan's music establishment at that time. Born in 1893, Ōtaguro himself grew up in a wealthy family as the son of Ōtaguro Jūgoro, the pioneer of hydroelectric generation in Japan, and used his means to freely pursue his interest in the arts to the point of becoming one of the nation's first influential music critics. Through Ōtaguro, Horiuchi gained not only a deeper appreciation of the finer points of Western art music but also the acquaintance to other young music fans, several of whom would later become musicians and critics themselves.[18]

In September 1923, Horiuchi returned to Japan from his studies in the United States, shortly after Tokyo was ravaged by the Great Kantō Earthquake. As he put it himself, Horiuchi spent a period of time after his return to Japan "dithering," in the wake of which he definitively abandoned his pursuit of a career in engineering, which was the focus of his American education, by becoming employed as an instructor at the Tōyō Conservatory of Music in 1925.[19] While teaching subjects such as music theory and music history, Horiuchi also pursued a career as a music critic, contributing music-related

Ōtaguro (seated cross-legged in the front row), Horiuchi (seated immediately to the left of Ōtaguro), and others gathered for one of the regular home concerts held at the Ōtaguro residence (courtesy of the Archives of Modern Japanese Music, Meiji Gakuin University Library).

articles to newspapers and journals. At the same time, he also began to make appearances in radio broadcasts that had just begun in Tokyo, starting with a role as accompanist for broadcasts of the Tōyō Conservatory choir and formally joining NHK as the head of programming for Western art music the following year. By all accounts, Horiuchi flourished in his position at the heart of the new medium. From that time until his departure from NHK in 1933, Horiuchi's programming included not only broadcasts of performances by leading Japanese musicians of Western art music but also innovative attempts at popularizing opera and jazz.

Horiuchi did not limit himself just to the radio, perhaps, as he recalled in 1947, because the future of mass media remained unclear in the initial stages: "It looks funny from today's perspective, but our imagination back then could not have possibly envisioned the flourishing [of radio] today. The same could be said for phonograph records or talkies [sound films]. These provided new and interesting opportunities for work, but they also prompted anxieties about what any of them would amount to in the end."[20] Prompted apparently by this mix of curiosity and anxiety, Horiuchi involved himself in other forms of new media, including the newly expanded recording industry, talkies, and, eventually, journal publication. In hindsight, Horiuchi did not have much to worry about. In 1928, "My Blue Heaven" and the "Song of Araby," two American pop songs whose lyrics were translated by Horiuchi, were sold by Japan Columbia as two sides of a single record and became some of the first major hits for the newly formed company. The place of "My Blue Heaven" within Japanese media history was further solidified in 1931, when it featured as the theme song for Japan's first sound film, *My Neighbor's Wife and Mine* (*Madamu to nyōbō*). In fact, the melody and Horiuchi's cheerful lyrics about the joys of domestic life are both well remembered by many Japanese today, long after their American originals have been forgotten. In 1935, Horiuchi joined the Kamata studio of the Shōchiku Film Company as the head of its music department—a pioneering film studio renowned for its work on sound films as well as its luminaries including the director Ozu Yasujirō. During the next several years, Horiuchi's activity shifted toward journal publication, starting with him becoming the publisher of *Music Score Monthly* (*Gekkan gakufu*) in 1936 and that of *Music World* in 1938. When the two journals were forced to merge with another publication to form *Friend of Music* (*Ongaku no tomo*) in 1941, due in part to the wartime limitation on paper use, Horiuchi became the president of the new journal's publisher—a company that grew in the postwar era to become a household name as a major source of music-related publications in general.[21]

Starting in the middle of the 1920s then, Horiuchi Keizō not only embarked on a path that ultimately allowed him to emerge as a central figure in Japan's Western music establishment, but did so by embracing the various forms of newly emerging mass media and leveraging them to promote the aesthetic priorities of his broader artistic community to his ever-growing audience. In particular, Horiuchi's experience highlights the significant role played by radio broadcasting in the prewar era not only in launching his career in the music establishment but also in acting as a cultural gatekeeper that, in effect, worked to limit the dominance of popular songs in the Japanese soundscape. Working within the framework of state monopoly, Horiuchi and others ensured that the NHK's musical priority was the promotion of Western art music to the Japanese audience throughout the 1930s and 1940s. In line with Horiuchi's fear that even radio was not entirely immune to the popularity of popular songs, NHK kept popular music at arm's length throughout the prewar era, focusing instead, as Horiuchi put it, on "taking on the role of cultural leadership and working to elevate the tastes of the citizens."[22] Looking back at this period, Horiuchi later boasted: "We continued to play much highbrow (kōkyū) Western music despite the numerous letters we received [from listeners] who opposed its broadcast, and eventually such letters decreased."[23] Horiuchi resumed his career at NHK after the end of World War II, when he was invited to join a panel of expert contestants as a specialist in music in one of the first quiz shows to appear on the Japanese airwaves, The Fountain of Conversation (Hanashi no izumi), which was directly modeled on the American show Information Please.[24] Perhaps in response to his popularity among the listeners, NHK gave Horiuchi his own show in 1948, The Fountain of Music (Ongaku no izumi), which focused on introducing a broad range of Western art music—a program that continues to this day, long after Horiuchi's retirement in 1959.

Policing Culture

As already noted, the relationship between the state and NHK was one that was marked by ongoing intrastate competition among bureaucratic stakeholders, each of which claimed aspects of broadcasting that were deemed to be under its jurisdiction. However, Horiuchi's story further complicates this vision by revealing how NHK was also significantly dependent on the expertise of nonbureaucratic specialists and members of existing cultural establishments in its day-to-day work of producing and broadcasting a broad range of programs. In the case of music broadcasts, this also clearly presented an opportunity for entrepreneurial figures like Horiuchi and Iba not only to advance their own careers but also to promote their long-held cultural priorities within the context a promising new medium. As such, the "state" that was involved in music through radio was one that was arguably significantly more complex and multilayered than, for example, the one that had introduced Western music into the compulsory education system during the Meiji period. In such a context, it becomes increasingly difficult to clearly differentiate between the extent to which the musical priorities of NHK were ultimately the product of government directives or the aesthetic commitments of "experts" like Horiuchi. In contrast, censorship arguably presented clear-cut opportunities for a more direct intervention on the part of government officials.

As the modern Japanese state pursued its nation-building project in these decades, it successfully widened its reach into the practices of everyday life.[25] For the Japanese police, which stood at the forefront in much of this effort, the focus of activity was on the prevention of crime, rather than dealing with its aftermath. As such, their ultimate aim was to reorder the everyday lives of subjects so that they would increasingly conform to the "national order."[26] To that end, policing extended well beyond dealing with criminals to a growing concern for public mores, hygiene, commerce, and entertainment.

Placed largely within the framework of "public mores policing" (*fūzoku keisatsu*), the policing of culture in the Meiji period had extended from prostitution to theater and street performances. In the case of theater, the state not only urged theaters to focus on themes of "encouraging virtue and punishing vice" (*kanzen chōaku*) but, in 1882, established the Theater Regulation Code, which regulated the allowable number and size of theaters within its jurisdiction.[27] More important, the code also instituted mandatory precensorship of scripts as well as police surveillance of actual performances. In 1891, the state created a similar code governing street performance in general, requiring each performance to be registered with the local police, who reserved the right to halt any performance that was deemed to be harmful to public mores.

The advent of an increasingly complex and cosmopolitan lifestyle in the early twentieth century brought new challenges as well as new opportunities for the state. In particular, the rapid transformation of Tokyo after the devastation of the Great Kantō Earthquake of 1923 facilitated the flowering of an urban consumer culture that catered to the growing demands of Tokyoites, who availed themselves of a widening array of entertainment venues and services, including cafés, dance halls, and jazz music. Desires for consumer goods were, in turn, amplified and disseminated through the rapid growth of mass media including mass magazines, inexpensive publications, domestic as well as foreign films, radio, and phonograph records.[28] Among some critics, the growing consumer choice was associated with rampant materialism and capitalist excess, while the seeming Americanization of everyday life raised the specter of radical individualism and the breakdown of Japanese aesthetic and cultural values. In response, the police extended the regulations that they pioneered in relation to theater to other forms of media and entertainment, including cafés and dance halls. One of the most spectacular examples of these efforts occurred in July 1937, when the police raided cafés, movie theaters, and other entertainment centers and arrested 7,373 youths, accusing them of truancy and other forms of delinquency.[29]

It was within such a context that government officials became increasingly aware of the chorus of criticism surrounding popular songs since the late 1920s. Educators in primary and secondary schools were especially vocal in articulating their misgivings about this new form of mass entertainment. In particular, they were fearful of the moral degradation that these "plaintive, lewd, and lustful tunes" (*aichō to inranteki seiyokuteki senritsu*) allegedly caused among their students.[30] Reflecting such concern, the Ministry of Education established the Committee of Popular Culture in 1931, which was designed to discuss and combat the negative social effects of mass entertainment, including film, theater, radio, and popular songs.[31] One of the first activities of the committee was to create a list of approved phonograph records that were deemed to be suitable for popular consumption. Tanabe Hisao, a member of the committee and a musicologist, also published *How to Choose and Listen to Phonographs and Records* (*Chikuonki to rekōdo no erabikata kikikata*) in the same year, in which he argued that the Home Ministry should join the fight against popular songs through censorship.[32] Tanabe's opinion was shared by Education Ministry officials, who reportedly approached their Home Ministry counterparts in the same year to begin discussing precisely such measures.[33] It took another three years for phonograph records to formally come under state censorship when, as noted earlier, the Publications Law was revised and put into effect in May 1934. As a result, records were subjected to censorship by the Home Ministry's Criminal Affairs Bureau, which not only controlled the bulk of the government's censorship activities but also formed the core of

Japan's police apparatus as a whole. Internal reports circulated within the Home Ministry indicated that, by then, police officials were not only convinced of the importance of adding the new medium under their jurisdiction but also well aware of the significance of the popular song genre as an increasingly popular cultural phenomenon. At the end of 1935, one such report made a point of noting that the number of new records featuring popular songs produced in that year easily outnumbered that of other genres of music.[34]

It is important to note that the broader revision of the law also occurred within the context of an increasing tendency toward statism not only among police bureaucrats but also party politicians, who called for increased vigilance against radical ideas in the years following Japan's invasion of Manchuria in 1931.[35] Notably, the law included a revision to Article 26, which had originally criminalized the publication of materials that were deemed to advocate "the destruction of the existing form of government and cause disorder within the constitutional order"; the same article now also criminalized publications that were deemed to "violate the dignity of the imperial household."[36] The revised Publication Law was one of the statutes used a year later by right-wing activists and their allies in the Diet as well as the military in their sustained public persecution of leading legal theorist Minobe Tatsukichi (1873–1948), who was targeted for his advocacy of the liberal constitutional order as well as his critique of the military. In particular, Minobe's critics were incensed by his "Emperor-as-organ-theory," which posited that sovereignty resided in the state as opposed to the person of the emperor, who merely exercised power as the highest organ of the state, leading them to accuse Minobe of lèse-majesté.[37] While the inclusion of phonograph censorship in the Publication Law was likely a direct product of the increasing profile of the recording industry and popular songs within Japan's mediascape, the revision of the law as a whole also pointed to growing tensions within domestic as well as international politics.

The Record Censor at Work

One might presume that the relationship between the state and the music establishment as seen in the context of radio broadcasts would be different in the context of record censorship. On the surface, the greatest and most obvious point of difference stems from the fact that NHK *broadcasted* music, while the censor effectively *deleted* objectionable content and, in the most extreme cases, banned offending records outright. And yet, the case of "Tokyo March" and the broader musical preference of NHK in the prewar era suggests that radio played as great a role in suppressing objectionable music as the phonograph record censor, especially given the sensitivity of the Communications Ministry as well as the priorities articulated by members of the music establishment such as Iba and Horiuchi. Such commonality in the approach of the public radio broadcaster as well as the record censor toward popular music suggests further conclusions that may well be analogous to the relationship that literature scholar Jonathan Abel identifies between the archivist and the censor in his study of publication censorship in Japan during the same period: "Despite their stated institutional responsibility to remove and destroy, censors historically have collected and preserved for posterity the very material deemed dangerous to society. Conversely, despite their overt purposes of collection and preservation, archivists have historically excluded, removed, and destroyed material deemed unworthy or unwieldy."[38] Abel points out that censorship itself spurred a variety of cultural production, including publications "about, against, and in favor of censorship" written by spurned authors, defensive censors, and even those seeking to capitalize on prurient interests in the presumably titillating objects of censorship. The question, then, is to what extent the Home Ministry record censor also followed such a pattern. What might, in other words, be considered to be the cultural products of the phonograph record censorship, and to what extent was the censor conscious of this process?

Home Ministry officials started to censor phonograph records August 1, 1934, three months after the revised Publications Law was promulgated. Records were now censored according to a provision in Article 19 of the law, which stipulated that any material that "disturbed public order" or "endangered manners and morals" was liable to be banned from sale and distribution.[39] The revised law also required record companies to submit to the Home Ministry two copies of each new record three days prior to the date of release, thus placing records under a form of precensorship. In practice, the recording industry typically completed the production of new records by the second week of a given month in preparation for release on the twentieth day of the same month.[40] Consequently, records were typically submitted for censorship long before the three days required. The most direct evidence documenting how record censorship was practiced comes from sources published by none other than the Home Ministry itself, including the *Publication Police Report* (*Shuppan keisatsuhō*) and the *Publication Police Summary* (*Shuppan keisatsu gaikan*), both of which were internal reports of censorship activities and were circulated within the ministry.[41] Notably, these sources indicate that relatively few popular songs were actually banned from sale and distribution under Article 19 throughout the period the Publication Law was in effect. Between August 1934 and December 1937, only twenty records featuring popular songs were actually banned from sale. Given that 2,166 such records were submitted for censorship in 1935 alone, this is a remarkably small number.

All twenty records that were banned outright under Article 19 were prohibited for "endangering manners and morals" rather than endangering public order. The majority of these records were banned under one of two specific circumstances. The first of these emerged in 1936, when Victor's "Don't You Forget Me" ("Wasurecha iyayo") became a runaway hit after its release in March. The song featured Watanabe Hamako (1910–1999), one of the most celebrated female singers in the early to mid-Shōwa era, who ended each verse by pleading with her lover in a sugary voice, "Oh, don't forget me. Don't you forget me." While the song initially passed the censor's inspection, its growing popularity alarmed Home Ministry officials and prompted them to prohibit its public performance after May.[42] Even more problematic for these officials, however, were the numerous imitations that "Don't You Forget Me" spawned, most of which accentuated the original song's amorous tone. In the words of the Home Ministry report, these songs featured sections "resembling an actual interaction [between a man and a woman], creating an extremely lascivious sensation that brings to mind a woman's coquetry."[43] Consequently, the Home Ministry banned eight such records between June 1936 and June 1937 under Article 19, while Victor was also ordered to suspend production of the original record. Record censor Ogawa Chikagorō later recalled that, when he first examined the song in March 1936, he did not feel that anything was particularly wrong with it, "except for the very last line of each verse, which felt a little too sweet."[44] This initial impression apparently gave way to alarm as the song became a massive hit.

The second set of circumstances emerged as a direct consequence of the Second Sino-Japanese War (1937–1945), which began with skirmishes surrounding the Marco Polo Bridge near Beijing on July 7, 1937, and quickly turned into a full-scale offensive by the Japanese forces in Northern China. As the military operation escalated overseas, the government used the rhetoric of "time of national emergency" (*hijō jikyoku*) to assert greater control and demand a new sense of urgency among the inhabitants of what was increasingly seen as the home front. Almost immediately, the Home Ministry strengthened its censorship standards, beginning with newspaper coverage of the war and quickly expanding to all other forms of media, including records. As a result, six records were banned for featuring popular songs that were deemed to be "unsuitable to the current emergency situation" between September and December 1937.[45] Most of these featured songs that, while not as directly sensual as the likes of "Don't You Forget Me," were nevertheless accused of being inappropriately focused on romance in such serious times.

The ban on the twenty records featuring popular songs was not the full extent of record censorship, however, as other records were in fact banned under Article 19 in the years 1934–1937. Most of these songs were *manzai* (comic dialogue), *rakugo* (traditional comic storytelling), and other forms of speech-based entertainment. These records largely fell into two categories: 1) those that contained language and themes that were deemed to be overtly erotic; and 2) those that were seen to disturb public order by using the key institutions of the nation for comic relief, including the military, the Yasukuni Shrine, and, in one case, Prince Shōtoku, an ancient imperial prince long venerated as one of the key figures in Japanese history.[46] All together, twenty-two such records were banned from sale and distribution during this period.[47]

In the early years of record censorship, there were many other records that also came under the sanction of the Home Ministry but not under the provision of the Publication Law. These were records that were originally produced before the implementation of the new law and were regulated by Article 16 of the Public Peace Police Law. This article gave police the authority to ban public performances that were deemed to "violate public order" (*an'nei chitsujo wo midashi*) or "endanger manners and morals" (*fūzoku wo gaisu*). After August 1934, records within this category that were deemed to be harmful continued to be regulated under the Public Peace Police Law, while further production of those records was suspended. Between 1934 and 1935, 128 records in this category were banned. However, the effect that this particular provision had on the production of popular songs was negligible. As was true in the case of records that were produced after August 1934, most of these banned records did not feature popular songs, and, when they did, the producers had typically already collected as much profit as they could from the older hits. Consequently, the recording companies tended to be much more focused on producing new hits rather than reproducing old ones.

In short, outright banning of songs never emerged as the central function of popular song censorship in practice. What, instead, lay at the heart of the censor's task was what Home Ministry officials termed "consultation" (*kondan*), an extralegal system involving an ongoing contact between the censor and record producers.[48] A report in the 1936 *Publication Police Summary* expressed satisfaction with the small number of banned songs and attributed this to the "communication and cooperation" that they had established with the record companies.[49] Indeed, the record companies cooperated with the Home Ministry by discussing the viability of their new songs with the censor during the planning phase, a practice known as "internal review" (*naietsu*).[50] There are indications that this was occurring as early as September 1934.[51] From the Home Ministry's perspective, the task of the censor was not only to implement the law but also, more importantly, to give direct guidance to record companies in order to prevent them from producing songs that would eventually have to be banned.[52] There was also a clear financial incentive for record companies to cooperate, since they faced significant losses whenever songs were banned. Understandably, and as noted above, most major recording companies submitted their records for formal censorship long before the legally mandated date.[53] The outbreak of the war with China in 1937 quickly led to further intensification of this process. On August 28 that year, the home minister summoned executives from film and record companies in order to discuss how to make entertainment media adhere to the "aims of the total mobilization of the national spirit which have emerged in this state of emergency."[54] Three days later, on August 31, the director of the Criminal Affairs Bureau convened a similar meeting, this time inviting record company officials, musicians, critics, journalists, and other bureaucrats to discuss specific steps to implement changes in the production of popular songs. The discussion covered a diverse range of topics, including choice of theme in lyrics, choice of tunes, performers, methods of advertisement, and the need for further coordination between record producers and censors. As one Home Ministry official put it, all of this amounted to a demand for the record companies to shift their "singular focus on making profit" to "public service for the sake of overcoming the current emergency."[55] In an internal report written shortly after these consultation meetings, the record censor noted, with satisfaction, how very few records had proven to be problematic since the outbreak of the war.[56] This was in part due to the fact that the record companies were increasingly focused on producing songs with war-related themes, which displaced songs like "Don't You Forget Me." As one record company official recalled in the postwar period, war songs sold well in the early years of the war against China, helping to revitalize an industry that was struggling to produce new hits.[57] In other words, the change of course demanded of them by the Home Ministry coincided with their business interest.

At the same time, the day-to-day consultation process undeniably became even more thorough in the last months of 1937, as the censor came to be more consistently involved with such basic aspects of song making as the choice of words in the lyrics and the singers who were assigned to each song.[58] Maruya Yoshizō, who worked at Columbia during this period, recalled in a postwar memoir how one of his colleagues visited the censor's office almost every day to discuss ongoing projects.[59] One example of the songs that emerged out of this process was "China Nights" ("Shina no yoru"), which became a major hit after its release in 1938 and a popular souvenir among American soldiers stationed in Japan during the occupation period. Sung yet again by Watanabe Hamako, the song featured melody and lyrics that evoked sweet, exotic memories of a romantic night in China:

> China nights, China nights.
> In the harbor light, in the purple night,
> A dream-like Chinese boat emerges.
> I hear the unforgettable sound of *kokyū*.
> China nights, nights of dream.[60]

While the censor did not object to the general content of the song, Maruya was nonetheless forced to change certain parts of the original lyrics, such as "opium smoke," which became "harbor light"; and "nights of love," which became "nights of dream."

Censorship as Cultural Critique

The history of the nascent record censorship in Japan could, on the one hand, certainly be seen as being primarily characterized by the increasing intensification of both consultation and banning of records after the outbreak of the Second Sino-Japanese War in

1937. In this light, record censorship was seemingly shaped inexorably by the escalating political circumstances within and outside of Japan. For its part, the state was clearly determined to remold mass media in the context of wartime mobilization. On the other hand, it is the very centrality of the consultation system that also complicates such an understanding of record censorship that emphasizes a linear chronology of intensifying control by the state. For one thing, consultation was likely seen as preferable not only by Home Ministry officials but also by their counterparts in the recording companies, given the fact that the alternative would have left the latter without any mechanism to understand the actual standards of censorship. In fact, this was the case for the censorship of published materials as the censors abandoned the consultation system in 1927, when they could no longer keep pace with the explosive increase in the sheer volume of publications during those years.[61] As a result, authors were left guessing as to what would ultimately raise the ire of the censors and, not surprisingly, bans and reductions of books spiked from 1927 through 1936—a situation that was only somewhat mitigated when the Home Ministry invited leading authors and publishers for group meetings in the same way that it did for the film and music industries.[62] In contrast, the recording companies were able to rely on an ongoing conversation with the censor that gave them access to a more precise understanding of censorship standards as well as some room for negotiation over specific aspects of recorded materials.

However, an even more important consequence of the centrality of consultation in the censorship of popular songs was the fact that it amplified the importance of the censor, who was, after all, at the forefront of such interactions with record producers. This is especially true in the case of record censorship, which was, for all intents and purposes, conducted by a single censor for much of its existence. From 1934 to 1942, this censor was the aforementioned Ogawa Chikagorō.[63] While he worked along with a supervisor as well as two subordinates who helped with the organization of the numerous records that came into his office, Ogawa was primarily in charge of the actual task of censoring records. Notably, Ogawa defied the stereotypical image of the censor as a faceless, taciturn official. During his tenure, he wrote numerous journal articles and participated in roundtable discussions (*zadankai*) hosted by music journals. In 1941, just as Japan was heading toward open military conflict with the United States, he published a two-hundred-page monograph on the history of popular songs and censorship. In addition, he was interviewed by newspapers and journals on multiple occasions, where he described his work.[64] As already noted, relatively few popular songs faced an outright ban under the Home Ministry's censorship of phonograph records. That this did not stem from indifference on the part of the censor becomes apparent from the fact that an overwhelming majority of Ogawa's writings and media appearances were related to popular songs. In these, we see a censor who not only sought to intervene in the broader public discourse on popular songs but also expressed his appreciation for the songs that were the very objects of his censorship quite freely.

While very little is known about Ogawa's personal life, there is little indication in what is known about his life before the Home Ministry that he was destined to become a record censor. Born in Oita prefecture in 1896, Ogawa did not go directly into the government after his graduation from Senshū University in Tokyo but instead worked in other fields for about ten years, including stints at a trading company in Tokyo and the Taiwan Electric Company. In 1928, he joined the Bureau of Reconstruction, an organization established under the Home Ministry that was responsible for the ongoing reconstruction of the imperial capital in the years following the Great Kantō Earthquake. In the following year he was transferred to the ministry's Criminal Affairs Bureau. In one of the magazine-sponsored roundtable discussions in which he participated, Ogawa emphasizes the more or less coincidental nature of his appointment as a record censor: "I didn't 'understand' music but I liked it. I liked it but I had no academic knowledge of it. I understood music as sensation but not in a logical way. And then, by coincidence, it was decided that I was the one who had a musical sense (*ongakuteki kankaku*) within the Home Ministry. As I've mentioned before, this was at a time when the world of popular songs was in chaos. The question, then, was how I would bring order to it."[65] Perhaps liking music was a natural prerequisite for a job that required one to listen to hundreds of records every month. At the height of record production in the 1930s, the recording industry sometimes released over 800 new records in a given month, bringing as many as 150 records into Ogawa's office per day.[66] In another roundtable on the so-called light music (*keiongaku*), Ogawa confessed that he even grew to appreciate jazz as a form of music, after persevering through the initial shock.[67] What is important to note is not only the fact that Ogawa was most likely the only Japanese of his time who had listened to as many newly released records but also, more significantly, the fact that his selection as a record censor was not based on any formal musical education or credentials but, instead, on his appreciation of music as a lay consumer.

Ogawa's enthusiasm for recorded music is further substantiated by the entries regarding record censorship within the Home Ministry's monthly censorship report, which reveal a censor who not only increased his knowledge of music on the job, as it were, but also carved out opportunities to demonstrate his newly acquired expertise within the context of the secret reports that were only circulated within the ministry. In articles that were almost certainly authored by Ogawa between 1934 and 1935, the monthly reports on record censorship featured lists of songs, ranging from

Ogawa Chikagorō at work (courtesy of the National Diet Library).

Western art music to popular songs, that were deemed to be "particularly excellent" by the censor. These lists featured several popular songs sung by some of the most famous popular singers of the time, including Kouta Katsutarō, Shōji Tarō, Fujiyama Ichirō, and even Watanabe Hamako, whose hit "Don't You Forget Me" (1936) had the dubious distinction of becoming one of the few songs that was banned by Ogawa. Special commentaries were attached to songs that were considered to be particularly noteworthy, as was the case for "Hidden Tears" ("Himeshi namida"), a 1935 hit by Katsutarō, who had gained fame as a geisha singer. Ogawa noted, "Featuring lyrics and tune that are calm yet full of sentiment, this is a very suitable piece for Katsutarō."[68] Ogawa's lists also included in-depth discussions of recordings of Western art music that featured record reviews from leading music journals, suggesting that his enthusiasm most likely prompted him to familiarize himself with music-related publications.[69] Taken together, these lists not only demonstrate Ogawa's eclectic appreciation of music but also point to the infiltration of a consumer's pleasure into the realm of censorship. Within the pages of the monthly censorship reports, Ogawa seemingly relished the opportunities to slip into the role of a music critic. At the same time, his eclectic taste also hints at the possibility that he was not especially wedded to the cultural hierarchies we saw at work in the debates surrounding "Tokyo March."

In fact, Ogawa demonstrated an even more sophisticated appreciation of popular songs in the context of his media appearances. In 1936, Ogawa participated in his first roundtable discussion, hosted by the music journal *Music World*. In this discussion, entitled "Tendencies of Popular Songs and the Problem of Censorship," Ogawa argued that the essence of popular songs lay in the fact that they were easily accessible to a mass audience, featuring tunes that were not placed in rigid form and, instead, maintained "softness" and common sensibility.[70] Consequently, he argued, it would be a mistake to try to insert anything solemn in their content. In his opinion, "it would be unavoidable to have some amount of sensuality in them, like jazz."[71] Ogawa declared that careful consideration of such fundamental characteristics of popular songs was indispensible in his work as a censor. Yet, almost defensively, he explained that his work as a censor necessarily reflected what he called "the opinion of the dominant forces within society."[72] While it was his personal opinion and hope that he would not have to crack down on most songs, such actions were inevitable given the relationship between "politics, government administration, and the trend of the times."[73] In fact, the tension he articulated here—between his fundamental understanding of the nature of popular songs and his role as a censor—remained a consistent feature in his writings throughout his career.

In an article written in October 1937, following the Marco Polo Bridge Incident, Ogawa reiterated the stance that he had taken since the inception of record censorship. In his belief, all popular songs emerged as a reflection of the social realities of the time of its birth and, in particular, the sentiment of the masses.[74] Consequently, it was natural for songs to reflect the times of decadence as well as discipline. His policy had been to accept such natural tendencies of popular songs as much as possible, while simultaneously working gradually to improve their quality. In other words, while it was his ultimate aim to "elevate the tastes of the masses," he had to allow for some amount of low taste if he was to preserve the natural characteristics of popular songs. Almost defiantly, he acknowledged that such a policy would not lead to the production of songs that would please or match the tastes of the educated social elites of his time. Given the recent political developments, however, he admitted that such a policy was no longer entirely viable and that it was necessary to base the standard of censorship on a "political consideration" instead of the natural characteristics of the songs. According to him, the state of national emergency now required "popular songs that could be sung by anyone, anywhere, and at any time."[75] In other words, the home front required what he later called "public popular songs" (*kōteki ryūkōka*) that positively motivated the masses as they were mobilized in the war effort.[76] Nonetheless, Ogawa closed the article by suggesting that, even in time of war, "human sentiments, melancholy, and even love" could continue to exist as themes in popular songs, "so long as they do not lose a sense of cleanness and wholesomeness." Rather than demanding that all popular songs become like military marches, Ogawa argued that the ideal song would continue to express realities of life "without falling into nihilistic hedonism."[77]

Ogawa reiterated the tension between the demands of national emergency and what he saw as the immutable characteristics of popular songs in the book he published in January 1941 entitled *Popular Songs and Social Currents* (*Ryūkōka to sesō*). At the first glance, the book's content resembles what one might expect from a survey of music history written by contemporary music critics and scholars, with many of the pages devoted to narrating the history of popular music in Japan from the time of the Meiji Restoration to his own. The book even included a fifty-eight-page appendix that not only listed the titles of what were deemed to be "representative popular songs" from 1868 through 1939 but, for each entry, also included the release date, a lyric excerpt, and the names of the composer, lyricist, and recording artist. As might be expected from an account written by a censor, the book also included a discussion of the history of Ogawa's work as a record censor, along with passages that discussed popular songs as the object of the state's cultural policies. While the mixture of music history and the nature of censorship is one of the most striking features of this fascinating artifact of wartime cultural politics, it is important to note that the book was also unique for the fact that it made popular songs its central subject. During the prewar decades, very few monographs on the history of music in Japan were published, and those that were focused either on pre-Meiji musical culture or the development of Western art music in Japan since the Restoration.[78] In contrast, Ogawa's work stood out for the seriousness with which it dealt with popular songs, making it reasonable to consider the book as the culmination of Ogawa's development not only as a censor but also as a would-be music critic.

At times, *Popular Songs and Social Currents* does read like a litany of regrets regarding songs that Ogawa did not but *should have* censored in hindsight—a perception that was undoubtedly colored by an increasingly palpable transformation of Japanese society into a home front at the turn of the decade. For example, he gave a particularly lengthy explanation for why he failed to censor Watanabe Hamako's "Don't You Forget Me" before it became a hit: "Under the circumstances of that time . . . this particular song did not stand out to me when popular songs in general were naturally increasing in unhealthy elements, given the social currents. It did not strike me as being especially terrible; my only impression was that it was a popular song that featured a somewhat strange way of singing. In hindsight, I was extremely careless and I regret knowing that the crime of allowing such a song to spread widely deserves thousands of deaths (*banshi ni ataisuru*). But—and this is not an excuse—I simply thought very lightly of it at that time. The song was examined, of course, but it only caused a little bit of wry smile before it was decided that passing it would cause no harm. [A colleague] even joked that the song was amusing."[79]

While his crime of omission apparently deserved "thousands of deaths," it is noteworthy that Ogawa's defense of himself ultimately appealed to the historical context within which he made his decision. In fact, as the very title of the book indicates, the substance of Ogawa's stance toward popular songs had not changed significantly. As in his previous writings, Ogawa took care to emphasize that in every historical period popular songs reflected the social climate and the sentiments of the masses, leading him to insist that popular songs, with all of their "natural characteristics," would always be sung by the people. Toward the end of the book, Ogawa juxtaposed "public popular songs," which were meant to be promoted under the wartime regime, with the unreformed "private popular songs."[80] Ogawa argued that, despite the best efforts of educators and police officials, the former will never succeed in eliminating the latter. Consequently he suggested that, while people should be encouraged in their singing of patriotic songs in public, they should also be left alone to sing songs like "China Nights" in private.

Ogawa's rhetorical shuffle between his sympathy for what he identified as the "fundamental characteristics" of popular songs and the need to regulate their perceived negative effects remained a constant feature of his writings throughout his career, even as censorship standards were tightened steadily. This was not, however, the only evidence that suggested that Ogawa's affinity toward "private popular songs" remained remarkably consistent, even amidst the escalating climate of wartime emergency. A survey of Ogawa's writings on popular songs reveals not only his expression of sympathy for the genre but also the fact that they almost never repeated the critical tropes that emerged around "Tokyo March" and similar songs. In the end, Ogawa never censored, or for that matter even criticized, songs for being too sentimental or inappropriately traditional. Such a stance is even more remarkable when one considers the fact that the Japanese colonial authorities in Korea *did* censor popular songs for being precisely "all too old fashioned and sentimental."[81] On the one hand, such a discrepancy was clearly the product, at least in part, of a Japanese colonial discourse that identified Korean culture with a set of characteristics such as primitiveness and melancholy.[82] As such, Korean songs such as the famous

"Arirang" came to be seen as a problematic embodiment not only of backwardness but also of latent anticolonial nationalist sentiment that needed to be restrained. Colonial censors successfully solicited the cooperation of Korean intellectuals in leading movements to "eradicate decadent, evil song," who, for their part, problematized popular songs as well as some traditional genres. Using a remarkably similar set of vocabulary as many of their Japanese counterparts, leading Korean-language newspapers and journals of the 1920s and 1930s featured calls for initiatives against "decadent, melancholic, degenerate, nation-ruining" songs, to quote a 1929 editorial in the national daily *Dong-a Ilbo*, which expressed the nihilism and pessimism of a people who had been oppressed ever since the "absolutist monarchical rule" of the Yi dynasty.[83] Such instances of shared concerns among the Korean intellectual elite and the colonial censors further highlight Ogawa's distance from a similar critical discourse surrounding popular songs that had emerged in Japan.

At the same time, Ogawa's stance was undeniably a self-serving one in that it created an opportunity to amplify his position, and therefore that of the state, as arbiter of the contemporary discourse on popular songs. He recognized that many of the social and political elites of his time considered popular songs to be fundamentally problematic. In his view, public opinion in 1934 was divided between supporters of popular songs who dismissed any potential for harm and critics who seemed to "criticize for the sake of criticizing."[84] Acknowledging the limitations of the arguments of both sides, Ogawa suggested that his task as a government censor was to find a middle ground between these opinions. To that end, Ogawa also sought to build connections with Japan's music establishment throughout his tenure as the record censor, as is apparent in the first and last roundtables in which he participated in 1936 and 1942, respectively.[85] Hosted by prominent music journals, both meetings featured some of the leading practitioners as well as critics of music at that time, including Yoshida Shin (composer, 1904–1988),

Yoshimoto Akimitsu (critic, 1899–1960), Shioiri Kamesuke (critic and editor of *Music World*, 1900–1938), Nakayama Shimpei (composer, 1887–1952), Sonobe Saburō (critic, 1906–1980), and Yamane Ginji (critic, 1906–1982). In these roundtables, Ogawa called on the critics who sat with him to join him in his work by "entering into the politics" of the censorship of popular songs as social and cultural leaders.[86]

On both occasions, the critics who participated in the discussion responded positively to such calls for involvement. At least two of the participants in the last roundtable, Yamane Ginji and Sonobe Saburō, continued to be involved in the critique of popular songs well into the postwar period, suggesting that they were not merely paying lip service to wartime government rhetoric. The broad range of connections Ogawa constructed during the course of his work were also apparent in the three forewords that were included in *Popular Songs and Social Currents*, which were written by figures who represented three distinct groups within Japan's musicscape at the time: Kyōgoku Takatoshi (1900–1974), Saijō Yaso (1892–1970), and Mutō Yoichi (1880–1966). Kyōgoku was then a member of the House of Peers and in that capacity was known for his work incorporating Western art music in wartime propaganda and other domestic initiatives. Mutō was then a Columbia executive, who eventually served as the company's president and chairman in the immediate postwar years. While one is tempted to dismiss their praise for Ogawa and his book out of hand as coming from those who had a distinct interest in maintaining good relations with the author, this need not invalidate Saijō's description of Ogawa as having "the greatest understanding for the spirit of popular songs within the bureaucratic world"—a characterization that seems reasonable enough, coming as it did from the lyricist who had faced far more overtly hostile critics in the world of music.[87] Saijō's compliment was repeated by Horiuchi Keizō, who included a description of Ogawa's work in his *Fifty-Year History of Music (Ongaku gojūnenshi)*, a general survey of the history of modern Japanese musical culture that was originally published in 1942: "The Home Ministry had already begun its record censorship in 1934, with the stated goal of removing songs that were against the morals or those that were deemed to be incompatible with statism and encouraging the growth of moderate (*onken na*) music. But this was an age when there was hardly any political or ideological content in records; the only records banned in the early years of censorship fell into the category of those that threatened manners and morals. Censorship reflected the warm and gentle personality of Ogawa Chikagorō, the censor, who proceeded under the policy of preserving good morals and beautiful manners (*ryōfū bizoku*) and encouraging beautiful music. He was doing commonsensical, reasonable work."[88]

While Horiuchi's book was first published during the war, this passage comes from a chapter on wartime musical culture that was added to the second edition published in 1948.[89] By then, Japan was under Allied occupation and Home Ministry censorship had ended, leaving Horiuchi free from any need to curry favor with Ogawa. In fact, it may well have been more politically expedient to denounce the censor as part of the wartime oppression of music. However, Horiuchi's positive description of censorship under Ogawa appears less surprising when one keeps in mind the nature of the latter's work and relationship with critics. If anything, Horiuchi and his colleagues proved to be far harsher critics of popular songs and may well had preferred the censor to act more directly on their ire against certain types of music.

The State as Facilitator and Mobilizer

Ogawa was not, in fact, the only censor who ventured into the realm of cultural critique. A more notable example of this can be seen in

the career of Tachibana Takahiro (d. 1938), who started at the Tokyo
Metropolitan Police as a film censor in 1917 and eventually became
the head of a police station in Tokyo. Throughout his time as a
censor, Tachibana maintained a parallel career as a film critic,
starting in the late Meiji period.[90] During that time, Tachibana contributed articles to several film journals in which he discussed
various aspects of film and filmmaking, including discussions of
actors, technical issues in filming, and the educational merits of film.
Tachibana also hosted a film study group called the Square Table
Society (STS) at his home. The group attracted university students
in the Tokyo area, many of whom went on to become filmmakers or
critics.[91] While Tachibana did the most to cross over into the world
of film critique, another of his film censor colleagues at the Metropolitan Police, Tajima Tarō, also published a collection of journal
and newspaper articles and lecture notes, evocatively titled *Muttering
in the Darkness of the Censor's Office* (*Ken'etsu shitsu no yami ni
tsubuyaku*), in 1938. The book was a hodgepodge ranging from a
discussion of film's effect on children to a short explanation of how
animated films are made. A major theme that cuts across much of
his writing, however, is the desire to counter what he perceived to
be the public's misunderstandings regarding the work of censors.
In one article, Tajima argued that censors were "the same as sur-
geons; we don't cut indiscriminately."[92] He stated that his goal was,
instead, to make only necessary cuts while doing the utmost to
maintain the integrity of the film in a way that the changes he made
would be undetectable by the audience. While Ogawa and Tajima
never gained the same level of prominence as Tachibana in the realm
of cultural production, their writings nonetheless betrayed Japanese
censors' desire to directly intervene in the contemporary cultural
discourse, pushing censorship beyond the act of simply removing
objectionable materials.

Beyond the censors, it is also important to note that the Home Ministry at times also played the role of not only facilitating the business of the recording industry but also defending its interests. This was especially evident when the Home Ministry took the initiative in streamlining the underdeveloped and often chaotic practices surrounding copyright in the early 1930s.[93] This issue came to a head after the Copyright Law was revised to accommodate broadcasting rights in 1931, creating a conflict between NHK and the music rights holders over the terms by which the radio broadcaster would make use of recorded music. Shortly after that conflict, Wilhelm Prage (1888–1969), a German teacher living in Tokyo, began making copyright claims on behalf of European rights holders, demanding payment not only from NHK but also from the recording industry, individual musicians, sheet music publishers, and any others who were deemed to be making use of the music that Prage claimed for his clients. The outcry over his activities was such that newspapers began to refer to this development as the "Prage Whirlwind," casting it as an attack on Japan's budding musical culture. In response, the Home Ministry mediated a truce between NHK and the recording industry, which was reflected in the revised Copyright Law of 1934. Five years later, the Home Ministry revised the Copyright Law once again, this time to create the Greater Japan Music Copyright Holders' Association, which effectively brought to an end the "Prage Whirlwind" by mandating the association to take over all functions related to the collection of copyright fees.

At the other end of the decade, of course, the state sought to coordinate cultural producers in order to integrate them more directly into the war effort, as it infamously did for a broad range of social, cultural, economic, and political entities through the creation of centrally oriented umbrella organizations known as "control groups." In the case of film, an industry organization called the

Great Japan Film Association was created in 1944. While ostensibly aimed at strengthening and unifying the state's control over the film industry, it was actually established after government officials failed in their attempt to take control of the entire industry by merging major film companies into a single entity and placing it under the direct control of a government agency.[94] The association, made up of major film companies and others involved in the various stages of film production and distribution, was given sweeping authority to regulate the industry. Its tasks included the management of resources, guidance of individual projects, and precensorship. The control of an entire industry, in other words, was largely delegated to the companies that constituted it.

In the case of phonograph records, the establishment of the Japan Association of Phonograph Record Culture (JAPRC) in 1942 led at an even earlier juncture to a very similar delegation of authority to the recording companies. Like the film companies' association, its purpose was to facilitate greater state control and strengthen the record industry's cooperation with the war effort by coordinating all aspects of its operation, from song selection to product distribution. Board members included record company executives and representatives from related organizations, including the Japan Musical Culture Association, another control group set up to manage musicians.[95] Not surprisingly, several government officials also joined JAPRC as "councilors": Ogawa represented the Home Ministry, while Miyazawa Jūichi, who became a well-known music critic in the postwar period, represented the Cabinet Information Bureau. Soon after JAPRC's establishment, however, the Home Ministry delegated the additional task of inspecting product proposals submitted by record companies to the association. At this point, record companies were required to submit proposals to JAPRC prior to the recording of each song. While the Home Ministry monitored this through its representative, a JAPRC official involved in the process attributed what was effectively the delegation of the task of precensorship to the increasing shortage of personnel within the Home Ministry, which was, in turn, part of the broader shortage of manpower that plagued the Japanese war effort in the 1940s.[96] Indeed, shortly after the creation of JAPRC, Ogawa Chikagorō was transferred to head the Nara prefecture's Office of Labor Affairs.[97]

Notably, JAPRC continued its activities even after Japan's surrender to the Allies in 1945. While the Home Ministry and its censorship apparatus were dismantled by the Allied occupation forces, JAPRC continued to coordinate the music industry's efforts at recovering their production capacity, which were gravely damaged in the last years of the war. The end of Home Ministry censorship did signal the end of JAPRC's official censorship duties, but a growing coalition of mass culture critics not only revived the prewar critique of popular songs but also demanded the introduction of some form of content regulation for phonograph records in the early 1950s. The Record Industry Association of Japan, the postwar incarnation of JAPRC, responded by establishing the Record Production Standards Committee in 1955. Made up of record company officials as well as prominent music critics, the committee was given the authority, at least in theory, to examine all songs before they went on sale and, when deemed necessary, to order record companies to make changes. In other words, in the mid-1950s, some aspect of the regime of music censorship that had been developed during the war was resurrected, albeit in the name of "self-regulation" (*jishu kisei*) by the industry.

Conclusion

Both the history of the Home Ministry's cooperation with the recording industry and the postwar durability of the industry association that had its roots in wartime mobilization would not surprise students of modern Japanese history, given both the Home Ministry's historic peculiarity as a uniquely powerful ministry that both policed and collaborated with a wide range of actors in civil society and the postwar cooperation between the state and a broad range of industries in bringing about the meteoric rise of "Japan Inc." The continuing significance of state involvement in those industries and society in general, however, does not really explain why the music critics themselves continued to participate in what Ogawa called the "politics of music" long after the censor himself had disappeared from the public stage. The answer to this riddle, in the end, lies in the wartime activities of the critics and musicians themselves.

To take one example, what is just as noteworthy as Horiuchi Keizō's successful career in various new media outlets is the degree to which he, and for that matter other members of the music establishment, doggedly pursued the dream of popularizing Western art music in Japan—a goal that could in many ways be attributed to the very origins of *gakudan* (music establishment) in the Meiji period, as discussed in the Introduction. Scholars have pointed out that Horiuchi's love for Western music was severely challenged during World War II, when he wrote several scathing critiques of jazz and called for the expulsion of "Anglo-American music" from Japan, coming, as it did, from "the enemy."[98] And yet, taking such rhetoric as a sign of his rejection of the West would be a mistake. In the same article in which he attacked jazz, which was published in January 1942, Horiuchi also warned against "narrow-minded nationalists" who demanded the promotion of "domestic music" (*hōgaku*), arguing that "much of domestic music was produced by Edo culture and, given our circumstances today, should not be especially promoted." Echoing the words of Meiji-era education bureaucrats as well as contemporary critics, Horiuchi's solution was not to return Japan's musical culture to forms that were somehow untainted by the West, even at the height of domestic war fever when the Japanese military was seemingly unstoppable in its expansion from the Aleutians to the Dutch East Indies. Instead, he called for a more thoroughgoing popularization of Western art music.

If Horiuchi and other *gakudan* members had enemies in mind, they would have more likely been found among the popular songs that had gained widespread popularity since the late 1920s. As Japan moved to a war footing in the course of the 1930s, the members of the music establishment saw a genuine opportunity to overcome popular songs and broaden appreciation for what they considered to be a more refined musical culture. The dominance of the wartime rhetoric of total mobilization, "overcoming modernity," and the defeat of liberal, capitalist culture during this period all suggested the arrival of the best opportunity to challenge the growing hegemony of the recording industry over Japan's popular musical culture. Under the sponsorship of the mobilizing state, Japanese musicians and music critics sought to wage their own war starting in the 1930s—the war *for* Western music and *against* popular songs. As it turned out, this war did not end in 1945 with the collapse of the wartime state but continued into the period of Allied occupation and even beyond. It is to this long war that we now turn.

3

The Long War on Popular Song

Those who have spent extended time in Japan at some point during the postwar era would have most likely encountered vehicles on the streets known as *gaisensha,* oftentimes loosely translated into English as "sound trucks." Usually large buses or trucks painted in solid black, white, or military green and decorated with the golden chrysanthemum emblem of the imperial household as well as Japanese national and military flags, these vehicles have long been one of the favorite tools for Japan's right-wing, paramilitary activists (*uyoku*) in their efforts to spread their message and harass their political enemies.[1] In order to prevent the entrance of these vehicles, police barricades are commonly set up on the streets in downtown Tokyo districts that host foreign embassies, which can be raised at a moment's notice. As their English name suggests, however, the most striking feature of these vehicles are the massive speakers placed on top of them that blare out music and slogans at extremely high volumes.

Much of the music that comes out of these speakers is in the form of World War II–era "military songs" (*gunka*). In her study of the history and postwar manifestations of this genre in Japan, ethnomusicologist Junko Oba draws from the memory of her own childhood in Japan to describe the affect conveyed by these songs: "Although I now cherish these childhood memories, at the time I hated hearing such inconsolably sad melodies and the image of inevitable death that was depicted in the military song lyrics. They made me uneasy—even made me feel like crying. 'Is somebody going to die?' I once asked my mother, scared to hear my father and great-uncle bellowing out their favorite *gunka*, 'Dōki no sakura' ('My Comrade Cherry Blossom') down the hallway."[2] Oba's description matches many of the songs that are typically broadcasted by the sound trucks, including "Sending Off the Soldiers" ("Shussei heishi wo okuru uta," 1939). While the song's chorus seeks to spur the listener into action—"Go now, warriors, men of Japan!"—it was described by Horiuchi Keizō during the war as a "melancholic song in the minor key" which was "unprecedented for a song that was public in nature."[3] While we will shortly examine why this song stood out as "unprecedented" for Horiuchi, it is important to note at this point that Oba's and Horiuchi's descriptions of military songs largely match both lay and scholarly impressions of the wartime Japanese musicscape as being dominated by solemn, melancholy tunes that were promoted by the state. Such impressions, in turn, dovetail with the long-held understanding of wartime Japan as an aberrant period that was sandwiched between the more liberal, cosmopolitan Taishō and postwar eras—a "Dark Valley" in which cultural expressions that were deemed to be frivolous by the state were suppressed in favor of those that sufficiently conveyed the seriousness of the "national emergency."[4]

More recent historians of Japan, however, have articulated significant critiques of such a periodization by pointing to the ways in which many of the consumerist, cosmopolitan cultural trends of the 1920s continued well into the 1930s and 1940s, amidst the increasing domestic as well as global tensions created by economic depression and war. In an important overview of the fate of consumption and leisure patterns that defined the emerging middle-class lifeways during this period, Andrew Gordon points out that not only were "phenomena such as mass leisure, changes in dress or the revolution of household electronics" never completely interrupted by war, but many of these trends were "even accelerated" by it.[5] In a convincing analysis that connects the burgeoning mass media and the "war fever" that overwhelmed Japanese society in the immediate aftermath of the Manchurian Incident, Louise Young argues that media producers were "driven more directly by the opportunities for technological and commercial advance at a time when the national crisis stimulated demands for Manchurian-theme products," rather than by any coercion from the state.[6] Even as studies like these significantly complicate our understanding of wartime culture, however, discussion of Japan's wartime soundscape oftentimes appears to remain under the shadow of the "Dark Valley," typically relying on the juxtaposition of "cheery" American music and "somber or strident" Japanese military-themed music.[7] Such characterization, however, leaves unchallenged the presumption that locally produced music was not only defined by melancholy and the spirit of wartime austerity, but also that such music constituted the archetypal sound that was demanded by the state. And yet, we would do well to pay attention to Horiuchi's assertion that "Sending Off the Soldiers"—a stern and somber song if there ever was one—was, in fact, unusual for a song that was "public in nature"—a description that, not coincidentally, evokes Ogawa Chikagorō's distinction between "public" and "private" popular songs. As Oba notes in her study of military songs, wartime officials were in fact wary of war-themed popular songs "because of their often rather *memeshii* (pathetic or unmanly) tone and their negative and tragic depictions of war."[8]

How, then, did the wartime Japanese state actually seek to mobilize music and how is it that songs described as melancholy—a

description that was used predominantly to criticize popular songs—
came to define the soundscape of this period in the minds of
subsequent generations? An important clue lies in the fact that, for
Japan's musical culture, "the war," while originating in wartime
Japan, was one that ultimately lasted well into the Allied occupation period (1945–1952)—two periods that have been typically
understood more in terms of their distinctions rather than simi-
larities. While the term "wartime" has most often been used in the
Japanese historiography of this era to refer almost exclusively to
the imperial Japanese state up to the announcement of its acceptance of the Potsdam Declaration on August 15, 1945, more recent
scholarship has pointed to important continuities that existed between the Japanese regime and that of the Allied occupation that
followed it, making it instructive to consider both as fundamentally interconnected wartime regimes.[9]

This is especially true in the case of the media politics of this
period in general and censorship in particular. In the case of the
latter, the Allied occupation authorities, while officially ending
censorship by the Home Ministry, in fact continued to conduct rigorous and thoroughgoing censorship across a wide range of mass
media, including newspaper, film, and even postal mail. The key
commonality that the two wartime regimes ultimately shared in
regard to their respective relationship to music, however, was the
striking level of inconsistency and indifference demonstrated by
their officials toward a cultural form that they outwardly sought to
mobilize for their purposes, which became particularly evident in
the haphazard manner in which they sought to counter musical
forms that were officially denounced as undesirable.

Instead, the war on popular songs of the 1930s and 1940s was
largely conducted by those who saw in the wartime regimes an
opportunity to pursue an agenda that was quite external to the
stated political priorities of either the Japanese state or the Allied

occupation—namely, the promotion and popularization of Western art music among Japan's masses. This brings us back to the initial critique of popular songs that was led by members of Japan's music establishment who had, along with most of Japan's cultural elite, long been convinced of the superior status Western art music as the *true* music that ought to be popularized among their more benighted compatriots. It was the members of the same group to which the Japanese state largely delegated the wartime mobilization of music, the former seizing an unprecedented opportunity to leverage state power in order to not only promote Western art music but, in that process, counter popular songs and their capitalist might. While the spectacular reversal of Japanese military fortunes and the accompanying breakdown of domestic economic life ultimately cut the music establishment's state-sponsored war on popular songs short, the critique of these songs continued in no less of a militant vein during the occupation period. Notably, it was the critics who emerged among the resurgent ranks of leftist intellectuals and labor movements who rejuvenated the war on popular songs.

While the political rationale for these efforts underwent the obvious change from that of total war to socialist revolution, what remained remarkably consistent was the largely unquestioned status of Western art music as the universal standard for civilized, politically acceptable music. On one level, this highlights the enduring power of the geopolitical hierarchy of aesthetics, which had been adopted at the outset of Japan's modernity, and the ways in which it manifested itself even at the height of the age of mass mobilization and revolutionary fervor. At the same time, such continuity was made possible in no small part by the addition of new layers of critique against popular songs that now included their association with Japanese war efforts that had only recently been discredited. As such, both the continuity and transformation apparent in the critique of popular songs in the "long war" against them ultimately highlight the malleability of the premise, if not the object, of critique. And this malleability, perhaps more than anything else, was at the root of the postwar trope of wartime Japan's "dark" musicscape and its staying power in popular as well as scholarly imaginations.

The War for Western Music

On December 8, 1941, the day after Japan's attack on Pearl Harbor, the *Osaka Mainichi* and *Tokyo Nichinichi* newspapers announced that they were hosting a public song context for the war effort, inviting their readers to submit the lyrics for a song entitled "The Song of the Final Battle in Greater East Asia" ("Daitōa kessen no uta"). The song was released by both Columbia and Victor in March 1942, featuring some of the star singers from each company.[10] An advertisement for the Columbia version of the song prominently highlights the names of Kirishima Noboru (1914–1984) and Fujiyama Ichirō (1911–1993), the latter of whom became one of the best-known popular-song stars in the postwar period, as well as several noteworthy features of the song. Along with the song's title and its singers, the advertisement prominently lists the government ministries and other entities that supported the song's production, including the Army, Navy, and Education Ministries, the Imperial Rule Assistance Association, and the Japan Broadcasting Corporation (Nihon Hōsō Kyōkai, NHK). The song's main sponsor was the Cabinet Information Bureau (CIB), which was created in 1940 as an interministerial body that was tasked with streamlining the state's efforts in propaganda and censorship. The advertisement also includes an eye-catching and grisly slogan, "Slaughter the Americans and the British! They are our enemy!" followed by the first stanza of the song itself:

> Sounds of annihilation and shouts of victory
> Quickly rise above the Pacific Ocean.

Now is the time to overturn
Their hundred-year-long ambition to invade East Asia.
Now comes the hour of the final battle.[11]

Somewhat incongruously, one can also identify the Columbia logo, including the English name of the company, in the bottom corner of the advertisement, indicating that this was not yet considered to be inappropriate by the authorities as it would later on in the war. Musically, the song was very much an upbeat Western-style military march in the mold of the more famous "Battleship March" ("Gunkan māchi," 1900) and not surprisingly so, since both songs were composed by members of the Imperial Navy Band.

In fact, the template for a song like this was created as early as December 1937, when "Patriotic March" ("Aikoku kōshinkyoku") was released simultaneously by almost all major recording companies, a few months after the outbreak of Japan's war with the Chinese Nationalist forces. Among all the songs that were produced in wartime Japan, "Patriotic March" was the one the state was likely most heavily involved in terms of its production and promotion. As with "The Song of the Final Battle in Greater East Asia," the Cabinet Information Section (CIS), the predecessor of the CIB, hosted a public contest for the song's lyrics, promising a remarkable sum of 1,000 yen, roughly a year's income for an average white-collar household, to the winner of the contest; perhaps because of this, the context attracted nearly sixty thousand entries.[12] Judges for the contest included luminaries of Japan's literary world, including Kitahara Hakushū and Shimazaki Tōson, who also edited the contest winner's work.

While the CIS also hosted a contest for the song's music and attracted roughly ten thousand submissions, the selection committee, made up of the members of Japan's music establishment like Yamada Kōsaku and Nobutoki Kiyoshi (1887–1965), ultimately selected the

Columbia advertisement for "The Song of the Final Battle in Greater East Asia" (courtesy of the National Diet Library).

work of none other than Setoguchi Fujikichi (1868–1941), the former bandmaster of the Imperial Navy Band and the composer of the Meiji-era "Battleship March." Not surprisingly, the music for "Patriotic March" was also thoroughly within the conventions of Western military music. That this was quite intentional becomes apparent when we consider the activities of the song's impresario, Kyōgoku Takatoshi. Born into the aristocratic Kato family, Takatoshi joined another aristocratic family, that of Viscount Kyōgoku, as an adopted son-in-law in 1934.[13] After a long stint as a journalist reporting on musical culture as well as politics, Kyōgoku joined the CIS and took the lead in promoting "Patriotic March." According to a statement he made to a music journal to solicit submissions to the contests for the song's lyrics and music, what he had in mind was "a song that could be sung by the Japanese people in peacetime as well as wartime."[14] Kyōgoku also noted that the song should feature a "natural melody" that could be easily sung by "the masses," pointing to Western patriotic songs like "Rule, Britannia," "The British Grenadiers," and "Hail, Columbia" as the models for the Japanese song—the kind of songs that, in other words, so impressed the Iwakura Embassy's delegation to Boston. Not only was "Patriotic March" very much in the lineage of attempts by Japan's political and cultural elite to introduce a nation-minded musical culture into Japan, it also proved to be one of the more successful examples of such efforts, reportedly selling nearly a million copies.[15]

For the remainder of the war, Kyōgoku continued to promote "Patriotic March" and similar musical endeavors as a member of the CIS and, from 1939, of the House of Peers in the Imperial Diet. Throughout this period, Kyōgoku maintained close relationships with key figures within Japan's music establishment, including Yamada Kōsaku, Yamane Ginji, and Horiuchi Keizō.[16] What became apparent in these years was the fact that Kyōgoku represented the many members of Japan's musical establishment (*gakudan*) who felt that the war provided an unprecedented opportunity to popularize music that they considered to be superior to the commercial popular songs among all Japanese, by which they of course meant Western art music.

The *gakudan* members, on their part, articulated this vision in countless newspaper and journal articles throughout these years. In a February 1940 article published in *Music World,* Horiuchi called for the "execution of [a national] music policy," arguing that the time had come for the state to lead the effort in "fostering the social efficacy of music."[17] Later in the same year, Horiuchi argued in *Shūkan Asahi,* a weekly news magazine, that it was necessary to "suppress vulgar, lewd music" and that "we must newly re-create our music by making use of the best of the world's musical culture, along with contemporary Japanese ideology and emotion."[18] In a similar vein, Sonobe Saburō, the music critic, welcomed statements made by military officials that music ought to be considered akin to "munitions" and "provisions," seeing them as a sign that "music, which was previously considered to be mere 'amusement' . . . was now considered [by the state] to be of equal status as munitions, which are of the highest importance in Japan today."[19] At the same time, however, Sonobe criticized many of the war-themed songs that were produced before the attack on Pearl Harbor, noting that "while the lyrics of these songs contained words of patriotism and loyalty, their melodies were either age-old lascivious tunes or senti-mental ditties."[20] From his perspective, it was no longer acceptable to justify the existence of "vulgar music" by making the excuse that the masses lacked the capacity to appreciate better music; instead, the Japanese state ought to lead "based on the assumption that 'the masses are capable of responding to all good art.' "[21]

What is important to note is that, even as Japan entered into open warfare with its Anglo-American foes, the priority of Japan's music establishment was to promote the popularization of Western art music, and to the extent that the state intervened in music during this period, it was largely in support of this priority. To be sure, anti-Anglo-American rhetoric easily made its way into the writings of these critics as the war progressed. Most notoriously, Horiuchi was not above writing a scathing indictment of jazz, even as he carefully avoided mentioning the fact that he was one of the early promoters of jazz and American music in general.[22] As we saw in Chapter 2, however, it was in the same article that Horiuchi recommended "shutting out Anglo-American music" that he also warned against "narrow-minded nationalists" (*henkyō na kokusuironja*) who simply demanded the promotion of "domestic music" (*hōgaku*).[23] Using very similar terms, Sonobe warned against "a narrow nationalism (*semai kokusuishugiteki kan'nen*) that makes light of artistic works by foreigners, simply because they had not achieved mass appeal."[24] Even if works by Mozart or Beethoven had only been appreciated by a "narrow stratum" until then, Sonobe argued that "without the promotion and performance of such works, it would be impossible to enlighten and improve the musical taste [of the nation]."[25]

In the 1942 symposium "Overcoming Modernity" ("Kindai no chōkoku"), which gathered Japan's leading intellectuals to Tokyo for an interdisciplinary discussion on how they ought to conduct their own "war" against Western ideas, the composer Moroi Saburō (1903–1977) represented the *gakudan* and articulated a stance that was in line with that of Horiuchi and Sonobe. He argued that "we must first guard against any simple negation of the West."[26] Instead, Moroi suggested the following course of action: "The first step in overcoming modernity in our sense involves perceiving the essence of Western culture with our own eyes and thereby distinguishing between what of this culture must be truly adopted and what abandoned. That is to say, this involves adopting Western culture critically and systematically. Even in the field of music, there is much to put in order and yet still much to adopt."[27] At the same time, Moroi warned against advocates of indigenous music who, in his view, "ignore [the spirit of traditional Japanese music] in their excessive focus on its formal and sensual aspects."[28] As with Horiuchi and Sonobe, Moroi's belief was that the solution to creating a truly Japanese music was not to be found in the abandonment of the West and even less in an indiscriminate embrace of the traditional. As he put it, this endeavor was not about "simply modernizing *gagaku*," the traditional court music, or any other existing indigenous musical genre.[29]

To be sure, some of the most elite composers of this period, including Yamada Kōsaku, Nobutoki Kiyoshi, and even Moroi himself, actively pursued the creation of what they hoped would be a more authentically Japanese or Asian expression of art music. Nonetheless, it would be a mistake to conclude that such pursuits emerged as a result of the coercive pressure of wartime rhetoric, let alone an aversion to the Western classical tradition. Instead, they developed out of a current that was already visible in the late 1920s and throughout the 1930s, when Japanese composers sought to further authenticate Western tradition within the Japanese context by drawing inspiration from a wide range of non-Western sources, including Japanese traditional music and musical cultures within Japan's colonial empire, with some pursuing a pan-Asian aesthetic.[30]

In the end, for the musicians and critics involved in this wartime effort at mobilizing music, their chief enemy was none other than the commercial popular songs and, in particular, those that featured themes related to the war. Witness Horiuchi's hostility toward popular songs: "Since the Incident [the Second Sino-Japanese War], members of the music world have been in agreement in regard to the problems associated with songs that have taken advantage of the national emergency . . . songs that, while seemingly adapting to the emergency on the surface, actually include decadent or pessimistic content in order to cater to the mass taste for commercial purposes. Most of these make a pretense of the spirit of emergency with their lyrics, only to pursue commercialism with their melodies. Such music must be exterminated."[31] The words "pessimism" and the "decadence," along with the reference to the Edo roots of "domestic music" quoted above, clearly indict the popular songs that had dominated Japan's music market in the 1930s, namely songs that featured the "Japanesey"-sounding syncretic *yonanuki* minor scale. It was, above all, to overcome this kind of music that Horiuchi, Sonobe, Moroi, and other members of the *gakudan* sought to enlist the support of the state.

On the ground, such priorities on the part of critics were clearly reflected in the wartime state's policies regarding music education. The compulsory elementary schools were reorganized into "national schools" (*kokumin gakkō*) in 1941 for the purpose of streamlining the national education system into one that better matched the demands of the home front.[32] In particular, a key purpose of the national schools was to mold their pupils into loyal imperial subjects (*kōkokumin*). Music was included in the national school curriculum as part of the "arts" (*geinōka ongaku*), and was given the task of "beautifying the sentiments" and "fostering the morals" of the students.[33] While lip service was paid to the importance of fostering appreciation for traditional Japanese musical culture, the list of musical works recommended for use in the official teaching manual belied the overwhelming emphasis placed on Western music.[34] Of the seventy-one pieces recommended for use in teaching music appreciation, forty-one of them clearly fell into the category of Western music, fourteen of them unquestionably being works of Western art music in the Baroque, Classical, and Romantic styles. Only eleven pieces arguably fit into the category of works that fit in the mold of traditional Japanese musical, including "Spring Sea" ("Haru no umi") and "Cherry Blossoms" ("Sakura sakura"). However, even these were mostly rearranged into examples not of indigenous music but of Western musical conventions, through the addition of Western instrumentation as well as musical forms. As such, despite the explicitly nationalistic aim of these schools, the music that was taught in them did little to change the Western-centric system that had been established during the Meiji period.

The Mobilization of Music by a Tone-Deaf State

In comparison to almost all other realms of culture, Japan's music establishment enjoyed a remarkable amount of autonomy under the wartime regime, so much so that the progressive literary critic Nakajima Kenzō (1903–1979) confessed after the war that he was "extremely envious" of musicians who were seemingly able to pursue their craft with what seemed to him an astonishing level of freedom. "All they had to do," Nakajima complained, "was to play [the patriotic song] 'Going to the Sea' ('Umi yukaba') and, once they did that, they were free to perform Stravinsky or whatever else. We in literature would never have gotten away with that."[35] Yet, the repeated appeals from the members of *gakudan* for the state to take leadership in the nation's musical reform belied their acute sense that the line between autonomy and benign neglect was extremely thin. Horiuchi, for example, repeatedly complained of the incomplete and haphazard manner in which the state had approached music until then, even going as far as to declare that "Japan has yet to possess a single music hall or organization dedicated to popular entertainment that has been created under the auspices of the state or another public entity."[36] In other words, whether the state was a reliable partner remained very much an open question.

Perhaps the *gakudan* members should have expected what would ultimately prove to be the wartime state's ambivalence toward musical reform, especially in regard to the proposed "extermination" of popular songs, given Ogawa Chikagorō's repeated insistence that commercially produced songs could never be eradicated and that any attempt to do so by the state would ultimately fail. In fact, Ogawa's approach to censorship reflected the state's general pragmatism toward mass culture, as it sought to mobilize all cultural resources available to it, including popular songs. Of course, the state did have some history of sponsoring efforts that attempted to promote alternatives to commercially produced popular songs, including the effort to produce an entirely new musical genre known as "national songs" (*kokumin kayō*) in the early 1930s as well as the numerous lyric and composition contests for the production of patriotic songs along the line of "Patriotic March" and "The Song of the Final Battle in Greater East Asia," which were hosted by various government agencies and media companies.[37] However, even as such "public popular songs," as Ogawa called them, increasingly dominated the streets, airwaves, factories, and other public spaces, consumers continued to prefer songs that followed the pattern of the mainstream popular songs that had been popular through the 1930s.

A list of the best-selling records in November 1944 points to the continuing prominence of songs that were more akin to popular songs than the vigorous, military marches, including "Parting Ship" ("Wakarebune") and "Praying at Dawn" ("Akatsuki ni inoru"), both of which were hits from 1940.[38] "Parting Ship" was a plaintive tune that sang of the sadness of parting. While it is easy to imagine this parting as taking place between a deployed soldier and his family, the song itself actually makes no direct reference to the military and stays well within the conventions of similar songs that were produced earlier in the decade, most of which sang of partings between lovers. "Praying at Dawn" was the title song for a film made under the sponsorship of the army's War Horses Department; it told the story of two soldiers from a rural village who left for war with a horse while simultaneously forming a love triangle with a village girl they left behind. Despite the fact that both the film and the song were created under the auspices of the military, both retained the sentimental themes that had previously made their purely commercial counterparts so successful. In the case of the film, part of its attraction clearly came from the melodrama centering on the love triangle, while the song plaintively expressed the soldiers' longing for their loved ones back home.

The appearance of an increasing number of parodies of state-sponsored patriotic songs, produced anonymously and spread by word of mouth, also served as further signs of the limitations inherent to the state's efforts at mobilizing music. Starting in 1943, when the tide of war had clearly turned against Japan, alarmed reports by the Home Ministry's Criminal Affairs Bureau indicated that songs mocking Japan's defeat and complaining about the vicissitudes of war were spreading far and wide, from factories to schools.[39] Beyond music, similar limitations also emerged in the state's effort to mobilize other forms of arts and media, including the film industry. Throughout this period, the state allowed the film industry to remain as a commercial enterprise rather than nationalizing it, hoping to benefit from the existing fan base as well as the marketing know-how of the film companies. This decision, however, also left the state's propaganda efforts vulnerable to the influence of consumer tastes.[40] As in the case of popular songs, a survey of the most commercially successful films during 1943 and 1944 indicates the strong preference of audiences for entertainment films rather than those designed to boost morale.[41] The state was not ignorant of this trend and ultimately chose to make concessions to consumers in order to maintain the viability of an industry that it still considered necessary. Respect for the recording industry's commercial priorities also prevailed in the case of popular songs, with which the state took a pragmatic approach in order to maintain the popularity of the songs it sought to use, and avoided purging them of all undesirable elements at the risk of alienating listeners.

Ultimately, however, the pressures exerted by this concern for commercial viability was not the only thing that hampered the wartime state's efforts to mobilize music. If anything, they were doomed by what can only be characterized as the state's fundamental indifference to music as an aesthetic enterprise. More likely than not, those involved at the core of the wartime regime simply did not consider the reform of the nation's musical culture to be a priority. A telling fact that lends credence to such an interpretation can be seen in the state's stance toward jazz, which, as noted earlier, maintained its presence within Japanese society throughout much of the war, albeit oftentimes under the less problematic label of "light music" (*kei ongaku*). Also noteworthy is the fact that the ban on phonograph recordings of Anglo-American songs did not take effect until 1943, halfway into Japan's war with the Allies, by which time most Japanese were increasingly preoccupied with sheer survival. Even when the ban took place, the confusion and haphazardness that characterized the government's effort was such that it gave rise to downright comical anecdotes, including one involving the then prime minister Tōjō Hideki (1884–1948), who was surprised and angered by the inclusion of "Auld Lang Syne," better known to most Japanese then and now as "Light of the Firefly" ("Hotaru no hikari"), in the list of banned songs.[42]

A similar faux pas occurred when the editor of the music journal *Record Culture* (*Rekōdo bunka*) participated in a government gathering in early 1943 only to recognize, to his great distress, an American war song from World War I among the music that was being played there.[43] While the editor did not name the song, the song was almost certainly the Japanese cover of "Over There," which was recorded by the opera singer Fujiwara Yoshie and produced by Victor just a few years prior to this incident in 1939. While the Japanese version did not include the original refrain of the 1917 hit by George M. Cohan (1878–1942)—"The Yanks are coming! The

Yanks are coming!"—the Japanese editor was nonetheless aghast that the officials hosting the gathering had no idea where the music came from. Occurrences like these may well explain the freedom of Japan's musicians that Nakajima Kenzō so envied. While Nakajima described the state's stance toward music as "easygoing" (*nonki*), a more apt description might be that it was, quite literally, tone-deaf.[44] Such a state was not, in the end, capable of bringing about the kind of paradigm shift in the politics of mass culture that the critics of popular songs had hoped for. As Japan emerged from its defeat in August 1945, then, uncertainty reigned not only in regard to the future of Japan's musical culture but also, in particular, in regard to how the officials of Allied occupation would seek to shape music in the context of their broader plans for the country.

The Sound of Liberation?

Shōchiku Film Company's first postwar film, *Breeze (Soyokaze)*, appeared in theaters on October 11, 1945, less than two months after Japan capitulated to the Allied powers. The story of a girl who rises from obscurity to stardom in a musical revue theater, *Breeze* holds the distinction of being the first postwar film to pass the censorship of the newly arrived Allied occupation authorities. The film is best remembered, however, for its theme song called "Apple Song" ("Ringo no uta"), which became Japan's first postwar hit. Sung by Namiki Michiko (1921–2001), herself a member of the Shōchiku Revue Company, the song's carefree attitude, as seen in its opening verse, was as distinct as it could be from the pathos that had pervaded much of the military-themed popular songs that had dominated the record companies' repertoire in the last years of war:

Red apple to my lips,
Blue sky silently watching.

> The apple doesn't say a thing,
> But the apple's feeling is clear.
> The apple's lovable, lovable's the apple.[45]

Even starker, perhaps, was the contrast between the song's other-worldliness and the harsh realities that the war-weary and impoverished Japanese faced, many of whom could only dream of eating a fresh apple. Not surprisingly, the song survived this era and came to be passed on in the collective memories of subsequent postwar generations as a symbol of the hope that emerged in this period despite the challenges of everyday life.[46]

The actual circumstances in which this song became a hit, however, complicate our understanding of its significance as a symbol of hope. The original film was planned during the last months of the war as part of an effort to boost failing morale. After August 15, it was hastily converted into a musical drama and was generally panned by the critics when it arrived in theaters.[47] The national daily *Asahi shimbun,* for example, recommended that people view this film only if they "want to become nauseous" and, even then, "the first ten minutes of the film should be sufficient" to achieve that goal.[48] Noting that "it was obviously a crude product that was [remade] in the last minute," the reviewer went on to complain the film's general lackluster quality: "Not only is Namiki, the new actress, not especially attractive in either her appearance or talent, the film's cinematography is such that the face of every actress appears filthy. . . . Viewing this film gave the reporter a visceral sense of [Japan's] defeat. Even without directly touching on themes that relate to defeat, it nonetheless manages to make one experience it [all over again]." Far from being an unproblematic example of the liberation from the climate and limitations of wartime austerity, then, the film was accused by the *Asahi* reviewer of forcing the audience to relive their collective trauma, from which the country had barely even begun to recover in any meaningful way. The sensation of defeat that the reviewer so objected to became even more apparent as the popularity of the movie's theme song spawned a cynical parody:

> Red apple in a street stall
> Pale, blue face staring at it silently.
> I don't know the price of the apple,
> But I know how delicious it is.
> The apple's expensive, expensive's the apple.[49]

In a time of mass starvation and daily struggles to gather food and other necessities on the black market at severely inflated prices, the vision of a lovable apple was perhaps too cruel for some. The mixed reception of both the film and its theme song serves as a reminder not only of the enormity of destruction that the Japanese faced at the outset of the Allied occupation but also the uncertainty regarding the prospects for national reconstruction.

In the years between the outbreak of all-out war with China in 1937 and the conclusion of the occupation in 1952, the recording industry faced a series of challenges in its own recovery. The industry that emerged from the ashes of wartime destruction was a mere shell of its former self.[50] By 1945, Victor and Polydor had lost their company offices, factories, and recording studios to Allied air raids. Teichiku also lost its facilities to an earlier air raid in 1943, but it managed to rebuild some of its record production facilities in the following year. While most of Columbia's facilities escaped such destruction, the factories that survived were mostly requisitioned in the last years of the war by the government and transformed into munitions factories. These challenges were further compounded by the continued scarcity of raw materials needed for the production of records and phonographs, both of which were deemed luxury items in a 1940 law that severely limited their production.[51]

While the Allied officials under the command of General Douglas MacArthur (1880–1964), the supreme commander for the Allied powers (SCAP; the abbreviation was also used for the offices of the occupation), authorized Japanese industries to switch back to civilian production in October 1945, little else changed in their circumstances. Industrial raw materials, including shellac, remained under the control of SCAP's Economic and Scientific Section. Starting in 1947, the Japanese government adopted the "Priority Production" policy, which prioritized production in the steel and coal industries in the hope of laying the basis for growth in other fields. In the short term, however, this meant that the recording industry found itself as a low-priority producer of luxury items. Taxes on phonographs and records also remained high; the tax rate for records, for example, was set at 80 percent until it was lowered to 50 percent in 1948. Meanwhile, rapid inflation in the early years of the occupation largely ensured that relatively few Japanese would be able to afford their products.[52]

At the same time, the recording companies and more broadly those who were connected to the wartime mobilization of music seemingly faced an even more urgent threat. Immediately after MacArthur stepped onto the runway of the Atsugi air base, just south of Tokyo, on August 30, 1945, SCAP officials began their attempts at dismantling a broad range of the wartime state's policies as well as their ideological expressions in mass media, all of which were deemed to have contributed to Japanese aggression and militarism. Given the recording industry's heavy involvement in the war effort as producers of militaristic songs as well as munitions, many in the industry feared political reprisal, including Saijo Yasō. When the war had ended two weeks earlier, Saijō was still in Ibaraki prefecture, northeast of Tokyo, where he had evacuated to escape the air raids. Saijō wrote in his memoir that shortly after that day, he noticed a disturbing newspaper article that predicted that he would most likely be hanged as the creator of countless war songs.[53] In particular, the newspaper singled out his 1944 work, "Song of the Decisive Battle in the Philippines" ("Hitō kessen no uta"), which includes these lines:

> The dawn of Asia shines in the decisive battle.
> Young cherry blossoms willingly sacrifice their lives,
> Competing to blossom in the Philippines.
> Come here Nimitz, MacArthur!
> If you come, we'll send you straight down to hell![54]

While Saijō claimed that he was forced to add the unfortunate reference to the two most senior American commanders in the Pacific theater at the insistence of the army officers who oversaw the song's production, he nonetheless acknowledged that his role in the making of military songs extended well beyond this particular piece: "From 'Song of the Student Naval Aviators' ('Yokaren no uta') and 'That's Right, That's the Spirit!' ('Sōda sono iki') to the 'Song of the Decisive Battle in the Philippines,' there was almost no military song that I didn't touch, including songs that were sent into lyrics contests hosted by magazines—songs like the 'Song for Sending Off the Soldiers' and 'Song of the Yasukuni Shrine' ('Yasukunijinja no uta'). I wrote countless songs for the record company as well as magazines like *Friend of the Housewife* (*Shufu no tomo*) and others published by Kōdansha."[55]

Convinced that he would not escape the wrath of Japan's new masters, Saijō even went to a nearby dentist to fix his dentures before his anticipated arrest. In the end, however, those fears proved to be exaggerated and Saijō was not arrested by the occupation forces. He was, however, placed on a list of potential targets for the massive purge that SCAP was planning on executing in the early years of the occupation, which was aimed at removing those who

were deemed to have led the war effort from public offices and positions of influence. In all, over two hundred thousand individuals,
mostly political officials and businessmen, were purged during
the first three years of the occupation. However, Saijō once again
escaped reprisal and was ultimately removed from the list.

In fact, no one connected to Japan's music establishment or the
recording companies received any official punishment for their involvement in the war effort, including the composer Yamada Kōsaku
and music critic Horiuchi Keizō, both of whom were also initially
considered for the purge given their influential wartime positions.[56]
One of the few notable developments that constituted an attempt at
addressing the question of war guilt within the music establishment was in the form of a debate that took place between Yamada
Kōsaku and the critic Yamane Ginji in the pages of the daily *Tokyo
shimbun* in December 1945. In it, Yamane argued that Yamada,
who was arguably the most influential leader of the prewar and
wartime music establishment, ought to be considered a "war
criminal"—an argument that was perhaps somewhat understandable given Yamada's willingness to work with the wartime state
as the head of the Japan Musical Culture Association (JMCA).
However, Yamada countered this by pointing to the fact that Yamane could hardly absolve himself for wartime collaboration with
the state.[57] In the end, this debate did not widen into something
more substantive and, more generally, the question of wartime collaboration remained unanswered within the music establishment
as a whole.

Record Censorship and Radio under Allied Occupation

In contrast, some phonograph records did not escape the wrath of
the SCAP officials who replaced the Home Ministry's censor in
1945. From 1945 through 1949, SCAP officials in the Civil Cen-

sorship Detachment (CCD), with support from the Civil Information and Education Section (CI&E), established a powerful and expansive bureaucracy that oversaw all forms of media, including magazines, newspapers, private correspondence, film, and phonograph records.[58] For records, censorship was conducted by the Broadcasting Section of the Press, Pictorial, and Broadcast Division (PPB), which was the central organ of CCD. While the majority of the censorship was conducted by PPB's central office in Tokyo, CCD's district offices in Nagoya, Osaka, and Fukuoka also shared in the censorship of media outlets in their respective districts.

In a system that was, at least on the surface, more thorough than that of the Home Ministry, a record company that wished to produce a new record was first required to submit "two copies of the lyrics in both Japanese and English."[59] At this point, the censor approved, rejected, or ordered a revision of the lyrics based on the Radio Censorship Code, established to govern broadcasting under the occupation. Once approved, the record company produced a test record that was subjected to a final censorship, in which the record content was compared to the approved lyrics. In addition, CCD compiled and maintained various lists of banned and approved records throughout the duration of record censorship. The most important of these lists were the "Master Lists of Censored Phonograph Records Submitted by Firms Desiring to Produce and Distribute," which contained songs that had been approved for broadcast. These lists were actually given to NHK and distributed to its branches throughout Japan as a reference. However, the "Lists of Militaristic Phonograph Records" were not given to the Japanese broadcasters, effectively leaving them in the dark about what precisely was prohibited.[60]

Within the initial months of the occupation, CCD swiftly banned records that were deemed to express values that were antithetical to the Allied project of democratizing and demilitarizing Japan.

These not only included many military songs but also works of traditional forms of music and chants that were deemed to express "feudalistic" values like revenge and suicide, including narrative genres involving *shamisen* (three-stringed lute) such as *gidayū* and *naniwabushi*. Perhaps more surprisingly, the ban extended to seemingly innocuous modern works like "Moonlight on the Ruined Castle" ("Kōjō no tsuki"), "Eight-Mile Path over Mt. Hakone" ("Hakone hachiri"), and "China Nights," creating further challenges to the recording industry by making the boundary between what was acceptable and what was not far from unambiguous.[61] The music for both "Eight-Mile Path over Mt. Hakone" and "Moon on the Ruined Castle" was famously created during the Meiji era by Taki Rentarō, a graduate of Tokyo Music School who is, even today, revered as one of the most important Japanese composers in the early years of the development of Western art music in Japan. Taki's reputation as an early genius in the history of Japan's music establishment as well as his untimely death at the young age of twenty-three combined to give both songs the status of modern classics by the time their records were banned by SCAP. True to its title, the "Eight-Mile Path over Mt. Hakone" describes the difficult terrain of the Hakone Pass, near Mt. Fuji on the Tōkaido Highway, while the "Moon on the Ruined Castle" is a melancholic meditation on a ruined castle in northern Japan.

The lyrics for both songs harken back to Japan's premodern past, with references to samurai castles as well as Hakone's status as the location of an important barrier for the defense of the shogunal capital of Edo during the Tokugawa period. Such references constitute the only likely reason why the SCAP censors might have objected to these otherwise apolitical and more or less high-brow songs. Within a few months of the initial ban, however, censorship standards began to be relaxed in an apparent response to external pressure, as well as internal review. A notable article appeared in

Time magazine in December 1945, featuring an American report-er's critique of the ban of "Moon on the Ruined Castle," which sar-castically noted that news of the song ban "was likely to be calami-tous only among Japanese schoolgirls, who favor the special love and lavender of Kojo no Tsuki ('Moonlight on the Ruined Castle') above all other popular songs."[62] Perhaps even more disturbing, the ar-ticle went on to suggest that these actions only resulted in drawing unflattering parallels between the SCAP officials and the wartime Japanese authorities by making the Japanese wonder "whether U.S. authorities would be more successful than their generals" in their quest to ban songs that were deemed to be "too languid."

Such critique apparently stung. On April 1, 1946, a PPB officer submitted a report to his superiors recommending that the ban on "China Nights" be lifted. The report noted that the song had been banned initially "because it was 'a popular theme song of a movie of anti-Allied nature.'"[63] The report goes on to state, however, that the "words of the song are in themselves innocuous" and that "it is not believed that association of this song with a presumably objec-tionable film is sufficient to justify banning the song itself." In ad-dition, the report pointed to the *Time* article as an example of the "considerable publicity [that had] been given to the ban on this song." Major John J. Costello, the head of PPB, authorized the lifting of the ban, noting that this was the first instance of such a reversal by PPB. Within weeks, however, two additional recommendations were made to lift the ban on both "Moon on the Ruined Castle" and "Eight-Mile Path over Mt. Hakone." The report on "Moon on the Ruined Castle" described the song as "one of the most popular semi-classical Japanese songs" and suggested that "its suppression can only create the feeling among the Japanese that the American a[u]thorities have no real understanding of the purport of the lyrics."[64] On May 2, Costello authorized the lifting of the ban on both songs. His note suggested that "censorship in this case was both over-severe and over-sensitive," citing the *Time* article that criticized the original ban once again.[65]

In the end, SCAP officials' approach to music as it transpired was nowhere nearly as severe as what Saijō and others connected to the recording industry feared. Aside from the reflexive banning of "feudal" songs at the beginning of the occupation, the SCAP censor's attitude toward music was remarkably lenient. By contrast, other forms of media were censored far more strictly.[66] What emerges especially clearly from the internal reports of SCAP censors regarding the retractions of bans for songs like "Moonlight on the Ruined Castle" is the fact that, much like the wartime Japanese state, the American officials did not possess any critical grid that would have prompted them to approach music in a more systematic fashion. To the extent that they did have any opinion on the songs, they seemed to have largely settled on the assumption that they were overwhelmingly commercial and therefore essentially apolitical.

Such a perception placed the CCD censors in a position, on occasion, to even provide support for the recording industry, which faced other foes. A remarkable example of this occurred when an organization calling itself the "Chinese Young Men's Confederation" sent an ominous letter to Columbia in the summer of 1946: "A year already has passed since the surrender of Japan, yet, various phonograph records with Chinese terms are still on the market at various dealers in Kanto (Tokyo-Yokohama Area) as well as Kansai (Kyoto-Osaka Area). All of them contain the words "Shina" instead of "Chukoku" in calling [*sic*] our country. It is definitely a great insult to us Chinese. . . . We feel that you must stop the selling of the record at once. Depending upon your answer, the Chinese Young men's [*sic*] Confederation would take the matter into our own hands."[67] Columbia immediately responded by noting that "our factory has stopped manufacturing these records" and that it had ordered dealers to stop selling existing copies. In October that year, however, Columbia informed CCD of the incident, explaining that it still wanted to "continue the manufacturing and the selling of the record . . . if it is possible."[68] In a memorandum written in September, Costello had noted that, since the initial exchange with Columbia, the Chinese organization had been reorganized into another group called the Chinese Service Corps, which "enjoys a quasi-official standing" through its affiliation with the Chinese diplomatic mission in Tokyo. Nonetheless, Costello characterized the Chinese demand on Columbia as an act of "intimidation."[69]

During the following summer, Columbia sent a formal letter to CI&E, asking for permission to sell the sheet music of "China Nights" to "the Allied Personnel as a souvenir."[70] In September 1947, Costello submitted a final report to the head of CCD recommending that Columbia be authorized to produce the song and promptly received approval, with a note instructing him to "pass the song at all times."[71] In the end, both the record and sheet music of "China Nights" proved to be enormously popular among American soldiers, so much so that Saijō later noted bitterly in his memoir that the song was "stolen" by the Americans, who never bothered to pay him any royalties.[72] More importantly, the way the occupation censors placed themselves between Columbia and its Chinese critics was reminiscent of the way that the Home Ministry defended the recording industry against the "Prage Whirlwind," albeit on a smaller scale (see Chapter 2).

Under what ultimately ended up as benign neglect by SCAP as far as record censorship was concerned, the recording industry gradually took steps toward its own recovery in pace with the reconstruction of the broader Japanese economy. Within a decade, the industry recovered much of its prewar production capacity, during which it produced several notable hits. Following "Apple Song," these included "Tokyo Boogie-Woogie" (1947), "Spa Town Elegy" ("Yunomachi eregī," 1948), and "The Blue Mountain Range"

("Aoi sanmyaku," 1949). "Tokyo Boogie-Woogie" was an upbeat, swingy tune composed by Hattori Ryōichi (1907–1993) and sung by Kasagi Shizuko (1914–1985), while the other two songs highlighted the continuing popularity of two giants in the popular song world, Koga Masao and Saijō Yaso.

Notably, Allied media policies enabled the producers of popular songs to reach an unprecedented number of listeners by liberalizing the content of NHK radio broadcasts. Radio was not the most welcoming terrain for commercially produced popular songs for much of the pre-1945 era, as we have seen. Ironically, the wartime mobilization of both NHK and the recording industry did begin to force the broadcaster to include more of the latter's products in its programming, many of which were now being produced under the auspices of the military and other government entities.[73] Radio also achieved a remarkable reach in these years, as large numbers of Japanese bought receivers in order to gain information on the progress of Japan's war abroad. The SCAP officials accelerated this process by ordering NHK to "democratize" its programming almost immediately after the start of the occupation, seeking to use the broadcaster as a key asset in the democratization and demilitarization of the broader society. A major element of this initiative was the effort to reflect the "voice" of the ordinary Japanese in the broadcasts. This led to the creation of programs like *Sidewalk Interview* (*Gairoku*), which literally recorded the voices of people on the streets and famously began its broadcast in May 1946 with the question, "How do you manage to eat?"[74] Another popular program was the *The Fountain of Conversation* (*Hanashino izumi*), which, as we saw in Chapter 2, was a direct import of the American quiz show "Information Please," featuring various "experts" who would respond to queries sent in by the listeners.

More importantly, the liberalization prompted NHK to include more popular songs in its broadcasts. By 1949, its regular programming included a total of seven weekly slots solely dedicated to popular songs and another three programs that also featured them as part of their shows. While critics both within and outside the broadcaster lamented that it was becoming a significant purveyor of popular songs, NHK officials argued, "No matter how many times we poll our listeners, we always get an overwhelming demand for popular songs."[75] Indeed, among the ten most popular programs in 1949, those ranked fourth and ninth contained popular songs, competing with quiz shows, radio dramas, and *naniwabushi*. An NHK official noted, "We naturally have to put an emphasis on popular songs. . . . We can't ignore the musical level of average listeners."[76]

By far the most successful show in NHK's musical programming was *Amateur Singing Contest* (*Shirōto nodojiman*), which began in 1946. NHK invited listeners to come to the radio station to audition for the show. For the first broadcast, the nine hundred contestants who reportedly mobbed NHK were ultimately narrowed down to twenty-five singers who sang for the evening broadcast of the show.[77] The show gained even greater popularity, however, once it began to broadcast the audition process itself. As a result, listeners were now able to hear singers of all levels, often to highly comical effect. Maruyama Tetsuo (1910–1988), the producer of the show and the brother of the renowned postwar political theorist Maruyama Masao (1914–1996), guided NHK's conscious attempt to democratize music through this show. One way that Maruyama sought to achieve this was by emphasizing the amateurism of the singers who appeared on the program. While the show allowed singers to sing whatever type of music they liked, many of them chose their favorite popular song and were constantly admonished not to imitate professional singers.[78] The point of the show was not for singers to gain instant fame or a ticket into the music industry. Rather, it was considered to be more akin to a sports competition in which the contestants competed for the sake of the music alone.[79] The way in which the show presented and featured the performance of popular music provided a template for the first commercial radio stations, which began to be licensed in 1951. Free from NHK's self-imposed constraint to provide wholesome music, commercial stations aired an even larger quantity of popular songs from the outset, including shows that mimicked *Amateur Singing Contest* without the emphasis on amateurism. Either way, the popular song genre became a fundamental component of all broadcasting media by the 1950s, starting with radio, which was joined by television shortly thereafter.

The Leftist Turn in the War against Popular Song

Even before the commercial radio stations, however, there was another station that hit the Japanese airwaves almost as soon as the occupation began. This was WVTR, the U.S. Armed Forces Radio, which began broadcasting in September 1945. While it was primarily aimed at the Allied troops stationed in Japan, it soon found a following among Japanese listeners, whose access to American music had been limited at the height of the war. A 1948 article in *Free Women* (*Jiyū fujin*) exhorted readers to listen in: "We, too, should enjoy the WVTR broadcast."[80] The article listed the main musical offerings on the station's programming at that time, including "Hit Parade," featuring the top popular songs selected by an NBC poll and performed by singers like Frank Sinatra and Dinah Shore. Other shows featured jazz, classical music, and even Latin music. The breadth and quality of Western music available on this station was, not surprisingly, unmatched by NHK. Returning to his prewar role as an uninhibited promoter of Western music in general, Horiuchi Keizō was quick to extol the virtues of WVTR: "Nowadays we can always listen to the performance of

American popular music singers, thanks to the occupation forces radio. Even though the songs that are sung by Bing Crosby, Frank Sinatra, Dinah Shore, or Billie Holiday are not especially difficult, these singers have the charm to move you completely. This is a charm that is sorely lacking in Japanese singers of popular songs."[81] To Horiuchi, the songs performed by American singers were not only a welcome relief from what he saw as the stagnation of the Japanese popular music scene, but they also set a high bar for performance that cast his compatriots in far less favorable light. Recalling the time he spent in the United States as a student in the 1920s, Horiuchi argued that American performers possessed a level of "showmanship" that most Japanese did not.

Even as Horiuchi complained about Japanese performers, however, a growing number of Japanese jazz musicians were, indeed, learning such showmanship in the bars and clubs that catered to U.S. military personnel, who were stationed throughout Japan.[82] A network of establishments catering to this new clientele emerged throughout the country and eagerly employed what musicians they could find. While the sheer number of musicians required to meet the American demand allowed bands of questionable quality to find themselves performing in front of the GIs, this arrangement not only nurtured key musicians in the postwar Japanese jazz scene but also produced singers like Eri Chiemi (1937–1982) and Yukimura Izumi (b. 1937), who came to dominate the popular music scene in later years. Equally significant were the experiences of those like the jazz bassist Watanabe Shin (1927–1987), who would go on to build one of the most powerful artist-management companies in the postwar Japanese entertainment scene.

By 1949, newspapers were reporting the "massive popularity" of jazz and "cowboy songs" (*kaubōi songu*) that threatened to overtake the popularity of Koga melodies and other homegrown popular songs.[83] The national daily *Yomiuri shimbun* declared in a 1952 article that the record industry was, indeed, in a "time of transition," as companies aimed at "breaking the popular song style of the past" and "Americanizing" their offerings.[84] In reality, however, it took at least another decade for the American-style songs to gain the level of popularity that the more Japanese-style songs enjoyed. While the physical presence of the Allied forces clearly facilitated the introduction of American music to a growing number of Japanese, it did not immediately lead to a broader transformation of the popular music soundscape. Instead of innovating, Maruyama Tetsuo lamented in an article from 1948, the Japanese recording companies seemed to have gone back to the tried and true popular songs of the prewar period to restore their industry.[85] Indeed, much of what they produced indicated that this was the case. Musically, the Japanese-style tunes developed by Nakayama and perfected by Koga still held sway, despite the rise of composers like Hattori Ryōichi and his jazz-inspired pieces. Likewise, popular song lyric writing was also dominated by writers whose careers had started back in the golden days of the 1930s, chief among them being Saijō Yaso, who was joined by others like Nomura Toshio (1904–1966), Satō Hachirō (1903–1973), and Saeki Takao (1902–1981). Despite the seeming newness of songs like "Apple Song" and "Tokyo Boogie-Woogie," very little had, in fact, changed in the making of popular songs.

To the extent that it influenced Japan's popular music scene, then, media policies under the Allied occupation directly and indirectly reinforced continuity in the development of the postwar music industry, rather than causing any significant disruption. Perhaps because of popular songs' continued success after the war, their critics also reemerged quickly. Given that many of these critics had assisted the wartime efforts to mobilize music, one might expect that they would have hesitated before continuing with their oftentimes explicitly elitist critique of popular songs and mass culture in general. The NHK producer Maruyama Tetsuo was one of the few members of the wartime music establishment who directly addressed this dilemma. His 1946 article "Reflection on Wartime Music and the Music of the Future" listed numerous indictments against the *gakudan*'s collaboration with the war effort. These included the expulsion of prominent Jewish musicians from positions of leadership, control of musicians under the state-sponsored JMCA, and cooperation with the ban on what was deemed to be "enemy music."

According to Maruyama, however, their greatest failure was the "complete ineptitude" they displayed in gauging "the emotion of the masses" and in "cultivating it."[86] Maruyama blamed this fault on the Japanese musicians' traditional dependence on the political elites, which led them to ignore the masses even as they attempted to create music that would reach them. For Maruyama, the greatest example of this failure was the creation of numerous war-themed songs that he himself was deeply involved with as an official at NHK, almost all of which fell within the category of "public popular songs" in Ogawa Chikagorō's scheme. Noting that these songs mostly expressed abstract wartime platitudes like "Let's persevere" and "We will follow through," Maruyama suggested that, in the end, "they only succeeded in irritating the masses" instead of achieving the desired political goals.[87]

However, such self-criticisms of *gakudan* elitism did not lead Maruyama to embrace popular songs. Instead, he conceived the end of the war as an opportunity to chart a new course for Japan's popular musical culture: "We now face the challenge of freeing music from the economic limitations of the capitalist society and establishing its foundations within the working masses. From now on, music must eliminate its past self-righteousness and leisurely ways and be transformed into something that is truly attached to the everyday life of the masses."[88] Notably, Maruyama qualified this by saying that such a transformation need not "cater to the tastes and sensibilities of the vulgar stratum of society," but instead should "cultivate their sentiments and elevate their musical sense through enjoyment." Such would be the work of "the popular songs of the future," according to Maruyama.

Maruyama cast the end of the war not only as the moment in which music was freed from military prerogatives and bureaucratic control, but also as a historic opportunity to fundamentally change what popular songs had been in the preceding decades. Maruyama apparently saw no contradiction between renouncing his own wartime collaboration with the state and seeking to "cultivate" the masses in postwar Japan. In fact, another critic, Sonobe Saburō, faulted the wartime state precisely for failing to shape mass culture more directly: "In [wartime], the ignorance and anticultural nature of the militaristic ruling class led it to constantly pander to the tastes of the masses, rather than aiming to elevate their musical culture. They only conceived of the value of music in terms of diversion and entertainment."[89] While conveniently ignoring the fact that it was wartime rhetoric that gave rise to the hope among *gakudan* members that the state was willing to create a national policy for sweeping cultural reform, Sonobe now blamed what he saw as the continuing vulgarity of popular musical culture on the same regime—an argument that was understandable given the ambivalence of the wartime state toward popular songs.

Within this discourse, it was popular songs, and the industry that made them, that were clearly considered to have been collaborators in the war effort. As the composer Sonobe Tameyuki put it, the fact that the same "record companies who shook hands with the military clique" and the same "lyricists and composers who produced countless military songs" were now back in the business of making the same old songs went directly against the current of "free thought, constitutional reform, and democracy."[90]

Thus, largely unperturbed by their own wartime activities, the critics went about articulating features of popular songs they associated with an "old Japan" that they saw as being left behind by the democratizing reforms of postwar Japanese society. For example, in a 1946 article, "From Dark Songs to Bright Songs," Horiuchi Keizō outlined what he saw as the history of popular songs in Japan: "From the old days, melancholy has been the basis of Japanese popular songs. Since songs emerge from the realities of life, songs would naturally be sad, if life itself is sad. There was no chance for cheerful songs to emerge in a feudalistic society that took away the freedom of individuals."[91] According to Horiuchi, this had remained the state of affairs since the Meiji period, as Japanese experienced "extreme nationalism" and war. The melancholy of these songs, however, struck him as being unconstructive in the end: "The tunes of these songs are as dark as their lyrics. But this darkness is not the earnest darkness that touches the heart of human existence, like the one seen in American blues or French chanson, but something that is more escapist, merely covered by sweet sentimentality on the surface. . . . I think this reflects the honest feeling of the Japanese in the Shōwa era. While they seek happiness, darkness remains deep within them."

While suggesting that this is only to be expected during war and even in its aftermath, Horiuchi insists that things need to change: "Is has to be different from now on. Surely the Japanese have been freed from the oppressive feeling that has been over them for hundreds of years. . . . From now on, it is hoped that popular songs will change into something that cheerfully affirms life and sings of love as well as freedom." Here Horiuchi highlighted several common features of mainstream popular songs that had been produced since the 1930s, including the sentimentalism in the lyrics as well as the "dark" tunes, by which he very likely meant the frequent use of a minor *yonanuki* pentatonic scale. By suggesting that such musical and lyrical tendencies were the products of past social conditions, Horiuchi forcefully made the case for a change of musical culture, presumably along Western lines.

However, the resurgent popular song critique did exhibit significant postwar inflections. Horiuchi, Maruyama, and many of their fellow critics adopted in their critiques leftist political themes and language, including references to Japanese "feudalism" and the valorization of the "working masses" as the standard bearers of the "new Japan" and its musical culture. To be sure, critiques before 1945 also featured the association of problematic elements of popular songs with "feudal" premodernity. However, this association gained new currency within a historical context in which Japan's political left were enjoying increasing clout under the occupation. This was due, in part, to the early SCAP reforms, which encouraged unionization and the legalization of previously banned leftist parties, including the Japan Communist Party. At the same time, their influence was also due to the fact that the leftists offered what many Japanese saw as one of the most credible frameworks from which to critique the wartime and prewar society, given the history of their persecution by the state during those years.

Within such a context, music critics who explicitly identified their leftist political commitments became especially vocal both in their calls for the reform of Japanese musical culture and their critiques of popular songs. One such critic was Sonobe Saburō, who had occupied a key role in Japan's music establishment during the 1930s, along with his more famous colleagues like Horiuchi and Yamada Kōsaku. Sonobe, after all, was one of the critics who had interacted not only with Ogawa Chikagorō but also with the Japan Association of Phonograph Record Culture as a representative of the JMCA. While much of his prewar work centered on Western classical music and musical theory, he began to focus on what he called "people's music" (*minshū ongaku*) during the occupation period, publishing nearly twenty articles on the topic in newspapers and various journals in the period between 1946 and 1948.

At the heart of Sonobe's interest in popular music lay a single question: Why did the majority of Japanese, including "industrial workers, farmers, and even most of the salaried workers," seem incapable of "appreciating the superior arts of the West?"[92] Echoing the prewar Marxist debates between the Lecture Faction (*Kōza-ha*) and Labor-Farmer Faction (*Rōnō-ha*) regarding the nature of Japanese modernity and capitalism, Sonobe argued that the underlying problem lay in the continuing existence of feudal characteristics, not only within Japan's musical culture but in the very musicality of the individual Japanese. Such argument was, of course, not new in itself. Hoiruchi Keizō and, even earlier, those Meiji bureaucrats who had sought to create "national music," had also lamented that Japanese popular music was constrained by the historical legacy of what they identified as "feudalism." Nonetheless, Sonobe's analysis is notable not only for its relative sophistication but also for its single-mindedness in tying what he saw as the evils of popular songs to what he believed to be fundamentally *Japanese* elements of the nation's musical culture.

In an article published in 1947, entitled "The Path to the Popularization of Music," Sonobe pointed to the dominance of *katarimono* (speech-based arts) in Japan's musical tradition as evidence of its failure to mature into a more sophisticated art form that would be comparable to what emerged in the West.[93] Much of the music that would fall within the *katarimono* category, including narrative *shamisen* genres mentioned earlier, emerged from within the literary and theatrical arts. While its origins in literature and theatre had led to the development of a rich tradition that blurred the boundaries between artistic expressions based on speech and those based on sound, Sonobe believed that it also inhibited the emergence of a "*pure* musical tradition" in Japan that moved the listener solely on the merits of its musicality, rather than relying on the meaning imparted through words.[94] Sonobe argued that the dominance of *katarimono*, in turn, narrowed the possible range of musical expression, leaving Japanese music to be much less capable of expressing "a wide range of human emotions," unlike Western music. Sonobe attributed this fundamental limitation of Japanese music to a combination of what he understood to be Japan's feudal social structure as well as the Tokugawa policy of international isolation, which hindered the development of complex musical instruments as well as musical techniques. He bluntly concluded that musical development in Japan had never progressed beyond its own "Middle Ages."

Given this historical predicament, Sonobe argued that the deluge of Western music that had overwhelmed Japan since the Meiji period had only served to confuse most Japanese, whose own musical tradition had simply not developed to a stage that could make them capable of appreciating the new sounds they encountered.[95] According to Sonobe, the modern Japanese state ultimately failed to appreciate the need to modernize Japanese musicality, instead contenting itself with establishing a musical curriculum in schools that did little to free Japanese musical taste from the feudal past. The record companies, in turn, actively exploited this by producing the musically syncretic popular songs, which were specifically designed to appeal to the remaining feudal tendencies.[96]

However, now that the masses were "freed from the oppression of the feudalistic militarism," Sonobe saw an unprecedented opportunity to create songs that would enable the Japanese to "breathe deep the air of the new era."[97] Such songs, argued Sonobe, should be sung by individuals in communal contexts so that they would serve to develop the musicality of a greater number of Japanese. Placing Japan's musical culture within the contemporary political context, Sonobe suggested that "the music of the new era must emerge from the revolutionary situation," in which "new humans" were emerging as they "cast away all feudal practices" and recovered their "freedom as human beings."[98] While Sonobe cautioned that the new music should be careful to avoid political sloganeering or imitating the sterile seriousness of propaganda music, he nonetheless argued that such music should serve as a vanguard in the "democratic revolution" that was yet to be completed.

Conclusion

Thus, in the years immediately following Japan's defeat, members of Japan's music establishment continued their war *for* Western music and *against* popular songs by recasting themselves as proponents of democratic cultural change, couching their attacks on popular songs in terms of the broader calls for rebuilding "bright" (*akarui*), "New Japan" ("Atarashii Nippon") into a "cultural nation" (*bunka kokka*)—terms that were used by politicians, intellectuals, and others across Japanese society during the occupation. That they did so in order to maintain their prewar and wartime critique of popular songs was not, in the end, surprising or unique. The invocation of "change," "newness," and calls for "construction" within the discursive space of the immediate postwar period demonstrated profound continuities that stretched back not only to wartime but to the earlier decades of the twentieth century. As the historian John Dower put it, " 'Change,' in a word, was itself a continuity."[99]

What is perhaps more noteworthy is the fact that these arguments seemingly continued to be accepted within the broader public discourse, beyond the confines of the music establishment. On February 19, 1948, "Vox populi, vox dei" (*tensei jingo*), a serial front-page column penned by the editorial writers of the national daily *Asahi shimbun,* described the recent denunciation of musical and literary figures in the Soviet Union. The most famous individual among this group was Dmitri Shostakovich, whose works, denounced as "formalist," were banned by the Communist state. While the column did not support the purge, it nonetheless concluded with the following observation: "In contrast, the Japanese music world is a very easygoing place indeed. No matter how many disgusting popular songs are made and broadcasted ceaselessly, no one complains about it. Whether they are the producers and listeners of such songs, this is indeed a country of earless Kappa."[100] "Earless Kappa" was a reference to the 1927 satire *Kappa* written by the celebrated prewar author Akutagawa Ryunosuke, in which a man finds himself wandering into the magical world of the Kappa, mythical creatures in Japanese folklore, where the conventions of human society are turned upside down.[101] In one scene, the man attends a formal piano concert attended by the Kappa elite and featuring "a music program mostly written in German," just as it often was in Japan. However, the concert is suddenly interrupted when the police order the pianist to stop his performance. One Kappa explains to the confused human visitor: "Since the meaning of books or paintings should be clear to anyone, those things are never censored in our country. What we do have are concert bans. [This is because] no matter how much a song might be damaging to customs and morality, Kappa would not notice it, since we do not have ears."

While Akutagawa's description of this topsy-turvy world was a critique of government censorship in prewar Japan, the *Asahi* article turned it on its head to make a very different point. Three months later, *Song Stars* (*Kayō sta*), a journal for fans of popular songs, asked several public figures to discuss whether Japan really was a country of "earless Kappa." Notable critics, including Nii Itaru (1888–1951), Moroi Saburō, and Horiuchi Keizō, argued that popular songs embodied the various social malaises that plagued Japan. Insensitivity to the problems with popular songs, suggested Nii, was emblematic of the broader apathy toward many other forms of social ills.[102] The magazine also featured comments from the record industry, including the heads of the Literary Divisions from Columbia and Teichiku. Not surprisingly, they responded that popular songs merely reflected the sentiments of the mass audience and should not be subjected to moralistic judgment.[103] Critics, however, were not deterred. In the following year, Aragaki Hideo (1903–1989), a member of the *Asahi* editorial board, followed up the original column by summarizing his objection to popular songs in this way: "When I listen to those songs, I get depressed and the reconstruction of Japanese spirit seems totally impossible. Despair, melancholy, resignation, dreariness, weakness, stagnation, struggle, morass, and decadence are at their base. The words in these songs are all the same: tears, separation, silent weeping, night fog, ports, hills, deception, dream, journey—these are the nine principles of popular songs, a veritable flood of pitiful, tearful words of sentimentality."[104] Despite his hyperbole, Aragaki's list does encompass many of the common themes that appeared in the popular songs of this period. More importantly, Aragaki pointed to the broader significance of these songs he so dislikes by asking whether this is the music of a nation on an upswing or one that is destined to become "fourth-rate."[105]

The immediate postwar era, despite the ongoing paper shortage, also witnessed a publishing boom as a diverse range of Japanese demonstrated remarkable hunger for both producing and consuming words, taking advantage of the relaxed limits on the freedom of expression.[106] This is evident in the geographical diversity and breadth of the types of publications—ranging from major journals in Tokyo to the most obscure publications in provincial villages.[107] A typical example can be found in the April 1947 issue of the *New Road* (*Shindō*), published by the Culture Section of the Saeki North Village Youth League in Okayama prefecture. It contains an article on popular songs that described one member's impression of the music that could be heard on the streets: "After the war, songs like 'Apple Song' and 'Hill in a Foreign Land' ('Ikoku no oka') became popular. But when I sing them, I sense darkness lurking somewhere in these songs. The songs that become popular seem to be songs that have lost hope, reflecting the reality of defeat."[108] The writer suggests that "only when a more artistic and refined song becomes popular" will the process of a "building a hope-filled cultural Japan" move ahead.

Another writer, this one from Kagoshima in southern Kyushu, also complained about songs that were filled with "melancholy and nihilism," calling for songs that would suit the "renewed Japan."[109] An article in the *Literary Note* (*Bungaku nōto*), published by students in the Literature Club of the Yokosuka High School, took a more middle-of-the-road approach.[110] Its author, Yoshioka Shigeaki, suggested that people should not dismiss popular songs outright simply because many of them are "like the *enka* and vulgar"; people should recognize that these songs are aimed directly at the "general masses." Yoshioka notes that "as long as they [the masses] are musically ignorant, refined lyrics and tunes will never come out." The only solution, then, was to increase their musical literacy.

The greatest number of these "grassroots" critiques of popular songs came from clubs and unions located in various workplaces. These groups contained both critiques and defenses of popular songs that were very similar to those in other publications. Kawanishi Akira, a member of the National Railway Labor Union's Mihara subsection, published an article in his union's journal, the *Oak* (*Kashi*), to attack the record companies for being blinded by greed and abandoning their "cultural duties" as they produced popular songs that only catered to "reactionary mass psychology." While he acknowledges that popular songs express the "sensitivities of our age," Kawanishi also implores the masses to demand better music and thus "raise up our cultural standards."[111] Others, however, were less subtle. The inaugural issue of *Mine Workers*

(*Kōzan rodosha*), an organ of the All Japan Metal Mine Workers'
Union, carried a critique of popular songs that called on the readers
to "banish the erotic-grotesque popular songs and replace them with
our own songs!!" It continued: "Do we not have songs? No, we
must. What do we have? The melodies that we hear on the streets try
to drag us down toward decadence. Boogie-woogie stirs our hearts
and drags us down even further. Are those our songs? Not at all.
We hate them. . . . These are *eroguro* (erotic, grotesque) songs that
the ruling class created to drop us down in the abyss. We already
had fine songs of our own. Remember the 'Song of the Red Flag'
that we sang when the war ended and we felt the joy of freedom? We
have 'The Internationale.' And nowadays, we have 'From the Town,
from the Village, from the Factory' and 'Connect the World in a
Ring of Flowers.' There are many workers' songs. Let us sing our
song. Arm in arm, brother to brother. Sing and move forward."[112]
The last two songs mentioned became popular in the very early
years of the occupation when labor movements became extremely
active, organizing numerous strikes and large demonstrations in the
streets. In fact, both songs were broadcast on NHK with recordings
sold by Columbia and Victor. In the eyes of the more left-leaning
critics of popular songs, the success of these songs pointed to the
possibility that they themselves could create alternative music for
the workers.

While these critics outside the circle of the cultural establishment
in Tokyo demonstrated varying degrees of sophistication in their
writings, together they suggest that the Tokyo elite's discourse on
popular songs had a fairly wide geographic reach. What is less
certain, however, is whether or not these examples actually reflected
anything that could come close to being characterized as a broad-
based, national consensus on popular songs. Many of these opinions still came from the narrow well-educated stratum among the
Japanese of this period. In a society that was still overwhelmingly

agricultural and where, in an estimate based on the national census, the white-collar "new middle class" constituted just above 10 percent of the total population, it was highly unlikely that the critics' denunciation of "vulgar" songs represented a majority opinion.[113] If anything, the steady recovery of the recording industry and the proliferation of popular songs on the airwaves suggested otherwise. To some critics, however, the historical climate that saw the resurgence of the political left and the seemingly broad geographical research of elite cultural discourse suggested the existence of an opportunity to turn the critique of popular songs, and that of mass culture as a whole, into a broader movement. It was in the 1950s, as Japan regained its independence, that such a movement would materialize, somewhat ironically, in the name of democratizing culture.

4

Boogie-Woogie Democracy

Few singers, if any, embodied the hopes as well as the contradictions that emerged in Japan during the immediate postwar era as vividly as Kasagi Shizuko. After beginning her career in the 1920s as a dancer in the Osaka Shōchiku Girls Revue, Kasagi was already well known during the 1930s for her talent as a jazz singer, especially through her collaboration with the composer Hattori Ryōichi. An appreciative critic even crowned her the "Queen of Swing" in 1939, noting that "her swing feeling is something contemporary Japanese singers are unable to express."[1] For most Japanese of the postwar period, however, she came to be far better known as the "Queen of Boogie," thanks in large part to her best-known 1947 hit, "Tokyo Boogie-Woogie." An unabashedly upbeat dance song, "Tokyo Boogie-Woogie" contrasted sharply with both the government-sponsored marches of wartime as well the typically syncretic popular songs that remained the staple of the recording industry even after the war had ended. The song's distinct style derived in part from its unambiguously American sound, which can be heard in the energetic rhythm of the tune composed by Hattori as well as the song's lyrics:

Tokyo boogie-woogie, happy rhythm
Hearts throbbing, exciting sounds
What reverberates across the ocean: Tokyo boogie-woogie
The boogie dance is the world's dance[2]

As important as the song, however, was Kasagi's powerful singing, which emphasized her "natural voice" (*jigoe*) that was praised in the pre-1945 era as something that was seemingly impossible to replicate for an average Japanese, resembling the sound of foreign singers.[3] Buoyed by the song's popularity, Kasagi and Hattori followed up with several other "boogies," including "Jungle Boogie" (1948) and "Shopping Boogie" (1950). At the height of Kasagi's career in 1950, she and Hattori embarked on a U.S. tour that took them to Hawaii, California, and New York, which saw her sing to appreciative audiences made up mostly of Japanese Americans.

Not surprisingly, Kasagi's boogie-woogies have been enshrined in the postwar Japanese memory as an icon of social and cultural liberalization as well as the wave of Americanization that has been associated with the occupation era. In his trenchant analysis of the competing notions of freedom that were articulated by Japan's cultural producers during this period, Michael Bourdaghs examines the intersecting careers of Kasagi Shizuko, Hattori Ryōichi, and the film director Kurosawa Akira, who collaborated with the singer-composer duo in his 1948 film *Drunken Angel* (*Yoidore tenshi*). Whereas many of Kurosawa's films express an undercurrent of anxiety regarding the pitfalls of postwar consumerism—films in which "popular music defines the road not to freedom but to slavery"—Bourdaghs notes that many of Kasagi's songs not only explicitly equate freedom with the act of consumption but also suggest how such an emancipation could be gendered in significant ways.[4] Given both the sheer physicality of Kasagi's performance as well as the expression of female desires, be they sexual or material,

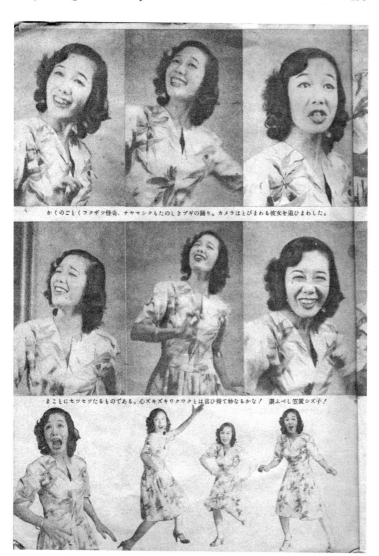

Expressions of Kasagi Shizuko performing the boogie-woogie (from *Salon* 3, no. 3 [1948]).

in many of her recordings, Kasagi's songs seemingly pointed to new opportunities for women in the postwar era to escape existing societal strictures on their behavior.

That Kasagi's boogie-woogies were emerging as symbols of newfound freedoms was not lost on many of contemporary observers, including the music critic Sonobe Saburō, who described Kasagi's performance of the song as an embodiment of a "primitive sensuality" that was being liberated following years of militaristic repression of all things sensual: "Kasagi uses every muscle to surrender her entire body to the rhythm, shaking it with abandon to squeeze out her natural voice, which is more wild than beautiful. This utterly physical performance, as if she is revealing everything to the masses, is what meets their demands completely."[5] According to Sonobe, the masses yearned for the "liberation of humanity" and the unleashing of "primitive instincts"—demands that he associated with what he saw as a growing tendency for "physical exposure" in literature and mass entertainment in general. While Sonobe acknowledged Kasagi's songs' potential to liberate the Japanese, he, like Kurosawa, was also quick to argue that such liberation was limited at best. Pointing to what he called the "Negro" (niguro) origin of boogie-woogie as a musical genre, Sonobe suggested that the songs only served to liberate "primitive instincts" in the end, which could be dangerous if it was not accompanied by "rational and scientific guidance."

Sonobe's explicit racialization of Kasagi's performance was far from accidental, given Hattori's tendency to draw on primitivism as well as Orientalism in his songs.[6] That Sonobe did so in discussing the potential dangers posed by such music, however, also reflected the increasingly turbulent cultural politics of a society that was not only beginning to be reconstructed under a foreign occupation but one that was also, as with many other parts of the world, entering into a period of intensifying political tensions that defined the Cold War era.

In this context, popular culture and media emerged as some of the key battlegrounds as competing domestic and international forces sought to shape the emerging mass society that was still in the process of recovering from wartime dislocations. It was in the 1950s, when Japan was in the process of regaining its formal independence, that popular songs and mass media in general experienced a set of political pressures of such magnitude that, by the end of the decade, most segments of the media industry were compelled to adopt formal frameworks of self-censorship, only a few years after government censorship had been completely phased out under the Allied occupation.

Not surprisingly, the overwhelming presence of America, as both a military and cultural force, loomed large over the politics of this decade in general and, in particular, over the process by which popular songs emerged as a lightning rod in its cultural politics. In this context, singers like Kasagi Shizuko, Eri Chiemi and Misora Hibari (1937–1989), all of whom started their musical careers as performers of American-style tunes, were perceived by some of their contemporaries with deep ambivalence even as they shot to stardom during this period. For other critics of popular songs, however, the songs and the industry that produced them proved to be deeply problematic not only because of their perceived role in what many identified as the "cultural colonization" of Japan but also because the genre emerged as the embodiment of the equally undesirable remnants of what they considered to be Japan's "feudal" past. In this context, the "Japanesey" syncretic tunes most famously exemplified by composers like Nakayama Shimpei and Koga Masao came under renewed criticism during the occupation era and its immediate aftermath for their allegedly reactionary characteristics.

Popular songs of this period stood out in Japan's cultural landscape for managing to so thoroughly embody what their critics saw as the problematic elements of "Americanism" as well as "feudalism" within their society. In fact, the critique of both perceived trends formed the core of the broader progressive politics of this decade, which fused nationalist anger at the ongoing presence of the American military in the Japanese archipelago with the attacks on a wide range of conservative government policies that were seen to be rolling back the more progressive reforms that were initiated in the early years of the occupation. As the sociologist Oguma Eiji has pointed out in his study of postwar Japanese politics, however, the progressive nationalism that emerged in the years surrounding the formal conclusion of the Allied occupation in 1952 embodied two significant currents of continuity with the pre-1945 era.[7] The more obvious of these was the fact that the rhetoric of postwar-era leftist nationalism—which saw its most obvious target, the United States, not only as an occupier but also as the dominant party in the U.S.-Japan alliance that was negotiated simultaneously with the latter's independence—not only displayed little shift from the wartime critique of the United States but also resurrected the wartime focus on "the nation" (*minzoku*) as the locus of identity and loyalty.

As important, however, was the continuity with the wartime state in terms of the economic and material circumstances that surrounded Japan, which, in the early 1950s, was not only a desperately poor country but also one that clung to its prewar self-image of a society that was deeply divided by social, economic, and cultural hierarchies. At the same time, it was these continuities that worked together to prompt many intellectuals of this period to attempt to overcome such hierarchies. With their renewed focus on the Japanese people as "the nation"—now relegitimized by the contemporary rise of anticolonial nationalism in Asia—thinkers like Maruyama Masao, Tsurumi Shunshuke (1922–2015), Shimizu

Ikutarō (1907–1988), and many others criticized what they saw as the ongoing isolation of Japan's Western-oriented intellectual elites from the broader society and sought to bridge that gap in order to transform Japan into a "unified and indivisible" (*tan'itsu fukabun*) nation constituted by citizens who had collectively overcome their hierarchical divisions.[8]

A notable example of this was the "Science of Thought" (Shisō no Kagaku) group that was founded by Tsurumi Shunsuke, along with his sister, the sociologist Tsurumi Kazuko (1918–2006), Maruyama, and others, in 1946. Science of Thought, which periodically published the results of collective research projects by its members, engaged with mass media and popular culture and self-consciously attempted to shed the elitism of their predecessors as they sought to foster a broad-based culture of democracy, and democratized cultures, within Japan. Another group, the Japanese Society for the Protection of Children (JSPC) was made up of a largely separate, though at times overlapping, set of intellectuals and activists who sought to support the ongoing process of democratizing Japanese culture by defending some of the most vulnerable members of society from what they saw as the vagaries of reactionary conservative politics and their cultural consequences. Both groups engaged with popular songs as a key element within Japan's cultural landscape, the former attempting to take the songs seriously as a social phenomenon while the latter sought to produce a genuine grassroots citizens' movement in critiquing popular songs and other forms of mass culture. Such attempts were complicated, however, by the fact that popular songs remained fundamentally déclassé even in the eyes of many of these would-be democratizers of Japanese culture. This revealed not only the limitations of the cultural egalitarianism of these intellectuals but also the enduring power of the very social and cultural hierarchies that they sought to overcome throughout the 1950s. Such limitations significantly undermined the progressive critique of popular songs, especially in the second half of the decade when changing political as well as economic circumstances placed increasing pressure on the Japanese left in general.

Mass Culture, Progressive Activism, and Children

In March 1952, the chamber of commerce in Yokosuka, a historic naval port south of Tokyo, commissioned the Columbia Record Company to create a song to promote tourism in the city. The chamber officials sought to highlight the city's increasingly cosmopolitan appearance as the U.S. Navy replaced the Imperial Japanese Navy as the city's political and economic core. Nomura Toshio, the lyricist who was selected for this song, was as good a choice as any. His previous works included the wartime hit "Praying at Dawn" (1940) and "Spa Town Elegy" (1948), a major postwar hit that he produced in collaboration with Koga Masao, one of the most dominant popular music composers since the 1930s. Perhaps confident of the popularity of a song produced by such an eminent lyricist, the chamber officials provided journalists with a draft of the song entitled "Yokosuka Dance: The It's-Too-Much Song" ("Yokosuka ondo tamaranbushi") even before it was officially approved by the chamber's board. The first verse of the song captures its cosmopolitan humor, dotted as it is with English loanwords transliterated into the Japanese katakana syllabary:

> *Japan* Yokosuka *wandafuru* (wonderful).
> *Biya* (beer) and *gāru* (girl), both *berinaisu* (very nice).
> On that hill where the *cherī* (cherry) blossoms bloom,
> I'd like to build myself a *suīto hōmu* (sweet home).
> It's too much! It's too much![9]

Contrary to what the chamber officials may have hoped, however, what ultimately resulted were waves of criticism, both locally and nationally, that not only forced them to abandon the original lyrics but also ultimately prompted radio broadcasters and record companies to adopt ethics codes banning "Yokosuka Dance" and similar songs. Notably, "Yokosuka Dance" caught the attention of a nascent coalition of critics, educators, teachers' unions, and mothers' groups, who would together form JSPC later that year. JSPC's preparatory committee targeted "Yokosuka Dance" as their very first public cause, and by doing so they placed the controversy within a context that went far beyond a single song or city.

Before examining the specifics reasons why JSPC targeted "Yokosuka Dance," it is worth considering the political and institutional contexts that gave birth not only to the group but also to the broader, loosely connected advocates for children's rights during this period. The years immediately following the end of World War II witnessed the emergence of a growing national concern for the welfare of children and, in particular, their plight within what was seen as a fundamentally degenerate social and cultural environment. Many Japanese across the political spectrum recognized that their society was entering into a period not only of democratization and peace but also of intense social, cultural, and moral upheaval. This anxiety found particularly strong expression in the renewed concern for the welfare of children shared by a wide range of observers including state officials, educators, and parents. In their view, children were living in an environment that threatened their healthy development and the broader project of national reconstruction. In particular, various forms of entertainment media—including popular music, film, and magazines—came under intense scrutiny, as critics sought to counter the alleged effects of "vulgar" and "decadent" entertainment.

On the one hand, such concerns clearly presented opportunities for the state to reestablish its authority over various aspects of Japanese life, including media and public welfare. As such, the government's postwar child welfare policies in many ways reflected the state's desire to "reconstruct and expand" the prewar and wartime efforts in juvenile policing, which largely focused on the prevention of delinquency.[10] On the other hand, scholarship on the emergence of various media regulations in the postwar period has pointed out that such an effort would not have been successful without the existence of alliances between the state and various groups within the civil society that called for media regulation.[11] In fact, the middle decades of the twentieth century witnessed numerous cases of collaboration between government bureaucrats and progressive middle-class activists, as members of both groups shared similar educational backgrounds as well as agendas.[12] The political reforms after 1945 increased the need for the state to solicit the cooperation of such nongovernmental allies, which, in turn, opened up new opportunities for a diverse range of civil society groups across the political spectrum to promote their agendas on the national political stage.

For many of its residents, Japan under Allied occupation was seemingly filled with evidence of society-wide exhaustion (*kyodatsu*) as well as the liberation that came with defeat.[13] On the streets and in the mass media, Japanese saw new and often disturbing images that signaled chaos as well as liberation. These included the prostitutes, known as *panpan*, who were accused of flaunting their fashionable dress, imported cosmetics, and other consumer goods as they walked hand in hand with their American clients; these women were seen as a particularly stinging example of Japan's national subservience to foreign powers. A complementary set of images was offered by the so-called *kasutori* culture, a conglomeration of erotic entertainments like striptease and pulp fiction that reintroduced some of the elements of the 1930s culture of "erotic grotesque non-sense" (*ero guro nansensu*) with more abandon. Named after a particularly unrefined form of moonshine, *kasutori* was a subculture that reveled in the decadent and tested the limits of newfound freedoms of sexuality and expression.

Such visions of the social and cultural climate of the immediate postwar years combined with other trends that, from the critics' perspective, collectively took on a decidedly more ominous tone that signaled outright social disintegration. One such trend was the emergence of an unprecedented number of children who had lost their homes and parents due to war, many of whom ended up on the streets. In 1948, their number totaled 123,510 according to a Ministry of Health and Welfare count.[14] To the alarmed public, these children were not only symbols of national suffering and economic hardship but also of chaos and threat to order, since many of them were suspected of turning into delinquents and petty criminals. In this context, *panpan* and *kasutori* culture not only offered images of liberty but of threats, both domestic and external, to the most vulnerable population within the nation.

In response, the Allied authorities ordered the Japanese government to pass a series of laws relating to child welfare, including the Fundamental Law of Education, School Education Law, Labor Standards Law, and the Child Welfare Law, all of which were enacted in 1947. As a complement to the Child Welfare Law, the Ministry of Health and Welfare also created the Child Bureau in the same year, which was designed to coordinate policies relating to children in general. In the following year, the Diet also passed the Juvenile Law, which governed criminal justice procedures for minors, raised the upper age limit for minors from eighteen to twenty, and designated May 5 as Children's Day.[15] In addition to such welfare-oriented legislations, the government also sought to deal directly with the perceived threat of juvenile delinquency at a national level. To that end, the cabinet drafted a "Basic Outline for Guiding Youths and Preventing Delinquency" in April 1949 and followed up by establishing the Council for Youth Problem Countermeasures within the cabinet secretariat three months later. Later in the year, directives were sent to prefectural governors, leading to the creation of similar councils at the prefectural level as well as at even more local levels.[16] These measures were given legal basis through a cabinet decree in 1950 and the Council for Youth Problem Countermeasures Establishment Law, which the Diet passed unanimously in 1953.

Such efforts culminated symbolically in the promulgation of the Children's Charter on May 5, 1951. Modeled on a similar document that was produced by Herbert Hoover's White House Conference on Child Health and Protection in 1931, the Japanese charter was not enacted as law but was instead, in the words of Prime Minister Yoshida Shigeru (1878–1967), a "moral pledge" and a "social pact" among adults vowing to defend the rights and welfare of children.[17] The final version of the charter was presented on May 5 in the presence of the prime minister, the speakers of the upper and lower houses of the Diet, representatives of Allied authorities, and the chief justice of the Supreme Court. The opening section of the charter read as follows:

> We hereby establish the Children's Charter, in accordance with the spirit of the Constitution, for the purpose of establishing the correct ideals for children and to ensure their happiness.
>   Children will be respected as human beings.
>   Children will be valued as members of the society.
>   Children will be raised in a good environment.[18]

This preamble was followed by twelve articles, including a vow to foster "moral" sentiment among the children and a declaration that every child will be encouraged to "contribute to human peace and culture as a good member of the nation." Another article of the charter declared that "all children will be provided with good places to play and good cultural materials, and they will be protected from bad environments." In the process of creating the charter, the Prime Minister's Office hosted the meeting of a Draft Preparation Committee for the Children's Charter in March 1951. Notably, the committee members included the writer and critic Kanzaki Kiyoshi (1904–1979), who was at that time already serving as the head of the Education Ministry's Subcommittee on Children's Culture. Following a period of student activism as a member of the Tokyo Imperial University's liberal student group "New Man Society" (Shinjinkai) in the late 1920s, Kanzaki became known in the postwar period as a social critic with strong interests in issues relating to children as well as prostitution. It was, in fact, Kanzaki who later personally led the protest against "Yokosuka Dance" as a founding member of JSPC.

The Children's Charter was produced in a period of deepening political polarization between the conservative government and the leftist opposition. By the late 1940s, the effects of Cold War had begun to make themselves felt domestically: leftists were purged from public offices, conservative politicians who had been banned from holding public office by the Allied authorities were rehabilitated, and the economy boomed as a result of the intensification of the Korean War in the early 1950s. This period came to be identified by contemporary critics as one of "reverse course" following a time of liberalization in the early years of the Allied occupation. Critiques of government policies relating children could, in fact, already be heard from the left before the establishment of the Children's Charter. In 1949, for example, the National Federation of Industrial Organizations, a federation of unions aligned with the Japan Communist Party, published a white paper on children in which it questioned the seriousness and sincerity of the Yoshida cabinet's concern for child welfare.[19] From their perspective, the creation of child welfare legislation was mere lip service from the very government that was "threatening the survival of working-class children." Likewise, the government's call for the public to show better understanding of children's rights was seen as being merely a ploy to shift responsibility to the populace.

Such critiques were shared by those who gathered at the House of Representative Members' Office Building on May 17, 1952, a year after the establishment of the Children's Charter, to establish JSPC. There, Kanzaki joined with like-minded critics and scholars to create "a national movement for the complete realization of the ideals expressed by the Children's Charter."[20] The founding members included Osada Arata (1887–1969), an education historian at Hiroshima University, Hani Setsuko (1903–1987), editor of the magazine *Women's Companion* (*Fujin no tomo*) and social critic, and Miyahara Seiichi (1909–1978), an education scholar at Tokyo University and the former head of the Education Ministry's Social Education Section. They were joined by various groups with an interest in child welfare, the most prominent being the Japan Teachers' Union, which continued to be the largest teachers' union as well as a stalwart in progressive activism for much of the postwar era.

While JSPC did not explicitly support a specific political party, what emerged was a coalition of left-leaning critics, scholars, educators, and unions, all of whom shared the worry Osada expressed in the first issue of the group's journal: "While it is well known that a lofty Children's Charter was promulgated recently, it has been all but betrayed by the state that refuses to achieve any concrete results. Instead, it focuses on armament even in contradiction to the constitution, spending 25 percent of the national budget on arms while leaving a meager 4 percent for education. Not only that, the sense of an impending war makes the protection of children a clearly urgent matter."[21] By the time JSPC was formed, then, the Children's Charter, like the constitution, had become a symbol of the postwar political reforms that the left sought to preserve in face of what they considered to be the onslaught of a reactionary state.

At this juncture, however, the group did not consider the state to be the primary target of confrontation but sought, instead, to build on the consensus that had emerged in the charter. This was apparent in the initial section of the statement just quoted, in which Osada emphasized that the focus of their activism was aimed at the social and cultural environment that surrounded Japanese children: "Throughout one's life, childhood is the period in which people are most susceptible to their environment. A child's development depends largely on whether the environment is good or bad . . . [and yet] in our nation, not only are our schools, families, and society terribly imperfect, children are also surrounded by various terrible environments that undermine their innocence." It was the chief aim of their group, then, to protect the children from their surroundings.

While schools and homes clearly needed reform, the group's initial "Statement of Purpose" argued that it was "impossible to protect a child with individual strength," surrounded as they were by aspects of a culture of decadence that "sprouted across this unhealthy society like poisonous flowers."[22] The list of such "flowers" included "decadent popular songs, radios that spread quiz shows, and westerns and samurai stories that glorify murder in the name of justice," along with magazines, cartoons, *kamishibai* (picture plays), and film.

Why "Yokosuka Dance" Was Too Much

It was within such a context that JSPC adopted the "Yokosuka Dance" protest as its own cause even before the group's official establishment. For the next several years in fact, JSPC continued to point to their "struggle" against "Yokosuka Dance" as a hallmark of their activism. But what precisely was it about "Yokosuka Dance" that JSPC so vehemently opposed? Its draft lyrics extolled various sights and destinations in and around Yokosuka as might be expected of a song that was meant to promote commerce and tourism. These included the scene of ships coming in and out of the port, Sarushima Island (an old navy fortress that now contained a beach), a lighthouse, and the red neon lights of downtown. However, two features—the song's perceived eroticism and its locale—stood out and suggested scenes with more problematic connotations. Critics of the song were quick to point to the song's erotic lyrics by citing references to a "rain of kisses," "ships of love," a "night job," a "pretty girl" waiting by the "red neon light," and taking a girl out to a hotel. The song's last stanza crooned:

> The deep port embraces the ships,
> The flower girl embraces her flowers,
> The bright lights embrace the city at night
> What will *you* embrace there?

Far from simply enumerating the sights to be enjoyed in Yokosuka, the song emphasized the amorous nature of the pleasures to be found in the city.[23]

Musically, "Yokosuka Dance" fit into a particular strand of popular songs known as "party songs" (*ozashiki songu*), which emerged as major hits in the early years of the 1950s. Drawing on the prewar precedents, these songs followed the now well-established pattern of combining Japanese-sounding tunes with Western instrumentation. More importantly, the lyrics of these songs mostly focused on the sexually charged pleasures of the geisha houses and were, in fact, oftentimes sung by geisha singers. Geisha singers had already established themselves in the 1930s as major stars and assets for the record industry, the most famous being Kouta Katsutarō, who, as we have seen, even earned the praise of the censor Ogawa Chikagorō.[24] In the postwar context, however, these songs were more immediately associated with the rush of wealth and prosperity that Japanese businesses experienced as the result of the Korean War, which enabled these "special procurements" nouveau riche (*tokuju narikin*) to indulge themselves in the geisha quarters. They were, in other words, suitable background music for a nation in "reverse course." The first and perhaps the most famous of these was "Tonko Song" ("Tonkobushi," 1949) by the famous Saijō Yaso-Koga Masao duo and sung by Kubo Yukie (1924–2010). The song features a conversation between a geisha and her client about their love, in suggestive terms. Before ending with the lines, "Is it my fault for falling for you? Or is it your fault for tempting me?" the geisha confesses her fears of eventual abandonment by comparing herself to *daruma,* a round traditional doll said to depict Bodhidharma, the founder of Zen Buddhism:

> That *daruma* doll on the sash clip you gave me worries me a bit.
> Once you've played and rolled me around as much as you want,
> Will you just as easily crush me?[25]

Kubo reached stardom after coming out with another hit, "Yatton Song" ("Yattonbushi," 1951), composed by Nomura Toshio (lyrics) and Hattori Itsurō (music). The Saijō-Koga duo, in turn, came out with another hit in the genre with their "Geisha Waltz" ("Geisha warutsu," 1952), sung by Kagurazaka Hanko who worked as a geisha in the famous geisha district of Kagurazaka in Tokyo.

It was, in fact, the Nomura-Hattori-Kubo trio that composed "Yokosuka Dance" in 1952. While this song is not set in the geisha quarters, it nevertheless followed the conventions of the party song genre in its musical style, in the centrality of erotic themes in the lyrics, and by featuring a singer who had come to be closely connected to the genre. In the eyes of the "Yokosuka Dance" critics, the close association of the song's musical and lyrical content with the party song genre ultimately pointed to a more serious and fundamental issue: these songs were products of the capitalist elite's dominance, both local and national. In an article recounting the controversy, Kanzaki Kiyoshi, who led the protest against "Yokosuka Dance" as a representative of JSPC, emphasized that the song originated with the local chamber of commerce, which was, in turn, run by the merchants who dominated the local economy by catering to their military clients, previously Japanese and now American.[26] It was their heedless greed, according to Kanzaki, that led them to commission a song that would place commoditized sex at the forefront of Yokosuka's identity. Similarly, critics of the party song genre accused the record industry, and especially figures like Saijō and Koga, of greedily marketing commercialized eroticism and sentimentality instead of innovating and composing songs that would be more appropriate to Japan's postwar renewal.

"Yokosuka Dance" was not, in fact, the only locally commissioned song that came under public criticism for its alleged intermingling of capitalist greed and eroticism. In May of the same year, the leaders of Hachiōji, a city located on the western end of Tokyo, commissioned Saijō to write a song to promote tourism, which he duly did. Encouraged by the developments in Yokosuka, members of women's groups and others moved to put pressure on the city to cease production of the song, "Hachiōji Dance" ("Hachiōji ondo"), which including the following lines:

> Like the colorful blossoms of the *Fujimori* cherry,
> I'm a simple girl but almost in full bloom.

Take me before the blossoms have completely fallen.
Take me before someone else does.[27]

To the critics' chagrin, however, the city resisted. While this led to an unsatisfactory compromise in which the city agreed to change the title of the song from "Hachiōji Dance" to "Tama Dance" ("Tama ondo"), which referred to the region in western Tokyo that surrounds Hachiōji, Kanzaki happily noted that the protest movement did have some effect on local consumption, where the song was "buried, for all intents and purposes, by the pressure of popular opinion and the citizens' conscience."[28] He noted that when he visited a café in Hachiōji shortly after the protest, he asked for "Hachioji Dance" to be played on the phonograph. The proprietor, however, refused to do so, citing the controversy.

Roughly a year later, Hiratsuka, a city on the southern shores of Kanagawa prefecture, came out with their own song, "Hiratsuka Dance" ("Hiratsuka ondo"), written by Saijō yet again. In an article entitled "An Advertisement That Will Doom the Nation" in the national daily *Yomiuri shimbun*, Yamakawa Kikue (1890–1980), the socialist critic and pioneer of Japanese feminism, attacked the city's officials and local economic elite for using the song to actively promote prostitution, despite the growing public criticism of "human trafficking" (*jinshin baibai*), a contemporary buzzword among social critics as well as state officials concerned with the allegedly decaying public mores of this period.[29]

For Yamakawa, the prevalence of songs like "Hiratsuka Dance" and "Yokosuka Dance" reflected not only commercial greed but also the enduring "feudal" tendency within Japanese society to undervalue the status of women and children. Referring to Hiratsuka's historical position as a rest stop on the Tōkaidō highway and, consequently, a center of prostitution in the Edo period, Yamakawa declared that "Hiratsuka Dance" suited the city as "a posting station that was established by a decadent feudal society that had lost its senses by viewing women and children as commodities." A few weeks later, Yamakawa reported that the Hiratsuka officials had backed down and had agreed not only to change the lyrics but also to limit the use of the song to geisha quarters.[30] Nevertheless, Yamakawa urged further civic vigilance against the official tendency to rely on vices like the geisha quarters, gambling, and even prostitution in developing urban commercial districts.

Masterpiece of Colonial Literature

Prostitution, however, was not the only thing that the cities of Yokosuka, Hiratsuka, and Hachiōji had in common. All three cities either hosted or were in very close proximity to U.S. military installations and their brothels catered to American soldiers. While the Allied occupation of Japan officially ended in 1952, the number and size of U.S. bases in Japan expanded throughout the 1950s. Kanagawa prefecture, which contained both Yokosuka and Hiratsuka and bordered Hachiōji, hosted one of the highest concentrations of U.S. military forces in Japan.[31] It is difficult to overstate the extent of the anxiety concerning prostitution and American military presence in this historical moment. Over the course of the decade, numerous works of both nonfiction and fiction on this theme were penned by Japanese (mostly male) writers, including Kanzaki, who led the "Yokosuka Dance" protest. Between 1949 and 1955, Kanzaki penned at least five separate monographs on prostitution, many of which contained lengthy discussions of prostitution near American bases.[32]

Not surprisingly, JSPC's objection to "Yokosuka Dance" also centered on the song's promotion of prostitution in a city that was dominated by American soldiers. As Kanzaki put it, "Yokosuka Dance" was a "masterpiece of colonial literature" that celebrated the city's subservience to America's military, economic, and sexual power.[33] From that perspective, the song easily evoked one of the most enduring and sensational symbols of the Allied occupation: that of the women who fraternized with American soldiers as prostitutes or lovers.[34] Known to contemporaries as *panpan*, these women alternately became the object of pity, envy, or outright hostility.

On the one hand, they were physical symbols of Japan's complete subservience to American might, especially in the eyes of the political elites. For some of these elites, however, these women were a necessary evil who acted as human shields protecting other Japanese women from the sexual threat posed by Americans. Infamously, within weeks of Japan's surrender to the Allied forces on August 15, 1945, the Japanese government enlisted more than one thousand women to become, in the words of an oath the women were asked to take, the "breakwater to hold back the raging waves and defend and nurture the purity of our race."[35] The "raging waves" referred to the imminent arrival of hundreds of thousands of Allied soldiers, for whom these women were hired to serve as prostitutes. On the other hand, *panpan* were some of the first Japanese in the postwar period to gain access to American consumer culture through their relationship with the soldiers. In a nation still reeling from the devastations of the war and its aftermath, these women embodied the fantasy of the kind of economic life that many Japanese aspired to—something that the lyrics of "Yokosuka Dance" directly touch on, with their reference to a desire for an American-style "sweet home."

For the critics of Americanization, the proliferation of English loan words like "Japan," *wandafuru, biya, gāru, berinaisu, cherī,* and *suīto hōmu* in "Yokosuka Dance" had the effect of evoking their worst fears about the state of Japanese society. In this regard, "Yokosuka Dance" was easily associated with other developments in popular music that were seen to be the products of Americanization. One of the most vivid examples of this is the career of Eri Chiemi, who started out as a child singer in the clubs that were located within various Allied bases in the Tokyo area during the late 1940s. While Kasagi sang almost exclusively in Japanese and seemingly remained uncomfortable with English throughout her career, Eri demonstrated an uncanny ability to sing covers of the latest American tunes. In 1952, Eri made her recording debut with a cover of the "Tennessee Waltz," which catapulted her to national stardom. In the following year, she traveled to the United States and even made a record with the major American label Capitol Records.

It was Eri's ability to sing in English, however, which drew the ire of the critics, including sociologist Minami Hiroshi (1914–2001). In an article published shortly after Eri's U.S. trip, Minami pointed to her as an example of singers who produced what he called "popular songs of dubious nationality" (*kokuseki fumei ryūkōka*): "The dubiousness of the nationality of these songs not only stems from the fact that many of them contain an excessive number of foreign words in their lyrics. It has even produced a grotesque phenomenon, in which young girls who sing jazz, like Eri Chiemi, . . . sing Japanese words with an English-style accent. This is not some Japanese American singer singing in broken Japanese but *real* Japanese girls singing in questionable Japanese, as if they have temporarily lost their homeland."[36]

Minami explicitly identified such development as the result of "Japan's colonization," echoing the fear of many other intellectuals of his time.[37] While Eri was hardly the only performer to sing such songs, it was one of her songs, recorded for Capitol Records that same year, that was damned by Minami in the same article as "a song of unprecedented national shame." This was "I'm Sorry" ("Gomennasai"), originally recorded by an American singer, Richard Bowers, for Columbia Records in 1952. Each verse of this English-language song starts out with the Japanese title, including the first:

> Gomennasai
> I am so sorry gomennasai
> I am so sorry I made you cry
> Won't you forgive me, dear?[38]

By flipping the pattern of linguistic mixture in "Yokosuka Dance," this song effectively evoked an intimate and presumably unequal relationship between a Japanese woman and an American soldier who had broken her heart. Copies of an album containing this song were apparently sold as souvenirs to Allied soldiers, along with songs like "China Nights" (1938) and "Orient Me to the Orient" (1951).[39]

While the song was initially ignored by the Japanese public, the news of Eri's recording and its reported success in the American charts ignited a storm of criticism that largely echoed Minami's lament about a "national shame." After *Yomiuri* featured a rebuttal to the critics by the song's composer, Hattori Itsurō, the newspaper company was flooded with letters of complaint against the song, causing them to feature another defense by Hattori. As one female reader wrote to the paper, "Perhaps a Japanese girl singing 'I'm sorry, Japanese ladies' in broken Japanese is something that is attractive to those who worship all things foreign . . . [but] such an insulting song should be boycotted by Japanese women."[40] In fact, Eri's recording of "I'm Sorry" was never sold in Japan, but the controversy it caused nonetheless attests to how deeply problematic it was for the Japanese public to even imagine the spectacle of a Japanese teenage girl singing the words of a fictional American soldier.

It is worth remembering at this point how musically incongruous "Yokosuka Dance" and the songs sung by Eri Chiemi were, with the former coming out of a genre closely associated with geisha singers and the latter emerging from a more thoroughly Americanized context. However, considering the career of a third singer, Misora Hibari (1937–1989), helps us to understand how both musical styles came be critiqued as the symptoms of the same social malaise. Hibari's career stands out in comparison to both Kasagi's and Eri's not only because of her stature as arguably the most successful singer in Japan's postwar popular music but also because of her reputation as the queen of *enka,* a popular music genre that came to be identified in the 1960s as the "most authentically Japanese."[41]

Hibari first gained prominence in the late 1940s as a child singer specializing in adult songs of various musical genres. In particular, she was celebrated for her covers of songs by none other than Kasagi Shizuko, including "Tokyo Boogie-Woogie." In 1949, the twelve-year-old Hibari scored her first major hit, "Mournful Whistle" ("Kanashiki kuchibue," Columbia Records), and also starred in a film of the same title. While the film contained Hibari's performance of "Carried Away by Boogie" ("Bugi ni ukarete") which clearly imitated Kasagi's signature style, her performance of "Mournful Whistle" at the film's climax is perhaps best remembered by Japanese today, especially because of her costume—top hat and tails.[42] While Kasagi seems to have initially taken a rather sanguine view of her young imitator, this was apparently no longer the case by 1950, when Hibari announced her plans to go on a U.S. tour shortly before Kasagi's visit. Fearing that the American audience would mistakenly identify her signature boogie-woogie songs with Hibari, Kasagi demanded that Hibari refrain from singing any of her songs on the tour. Not surprisingly, the spectacle of a twelve-year-old girl singing adult songs in adult settings did not sit well with the same critics who were disturbed by Kasagi and Eri. For some time in the 1950s in fact, film companies even promoted Hibari and Eri as part of the trio "Three Girls" (San'nin Musume) in several musical films. From the mid-1950s, however, Hibari's repertory increasingly focused on songs that contained elements that could be understood as indigenous, including the emphasis on the *yonanuki* pentatonic scale and native instruments like *shakuhachi* (flute) and *taiko* (drum). In this Hibari was, of course, orientating herself toward the mainstream of Japan's popular song genre, which, as we have seen, had been dominated by fundamentally syncretic music that incorporated Western instrumentation with native musical idioms since the prewar period. While Hibari's move toward more Japanese-sounding songs perhaps shielded her from the accusation of "dubious nationality" that Eri faced, such a shift did not make her entirely immune to the critics—far from it. Critics like Sonobe Saburō and Minami Hiroshi considered Hibari's newly adopted musical genre to be, in the end, worse than the outright Americanism exhibited by Kasagi and Eri.

This was even apparent in a landmark study of postwar popular culture that was conducted by Tsurumi Shunsuke's Science of Thought group and published in 1950. Entitled *Dreams and Memories* (*Yume to omokage*), the volume that came out of this project constituted a notable milestone in the postwar study of popular culture.[43] Intellectuals involved with Science of Thought aimed at not only discussing Japan's democratization but also practicing it in such ways as to close the gap between the nation's intellectual elite and the masses.[44] *Dreams and Memories* was part of the group's effort to seriously examine the everyday lives of their compatriots, including their entertainment—a fundamentally progressive mission that grew out of the group's broader objective during this period to take what they called the "philosophy of ordinary people" (*hitobito no tetsugaku*) seriously.[45]

The idea was to treat ideas that emerge out of the everyday lives of the "ordinary people" as seriously as one typically treated the works of professional philosophers and other intellectuals. As such, popular culture and entertainment media were seen as legitimate expressions of popular thought that should be considered carefully by intellectuals seeking to overcome their elitist isolation from the vast majority of their compatriots. At the same time, however, members of Science of Thought considered the project to be a two-way process, in which the culture of the people would also be "intellectualized" and, thus, elevated from its current state. The goal, as the historian Adam Bronson put it, was to "scramble traditional social distinctions they believed would impede the growth of a democratic culture."[46]

As contributors to *Dreams and Memories*, however, both Sonobe and Minami directed biting critiques against the popular music industry as a whole and, in particular, the Japanese-sounding tunes that dominated the scene. For Minami, these songs' overwhelming focus on melancholy and fate reflected the fundamental pessimism and lack of constructive attitude among the Japanese, while their emphasis on the traditional sense of justice and sentimentality exhibited "deformed humanism" that was, in his opinion, "laughable from a modern, rational perspective."[47] As such, Minami concluded that popular songs collectively constituted "a concentrated expression of the various misfortunes that Japan faces today."[48]

In the same volume, Sonobe aimed a more direct critique at Koga Masao, the composer who dominated the popular music industry from the 1930s through the 1960s and collaborated with Hibari after her stylistic shift. Noting that Koga's prewar hits only came out in a period "after the oppression of militarism clamped down on all liberal social trends," Sonobe suggested that his music was merely the product of the apathy and hopelessness felt by the masses.[49] His postwar works, in turn, could not have been made without the "degradation of the popular sentiment" caused by postwar strains in the everyday lives of the people living in a war-torn society.[50] In Sonobe's view, Koga's songs not only reflected such degradation but worsened it by offering no alternative. Far from making Hibari's music more socially acceptable, her shift toward Japanese-sounding songs arguably placed her right in the mass culture critics' crosshairs. At the same time, the vehemence of Minami's and Sonobe's critiques of popular songs revealed the fundamental limitations that existed within even the most progressive attempts at democratizing culture by reinscribing the very hierarchy that they and other intellectuals of their generation perceived and sought to overcome.[51]

Self-Censorship and Book Burning

The outrage against songs like "Yokosuka Dance" was not, however, limited to progressive critics and groups like JSPC. Their protests were covered by national newspapers in generally favorable tones and their critiques of mass culture were repeated, for example, at the National Conference on Children's Culture, a meeting hosted by the Education Ministry in August 1952. That conference called on the record companies to adopt an ethics code that would guide their song production and prevent a repeat of the "Yokosuka Dance" controversy. The calls for regulation succeeded in eliciting action on the part of the record industry and the broadcasting media within the year. In November, the Recording Industry Association of Japan (RIAJ), the industry organization that was created in 1942 as the Japan Association of Phonograph Record Culture, adopted an ethics code that was made up of the following four points:

1. Records will not feature items that will disturb public peace or the order of the nation and society, or harm the wholesomeness of the everyday life of its citizens by destroying good customs and encouraging bad customs.

2. Records will not feature items that will trample on justice or cause the listener to be attracted to crime.

3. Records will not feature items that will stimulate indecent sexual thoughts.

4. Record companies will respect child psychology and will pay special attention to their influence on the children, on whom the future rests.[52]

Taking a step beyond simply creating general guidelines, Nippon Cultural Broadcasting (NCB), one of several private radio broadcasters that had emerged after their legalization in 1951, created a list of forbidden songs, including "Tonko Song," "Geisha Waltz," "Yokosuka Dance," "Hachioji Dance," and eleven others that were deemed too vulgar.[53]

NCB's move was followed by the establishment of similar lists by other radio broadcasters and culminated in the establishment of an industry-wide ethics code by the National Association of Commercial Broadcasters in 1955. In the same year, RIAJ established a Record Production Standards Committee, which was given the task of examining all records before their production and making recommendations for changes or termination of songs that were deemed to violate the code. In order to assure the public of the committee's objectivity, it included nonindustry figures such as Horiuchi Keizō and Yoshimoto Akimitsu, both of whom had been prominent music critics since the prewar period, along with representatives from the major recording companies. This was not, of course, the first foray into censorship for RIAJ. As we saw in Chapter 2, one of the association's earliest tasks was to take over much of the actual wartime censorship that had been conducted by the Home Ministry until 1942. This time, however, RIAJ emphasized that their aim was not only to appease the protesters but also to preempt any attempt by local or central government to reestablish censorship. Indeed, a similar logic of defense against state-imposed censorship informed much of the private broadcasters' response to the controversy.

Encouraged by the initial success of their protest against "Yokosuka Dance" and similar songs, JSPC quickly expanded its critique to other species of "poisonous flowers" that they saw as threats to children. In October 1952, JSPC adopted the "movement to cleanse picture plays" as their cause.[54] Picture plays had long been a popular form of entertainment among children, usually involving a "picture plays man" who would come into the neighborhood, gather children, and tell them stories using colorfully painted pictures while selling sweets.[55] In the late 1940s, however, picture plays came under increased criticism for their allegedly vulgar themes, often involving violence and an emphasis on the grotesque.

Complaints eventually prompted the Tokyo Metropolitan Government to establish a Picture Play Ethics Management Council in 1950. The council, made up of educators, scholars, and representatives of the picture play industry, examined each play that was produced by member companies and placed stamps indicating the council's approval on those that passed their scrutiny. By the end of 1952, however, several companies had left the council, leaving it with a jurisdiction over only 36 percent of the plays that were actually being produced. Fearing that the council was becoming increasingly ineffective, JSPC invited representatives of the industry for discussion and sought to rehabilitate the movement for picture play reform by mobilizing their own network of mothers and child advocates to monitor the quality of the plays that were being shown to children. For example, the October issue of JSPC's journal included a picture of the council's seal of approval and called on mothers to report the name, content, and make of plays without the seal to the society, noting that such monitoring "could easily be done by kids themselves."[56]

JSPC also sought to educate mothers through meetings and through local chapters that were being established across the nation. A prime example of this was the "Mothers' Class" that they held in Tokyo on a monthly basis, to which they invited mothers as well as specialists on various topics relating to children.[57] The first Mothers' Class, held in November 1954 and cohosted by *Yomiuri shimbun,* featured none other than Sonobe Saburō, the music critic, who lectured on "Children and Popular Songs." Sonobe admonished his audience that children's tendency to mimic adults made them particularly vulnerable to adults, especially parents, who carelessly sang vulgar songs or listened to them on the radio. The seventh Mothers' Class, held in May 1955, focused on another form of mass culture that was becoming increasingly controversial, namely "bad books" (*akusho*). These included mass magazines that were aimed at children as well as comics with themes that included violence and eroticism. Calling for the "expulsion" of such publications, JSPC had created a research committee at its headquarters earlier that year, which in turn invited members and local chapters to submit reports of such books' content and influence on children.[58] What began as a protest against a single song in 1952 had expanded into a much broader campaign against mass culture within three years.

JSPC's critique of mass culture proved to be popular among wide sections of contemporary society, going well beyond the group's leftist allies to include local parent-teacher associations and mothers' groups, some of which were more politically conservative. Its voice of protest against "poisonous flowers" also found receptive ears among government officials as well as the editorial writers of the major dailies. *Yomiuri*'s editorial on November 24, 1954, for example, demanded that media industries exercise "self-restraint" (*jishuku*) in their production of "vulgar culture," and complained of popular songs that spread among the youth "like a contagious disease" along with erotic films and cheap magazines.[59] In the April 1955 issue of JSPC's journal, Osada acknowledged with some satisfaction that "the fire of the movement for the expulsion of bad magazines that JSPC lit has finally spread widely."[60] JSPC's "fire," however, was not always purely metaphorical. During the weeklong "Movement to Protect and Nurture the Youth" hosted by the government's Central Council for the Youth Problem (CCYP) in May 1954, the Akasaka Mothers' Group for Youth began burning "evil books" that members found in their homes in downtown Tokyo. By the time their activity was reported in the national daily *Asahi shimbun* in July, they had burned over five hundred books and magazines.[61] One of the leaders of the mothers' group characterized their actions as an "explosion of motherly anger against society" and an act of "self defense, since the authorities will not deal with these books." Notably, the *Asahi* article also carried a comment by a Tokyo Metropolitan Police official, who endorsed the book burning by suggesting that it was an expression of "motherly love" and declared the intent of the police to do their part in cracking down on such books.

Indeed, the involvement of the state went far beyond a simple expression of moral support for the mothers' outrage. For example, CCYP, which had evolved from the Council for Youth Problem Countermeasures (CYPC), acted as the state's chief coordinator for what quickly came to be known as the "Evil Books Expulsion Movement." Working with mothers' groups and other critics of mass culture, CCYP was particularly active in 1955, holding rallies, making recommendations to the government, and demanding the "self-restraint" of various media industries.[62] Underlying its activity, however, was a close cooperation with the national and local police forces, both in policy making as well as in implementation. The relationship, in fact, went back to the establishment of CYPC in 1949 and the subsequent founding of prefectural and local chapters. It was the police that took the initiative in mobilizing the citizens at both prefectural and local levels to create many of the provincial youth problem councils.[63]

The continued dominance of the police in these councils became apparent in 1950, when representatives of provincial councils gathered at the prime minister's residence for a National Meeting on Youth Problems, which was hosted by CCYP. During the meeting, many of the prefectural representatives called for a more rigorous attack on "corrupt cultural materials," including the establishment of a national law against such materials which would be enforced by the police.[64] During a discussion on picture plays, the representative of the Tokyo Metropolitan Police acknowledged the necessity of a national law to govern picture plays that would provide for a system of censorship.

The presence of the police was also felt in their close relationship to local mothers' groups, some of which were in fact created by the police in the first place, as in the case of local youth problem councils. The most notable examples of police involvement, however, were the establishment of prefectural ordinances against mass culture during the 1950s. Starting with Okayama in 1950, Kanagawa, Hokkaido, Hyogo, and Osaka prefectures would all adopt or plan for such ordinances by the end of 1956. Mostly entitled "Ordinance for Nurturing the Youth" or something similar, these laws gave provincial governments the authority to designate certain mass cultural products as "harmful" to youth and, in some cases, to ban their sale to youth, as was the case in Kanagawa. Within the subsequent decade, most prefectures would adopt similar measures.[65]

Conclusion

JSPC's response to growing prominence of the state, and especially the police, in the movement against vulgar culture was characterized by ambivalence that gradually grew into outright hostility. Signs of the rift became apparent as early as 1953, when the group sponsored a "Culture Conference for the Protection of Children," which was designed as a nongovernmental alternative to the Education Ministry-sponsored National Conference on Children's Culture.

A call for the meeting, published in the JSPC journal's October 1953 issue, acknowledged the value of the original conference held by the state, but criticized its second iteration by pointing out that nongovernmental organizations were largely shut out and that the discussion focused on issues of controlling culture (*bunka tōsei*)— language the evoked the wartime mobilization of culture.[66]

As the Evil Books Expulsion Movement began to escalate in 1954, the journal's tone became even more critical of state-sponsored initiatives. An article from December 1954 chronicling the group's second Culture Conference for the Protection of Children reported that the participants resolved to "absolutely oppose bureaucratic control that comes from an authoritarian culture" and called for greater efforts to foster independence and self-reliance among children.[67] At the height of the Evil Books Expulsion Movement, JSPC also published an editorial which declared the group's clear opposition to the "state control of bad cultural materials," arguing that such measures were not only ineffective but also risked the return of prewar regulations on speech.[68] What was needed, it emphasized again, was a concerted effort to foster children's ability to judge such materials autonomously.

In the course of the latter half of the 1950s, JSPC increasingly found itself opposing direct state involvement in reforming the cultural environment of children. The growing distance between JSPC and other state-centered child protection efforts was further reinforced by the group's consistent opposition to various education policies by the state, including the Education Ministry's growing control over textbook contents and the attempts to reintroduce "morals" into the national curriculum. The issue that placed the group on the most direct course of confrontation with the state, however, was neither education nor "evil books" but the presence of the U.S. military in Japan and its effect on children. In this sense, JSPC remained true to the core set of issues that had prompted them to protest "Yokosuka Dance" in the first place. Throughout the decade after its inception, the group's harshest criticisms were reserved for the presence of numerous American military bases across Japan and the alleged cultural and social degradation they brought upon the communities that surrounded them. The group conducted two extensive studies of such effects, in 1953 and 1957 respectively, both of which culminated in meetings entitled "National Conference for the Protection of Children around Bases."[69] Both conferences featured representatives and reports from numerous military installations around the country, which all decried and characterized the plight of these communities as essentially being under a form of colonization.

The 1953 conference in particular focused on the issues surrounding the recreational activities of American soldiers, which were alleged to have given rise to various services catering to them, including bars, cabarets, and dance halls. The service that received the most attention from the attendees, however, was the rampant prostitution that these bases were reported to foster wherever they were established. Children who lived around these bases were, in turn, reported to be living in an environment that was saturated by erotic forms of entertainment. A report from Asaka base in Saitama, for example, featured stories of children witnessing American soldiers and their Japanese *panpan* companions kissing each other and even publicly engaging in sexual intercourse.[70] The same report also suggested that some parents were acting as pimps for the soldiers, forcing children to witness the sexualized culture of their community even more directly.

The 1957 conference explored additional concerns, including the physical toll that the noise from military planes was taking on children living near air bases and, more importantly, the general militarization of mass culture for children that the ongoing military presence was believed to foster. In the minds of JSPC members, it was clear that some of the worst features of mass culture as they saw it, including the glorification of violence and war, had their roots in Japan's military alliance with the United States.

JSPC's concerns about the American military presence in Japan ultimately ensured that the group's activities would not escape the larger dynamics of Cold War politics in the course of the 1950s. This culminated in JSPC's participation in the 1960 protests against the renewal of the U.S.-Japan Security Treaty, during which the group defended the actions of student protesters and ultimately participated in street demonstrations surrounding the Diet themselves. Going a step further later that year, Hani Setsuko, the vice-chairman of JSPC, ran for an open seat in the Diet's House of Councilors, on a platform that promised child protection, promotion of peace, and reform of political corruption. Within a decade, then, a movement that was originally centered on a critique of mass culture found itself participating in far more overt forms of political activism.

This transformation of JSPC was accompanied by growing alienation from many other members of the broad coalition of child protection advocates and, especially, from the state. In the course of the 1950s, a growing sense of political marginalization emerged among the members of JSPC's leadership as well as in its local branches. The group's publications and internal reports during the decade included several cases in which members, including mothers and teachers, were attacked and shunned by their colleagues and families as "reds."[71] While this clearly did not lead the group to change its increasingly confrontational stance toward the state,

it did indicate its waning power within the coalition of child protection advocates and mass culture critics, in which it had originally played a leading role.

By the end of 1950s, no trace of the national consensus that had
brought about the Children's Charter was anywhere to be seen.
While both JSPC and the government continued to invoke the
charter from time to time, the existence of such a document would
be largely forgotten among most Japanese during the subsequent
decades. More importantly, the breakdown of consensus within
Japan's child protection movement coincided with a similar fragmentation that took place within the politics of both popular songs
and mass culture in general during the same period. The decline of
the child protection movement as a whole from the 1960s onward
left a vacuum that was not filled by other groups with sufficient
clout to mount the kind of widespread critique of media that was
seen in the heyday of the movement.

While police and provincial government officials continued to
regulate media during the subsequent decades, they largely focused
their attention on depictions of sexually explicit materials within visual media which were deemed at risk of breaking the Criminal
Code's prohibition on displaying obscene materials. Within such a
context, popular songs gradually became less of a target for the kind
of sustained, rigorous critique that had accompanied their existence since the late 1920s. However, the decline of the critical
discourse surrounding popular songs, and mass culture in general,
signified a far more sweeping set of transformations that were taking
place within Japanese society as a whole—changes that, taken together, pointed to the end of the Popular Song Era itself.

5

The End of Popular Song and of Critique

In the *Economic White Paper* (*Keizai hakusho*) published in 1956, Japan's Economic Planning Agency famously declared, "Already, the postwar is over."[1] The aim of the declaration was to highlight what was perceived to be a shift in the nation's economic mode from one that was centered on recovery from wartime devastation to one that was aimed at a long-term growth. Both in the immediate aftermath of the *Economic White Paper*'s publication and in subsequent decades, however, the bold declaration took on a life of its own and came to be conceived as a signal of a new era—one in which Japan was less encumbered by the shadows of the imperial era and the Allied occupation that followed it.

Such a view seems understandable when the *Economic White Paper*'s declaration is seen in conjunction with the momentous political developments that took place during the 1950s, including not only the end of the occupation in 1952 but also the rise of a new political dynamic in 1955 dominated by the governing Liberal Democratic Party (LDP) and its opposition, the Japan Socialist Party (JSP). And yet, from the outset, the *Economic White Paper*'s declaration was countered by a flurry of responses that suggested that such an assertion was, in fact, quite premature. An article in a white paper issued by the Ministry of Health and Welfare later in the same year pointedly asked, "Is the postwar, in fact, over?"[2] The article went on to cite a variety of evidence for the continuing legacies of wartime social and economic dislocation, including the ongoing presence of a vast number of Japanese who, despite the postwar reconstruction, remained impoverished.

The first decade after the war clearly witnessed as many continuities as departures in regard to the politics of popular music and mass culture as a whole. Despite the influx of American music along with its soldiers, popular songs in the prewar mold continued to dominate the soundscape. The newer songs were produced by the same recording companies that had ruled the market before the war. The critics of such music, such as the members of the Japanese Society for the Protection of Children (JSPC), remained resolute in their belief both in the inherent vulgarity of popular songs and in the cultural hierarchy that led them to such a conclusion. Wartime institutions, like the Japan Association of Phonograph Record Culture (JAPRC) and its self-regulation regime, found a place in the postwar media landscape and were seemingly there to stay. No less significant were the more short-term continuities, the most important being the tensions surrounding the ongoing presence of America, both as a military and cultural force, which seemed far from being resolved.

It was in the two decades following the 1956 *Economic White Paper,* however, that many of these continuities were severed. During this period, the politics of popular songs as it had existed was fundamentally upended by three interconnected developments that reshaped Japanese cultural politics as a whole. One of these key changes was the dramatic transformation that took place in the Japanese mediascape during these decades, when television emerged as an increasingly hegemonic medium that encompassed a broad range of mass entertainment within its programming, including music. For the recording industry, this signaled the rapid loss of their control over much of the music production process, as television broadcasters as well as production companies such as Nabepuro took greater control over musicians and their music.

This fundamental shift in the ways that popular music was produced and distributed also signified the increasing diversification of the Japanese music market and the consequent demise of "popular songs" as a catch-all genre. During these decades, the range of musical genres that were easily accessible to the average Japanese consumer broadened dramatically, making Western music (*yōgaku*) in particular far more popular than it had been before—a trend that was demonstrated dramatically when Beatlemania arrived in Japan with the band's much publicized visit in 1966. Japanese musicians also became increasingly integrated into the global trends in popular music, which led to the unprecedented prominence of Japanese musicians such as Sakamoto Kyū, of "Sukiyaki" (1963) fame, in the Western music scene.

In such a context, not only did *ryūkōka* lose its relevance as a term that signified the mainstream of Japanese popular music, but the very notion that such a mainstream could, in fact, be defined appeared to be an increasingly tenuous proposition. The great irony of this development, however, was the fact that it was precisely at this juncture that the products of Japan's music industry, and mass culture in general, appeared to rapidly lose their previous notoriety among critics as vulgar entertainment. Instead, entities that had previously held mass culture at arm's length, such as the Japan Broadcasting Corporation (Nihon Hōsō Kyōkai, NHK), increasingly took part in institutionalizing mass entertainment as part of their vision for a national culture, to the point that the state came to include prominent pop stars among the recipients of national awards. In the wake of the political turmoil surrounding the renewal of U.S.-Japan Security Treaty in 1960, many leftist intellectuals also made a fundamental shift in their approach to mass culture that prompted them to take a more benign view of popular songs. Criticizing the mass culture critique of the 1950s and earlier decades as being overly elitist, the New Left critics actively sought out popular cultural forms, such as the newly invented quasi-traditional genre of *enka*, as examples of an indigenous culture that could be incorporated into their critique of the emerging corporate society, even as some of the most significant progressive critics of the previous decades recanted their own critiques of popular songs in response.

Underlying all of these changes in the positionality of Japan's cultural elites in relation to mass culture was the dramatic shift in the perception of the vast majority of Japan's inhabitants in regard to the existence of class-based social and cultural hierarchy within their own society. As evinced most famously in a 1970 government survey in which 90 percent of the respondents identified themselves as belonging to the "middle stratum" (*chūryū*), the vast majority of Japanese had come to see themselves as constituting what social critics and other observers had come to identify as the "mass middle-class society" (*sōchūryū shakai*). Even as economic and demographic realities pointed to the persistence of social hierarchies in subsequent decades, the self-perception of Japan as a middle-class nation strengthened its hold on the Japanese cultural and political imagination, effectively closing out the discursive space in which the critique of popular songs and other forms of mass culture had thrived—a space that was created by a broadly shared perception and concern for the hierarchies that had deeply divided Japan only a short while ago. Together, these changes constituted both the end of Japan's Popular Song Era and the end of a broader confluence of cultural politics that had dominated the middle decades of the twentieth century.

Popular Songs as Objects of Nostalgia

On December 31, 1969, Kubo Yukie reappeared on a stage to perform her signature tune, "Tonko Song," nearly two decades after its initial release and after almost a decade's absence from Japan's popular music scene. Despite her success with "Tonko Song," which was followed by a few more hits in the first half of the 1950s, Kubo's stardom quickly receded during the second half of the decade and she had retired completely by 1960. What was even more striking than her abrupt return to public performing, however, was the venue in which this occurred. Kubo's New Year's Eve performance was part of a television program broadcast by Tokyo Channel 12, a relatively new station that had just began to broadcast in color.[3]

Entitled *Songs of Nostalgia, New Year's Eve Grand March* (*Natsukashi no utagoe, toshiwasure daikōshin*), the program featured an impressive array of popular song stars singing their hit songs from the prewar and postwar periods. However, *Songs of Nostalgia* stood out among the plethora of music programs that had come to fill the television broadcasting timetables in Japan.[4] As the title suggests, the program focused on songs that were deemed to come from a time that was distant enough in the past to provoke a sense of nostalgia, unlike other programs that mostly featured current hits. Not only that, the program insisted on having the songs sung by the original performers, rather than having them covered by more recent stars. Given that most of these singers had long retired from their professional musical careers, the producers of the program were forced to go through what proved to be a painstaking process of *re-discovering* these singers, many of whom had slid into obscurity.[5]

The original iteration of *Songs of Nostalgia* was broadcast in April 1968 as a filler program that was only meant to last for four episodes. The positive reaction from the audience, however, led the program to be extended to a total of seventeen episodes that were broadcast through August of the same year; this ultimately led to the adoption of the program as part of Channel 12's regular schedule in October. Emboldened by the program's success, Channel 12 made the audacious move of scheduling a special New Year's Eve version of *Songs of Nostalgia* in the same year during a time slot that made it a direct competitor to NHK's *Red and White Year-End Song Festival* (*Toshiwasure kōhaku uta gassen*), which took the form of a competition between the biggest names in the music industry.[6] Starting shortly after the end of World War II as a radio program, *Red and White Year-End Song Festival* had, by 1968, established itself not only as a music program juggernaut but a fixture in the New Year's family ritual in many Japanese homes.

Channel 12's potentially risky move ultimately paid off, however, as both the regular and New Year's Eve broadcasts of *Songs of Nostalgia* consistently secured high ratings in the subsequent years, turning the program into a boon for a broadcaster that was struggling to make a profit in an already saturated media market. Aside from ratings, Channel 12 profited by syndicating *Songs of Nostalgia* to local broadcasters around the country, which in turn enabled the show to gain popularity among a truly national audience. Channel 12's success was such that it prompted competing broadcasters, including NHK, to produce similar musical programs that featured past hits and singers, resulting in some viewers disdaining them as copycats of Channel 12's "original" approach.[7] *Songs of Nostalgia* therefore inadvertently became a pioneer in a broader resurgence of older popular songs within a new media environment that contemporary observers came to identify as the "nostalgic melody boom" (*natsumero būmu*).

Along with reacquainting many Japanese with hits from the 1930s through to the 1950s, the nostalgic melody boom also elevated the public profile of many singers who had long been forgotten. For some, the boom offered an opportunity to restart their musical career. Kubo, for example, continued to appear on *Songs of Nostalgia* as well as other "nostalgic melody" (*natsumero*) programs, while giving singing lessons to numerous students. Others parlayed their rediscovered fame into lucrative gigs at clubs and cabarets in Tokyo. Many of the "A-list" singers from the prewar years also began to receive official accolades during this period. This included Shōji Taro (1898–1972), who received three awards, including the Order of the Rising Sun (1969), and the geisha singer Kouta Katsutarō, who was awarded the Order of the Precious Crown (1974).[8] Fujiyama Ichirō, a particularly well-decorated star from the early postwar period, even received the traditional court rank of *jushii* (junior fourth rank), an honor that had been reserved for aristocrats and high-ranking state officials in the prewar period.

Popular Music in the Television Era

The resurgence of nostalgic melody singers and their positive public reassessment from the late 1960s onward vividly illustrate how much had changed since the days of the "Yokosuka Dance" protest. From the late 1950s through the end of the 1960s, both the music industry and the critical discourse surrounding it were transformed in ways that set the subsequent period apart from the decades that have been examined thus far, just as the birth of popular songs in the late 1920s marked a fundamental shift from what preceded it. Just as the entrance of Western recording capital provided the catalyst for the prewar transformation of music making into a popular music industry, much of the change in the 1960s and 1970s owed its origin to the disruptive entrance of television as the predominant form of mass media of the era. In particular, the leading role played by Tokyo Channel 12 and other television broadcasters in the development of the nostalgic melody boom ultimately underscored a more fundamental shift that was taking place in the manner in which popular songs were consumed by the majority of the listeners.

In the occupation period radio had emerged as a major conduit of popular songs. Following the precedent set by NHK as well as private broadcasters in the 1950s, television broadcasters began to offer highly popular musical programs in the 1960s. Along with *Red and White Year-End Song Festival* and nostalgic melody shows, notable programs from this period include NHK's venerable *Amateur Singing Contest*, Fuji Television's *Hit Parade* (*Hitto parēdo*, 1959–1970), Nihon Television's *Soap Bubble Holiday* (*Shabondama horidē*, 1961–1977) and, later, its *A Star Is Born* (*Sutā tanjo*, 1971–1983).[9]

Music television programs transformed the consumption of popular songs by adding a visual element to what was originally primarily a listening experience—a mode of consumption that ultimately came to be dominant, as television sets proliferated in Japanese homes.[10] Television, however, reshaped Japan's popular music scene on an even more fundamental level within the realm of production. Record companies like Columbia and Victor had succeeded in establishing near-exclusive control over the entire process of the production of popular songs by the late 1920s. Under that system, which largely remained intact through the 1950s, major record companies monopolized the popular song market by placing every aspect of song production, from the selection of lyrics, music, and singers to the distribution of records, under their direct control. At the heart of their hegemony lay the exclusivity contracts that each company made with lyricists, composers, and singers, all of whom were essentially record company employees. In short, the popular music scene was synonymous with the record industry during these decades.

In the course of the 1960s, however, the iron grip that the record companies had hitherto had on the production of popular songs began to loosen rapidly with the emergence of new forces that began to vie for control. An especially significant new player was the jazz bassist Watanabe Shin's Watanabe Productions. Established in 1955, Nabepuro, as the company came to be known, initially specialized in managing jazz musicians amidst the "jazz boom" of the 1950s, successfully marketing the music that was previously confined to clubs inside American military bases among a growing audience of young Japanese.[11] From the late 1950s through the 1960s, Nabepuro quickly outgrew its initial focus on jazz and began to manage a wide range of musical talents that were emerging at that time. At the same time, Nabepuro developed close ties with television broadcasters, beginning with Fuji Television and its *Hit Parade*.[12]

Starting only a few months after Fuji Television began broadcasting in March 1959, the weekly live show *Hit Parade* featured the latest American pop tunes translated and sung by Japanese singers. Notably, Nabepuro supplied the majority of the performers on the show, since it had emerged as the only company that was able to secure and train enough musicians who could perform in the latest American styles week in and week out.[13] The show's success encouraged Watanabe's company to take an even more central role in the production of Nihon Television's *Soap Bubble Holiday* in 1961. Unlike the Fuji show, this one featured Nabepuro musicians performing Japanese popular songs rather than covers of American songs; this, too, became a major success. Perhaps the most famous star to emerge from this show was the comic singer Ueki Hitoshi (1926–2007), whose "Sūdara Song" ("Sūdarabushi"), which sang of the vicissitudes of the white-collar *salaryman* life, became a massive hit when it was released only a few months after the start of the *Soap Bubble Holiday*. By the early 1970s, Watanabe had succeeded in creating what one competitor referred to as the "Nabepuro Empire."[14]

The rise of Nabepuro points to three specific ways in which the record industry's hegemony over music making declined in these years. First, starting with "Sūdara Song," Nabepuro began to produce the original master recordings of songs within the company, a process that had been the exclusive domain of the record companies until then. While most of the existing record companies would have balked at such an arrangement, Watanabe found a willing collaborator in the Toshiba Record Company, a relative newcomer to the industry, which was struggling to make inroads into a popular music market dominated by well-established players.[15] Eager to make its mark, Toshiba agreed to produce "Sūdara Song" records under a license agreement with Nabepuro. This arrangement, which effectively separated what was arguably the most important aspect of the production of popular songs from the hitherto streamlined process within the record companies, increasingly became the norm in the subsequent decades, as other production companies, sheet music publishers, and even broadcasters began to produce their own master recordings, relegating the record companies to the position of merely manufacturing the physical records.[16]

Secondly, Nabepuro's work with television broadcasters and its production of master recordings meant it had to forge connections with a network of singers, lyricists, and composers who were not under exclusive contracts with major record companies.[17] While this would have been a major disadvantage in the 1930s and 1940s, when few talents could be found outside the record companies, Nabepuro was able to take advantage of a growing number of young and independent musicians as well as writers. One such writer was Aoshima Yukio (1932–2006), who wrote the lyrics for "Sūdara Song." Rather than being a career lyricist like Saijō Yaso, Aoshima was a multitalented artist who was eminently suited for the television era. He wrote screenplays, song lyrics, and novels; he acted in a successful television comedy series; and he even served one term as the governor of the Tokyo Metropolitan Government.[18] The growing profile of freelance artists could also be seen beyond Nabepuro, as was apparent in the case of Aku Yū (1937–2007). After a stint in an advertising firm, Aku began writing song lyrics in the mid-1960s and rose to prominence through his involvement with the creation of Nihon Television's *A Star Is Born,* a successful competitor to the Nabepuro-produced shows which showcased numerous singing stars in the 1970s, including Sakurada Junko (b. 1958), Yamaguchi

Momoe (b. 1959), and the duo Pink Lady.[19] Aku himself ultimately became one of the most prolific and successful lyricists of the postwar period, establishing a career that became nearly synonymous with the popular music scene of this era.

Finally, both the growing separation of master recording production from the record industry and the rise of freelance artists occurred within the context of a broader shift in the definition of what constituted a "popular song" or a "popular song star"—namely the growing diffusion of Western, and in particular American, music among a wider segment of the population. This process began under the Allied occupation, which facilitated new avenues of contact between the latest American hits and a growing number of Japanese fans. While this contact took a more direct form through Allied radio broadcasting, an arguably more influential interaction took place within the clubs inside U.S. military bases, in which hired Japanese musicians, including Watanabe Shin, learned the latest developments in the American music scene literally on the job.[20] At the same time, Japanese singers like Kasagi Shizuko and Eri Chiemi began to perform before the Japanese audience in self-consciously American styles during this period, whether boogie-woogie or jazz. By the late 1950s, the jazz boom that was noted by observers earlier in the decade had been overshadowed by the "rockabilly boom" that accompanied the arrival of music dominated by Elvis Presley, whose Japanese fans even created a highly publicized fan club that drew the attention of major media.[21]

While both the rockabilly boom and the earlier jazz boom were relatively short-lived, they not only spread the popularity of American musicians among Japanese listeners but also reshaped the Japanese popular music scene in both overt and subtle ways, establishing a pattern of interaction that would be repeated during subsequent decades, culminating with the arrival of the Beatles in 1966. The growing diversification of the popular music market with the influx of newer Western popular music genres, the increasing demand for such music among a widening audience, and the emergence of musicians, production companies, and broadcasters vying to meet such demands ultimately combined to force the first major paradigm shift in popular music industry since the 1920s.[22] In the face of such change, major record companies proved to be largely incapable of taking the initiative in ways that would have preserved their dominance, wedded as they were to an ossified system of popular song production as well as a musical style that was increasingly seen as dated.[23] Even *ryūkōka*, a term that embodied the fundamentally modern characteristic of the record industry in the 1930s, had a distinctly retro ring by the 1960s, attesting to the loss of near-universal appeal that it had once had.

The End of Critique

The decline of the record industry and the popular song genre as the dominant form of popular music in the course of the 1960s and 1970s did not, however, signify the complete disappearance of the latter from the Japanese musical landscape. After all, it was precisely during this period that Kubo Yukie resumed her long-dormant career within the context of the nostalgic melody boom. While this latest boom in the music industry gradually ebbed, the transformation of popular songs into objects of nostalgia produced more lasting fruit in the form of *enka*, a self-consciously nostalgic genre that had come to be regarded by fans and nonfans alike as the most "Japanese" in style. Musically, most *enka* songs featured the *yonanuki* minor scale and vocal techniques like *ko-bushi* (ornamentation), which oftentimes combined to give these songs a weepy, emotional tone. The lyrics in turn emphasized sentimental themes, including parting, longing, solitude, and tears.

While its name harkened back to the preindustrial popular song writers of the Meiji and Taishō periods, *enka* was very much an invented tradition that emerged between the late 1960s and early 1970s through a selective emphasis on musical features and lyrical themes that were regarded as the hallmarks of the more "Japanese-sounding" popular songs created by Nakayama Shimpei, Koga Masao, and others during the heyday of the popular song genre.[24] Nevertheless, *enka* ultimately succeeded in convincing many Japanese of its claim to represent traditional Japan, remaining a constant, if somewhat marginal, presence in the Japanese popular music scene to this day. The combination of nostalgia and nationalism that *enka* embodied also secured a place of respect for the genre not only in the mainstream media outlets but also in the political establishment.[25] As noted earlier, a growing number of singers associated with this genre were honored with national and imperial awards starting in the late 1960s.

Even more noteworthy, however, was the way in which the emergence of *enka* was also accompanied by a major shift in the critical discourse surrounding popular songs, especially among leftist critics who had gained prominence in the postwar period. One such advocate for the genre was Itsuki Hiroyuki (b. 1932), the writer who has been credited with popularizing the very use of the term *enka*.[26] In his 1966 short story, entitled "Enka," Itsuki described the battle within a record company between the advocates of the older, Japanese-style songs and those of Western-style tunes, based on his past stint as a contracted lyricist for Columbia. In one scene, Itsuki has the main character passionately defend an *enka* song in a televised debate with a representative from the "Federation of Mamas' Society," an organization closely resembling JSPC, who has decried the "vulgarity" of *enka*'s vocal technique: "Perhaps you're right to say that it's vulgar. But there is *something* in that way of singing.

It's like the sound of groaning coming from someone who is being oppressed, discriminated, and trampled on; someone who is suffering under that weight and yet is attempting to resist it with their whole body. That song is needed by people who don't belong to a large organization, religion, or other forms of solidarity—people who are dispersed and alone."[27] In this story and other writings, Itsuki emphasized the nature of *enka* as the sound of "sadness and bitterness" (*on'nen hishō*) emanating from the voiceless oppressed "commoners" (*shomin*).[28]

Implicit in Itsuki's defense of *enka* was the critique of the organized left, including groups like JSPC, and their elitist disdain for the "vulgar" mass culture. Itsuki, however, was not alone in making such a critique. In the same year, in an article on popular songs published in the *Monthly Socialist,* the JSP's journal, the author Tsuda Rui decried the "separation between the avant-garde and the masses" that, from his perspective, was already apparent in the early days of the Allied occupation.[29] Directly naming JSPC, Tsuda castigated the postwar leftist activists for their fundamental inability to relate to the Japanese masses and for "so easily falling into artistic colonialism." For Tsuda, singers like Misora Hibari, often described as the greatest female singer in twentieth-century Japan, sang songs that were "uniquely Japanese" and the left's failure to embrace such tunes doomed their attempts to mobilize the masses against the conservative state.

A more sustained and self-conscious reassessment of popular songs emerged among Tsurumi Shunshuke's Science of Thought group. In 1970 the group published *The Secret of Popular Songs* (*Ryūkōka no himitsu*), a book that was entirely dedicated to the genre, juxtaposing articles from their groundbreaking *Dreams and Memories,* first published in 1950, with more recent articles written by the same authors, including Sonobe Saburō and Minami Hiroshi, both of whom had begun as harsh critics of popular songs.

In a reassessment, Minami softened his original critique in a way that echoed Itsuki's defense of *enka* by arguing that popular songs actually served a valuable role in expressing the "sense of alienation" felt by many Japanese in an era of "mass society," pointing to songs that expressed the homesickness of the migrant workers to Tokyo as prime examples of this. While most songs were still too passive in their political potential for Minami, he nonetheless showered high praise on Ueki Hitoshi's comic songs, including "Sūdara Song" and other songs that satirized the vagaries of contemporary Japanese life. From Minami's perspective, Ueki's songs served as a "vivid expression" of the disgust that the masses felt toward the "political, economic, and cultural irresponsibility of the ruling class."[30]

The Secret of Popular Songs also contained a reprint of a round-table discussion featuring the critics Tada Michitarō (1924–2007), Terayama Shūji (1935–1983), and Mori Hideto (1933–2013), which was originally published in the October 1963 issue of the journal *Science of Thought*. Their discussion echoed the critiques of Itsuki, Tsuda, and Minami by emphasizing the subversive potential of songs that expressed the "soul of the alienated masses" as well as the chaotic power of "the young masses of the lowest class."[31] However, they also took a step further by attempting to place this potential within the immediate historical context, thus attaching a particular importance to the popular songs and their fans: "In today's Japan, which is witnessing the maturation of capitalism, many things are being overturned. The discriminators are being discriminated against, the discriminated discriminate, things national and international are intermingling, and revolutionaries are becoming reactionaries."[32]

According to Mori, it was the current generation of popular music fans who possessed the ability to "create the future" in such a world. In many ways, the upheaval of existing hierarchies and the collision of domestic and international politics, as articulated in the roundtable, also captured the transformation of Japan's left in the two decades immediately following the U.S.-Japan Security Treaty protest of 1960. Echoing the rise of the New Left across Western industrialized societies in the wake of the Soviet invasions of Hungary in 1956 and Czechoslovakia in 1968, a new generation of leftists emerged in Japan, who were deeply critical of the authority and elitism of the existing leftist institutions, including the Japan Communist Party. Japan's New Left, like its global counterpart, sought to circumvent such authorities primarily by focusing on the universities as the site of their activism, culminating in the dramatic confrontation between students and riot police at the University of Tokyo in 1969. At the same time, many of its ideologues sought to close the gap with the elite avant-garde and Japan's masses by searching for loci of resistance to the dominant capitalist regime among "native" (*dochaku*) elements in Japan's society and culture.[33] It was within this context that Itsuki championed *enka* as embodying the voice of the alienated masses and Minami saw a potential for resistance in some of the new breed of popular songs.

However, the most intriguing example of critical transformation was that of Sonobe Saburō, whose career as a music critic thrived before and after World War II. Born in 1906 in Osaka, Sonobe pursued a degree in French at the Tokyo University of Foreign Studies. He belonged to the same generation of music critics that included Horiuchi Keizō, Iba Takashi, and Moroi Saburō, writing nineteen books and countless articles on music throughout his long career.[34] Like most other music critics of his time, his interest was largely focused on Western classical music in a way that reflected his undergraduate education, including analyses of works by Bizet, Debussy, and Beethoven. Sonobe had already achieved some prominence in the prewar period, when he served as the chief editor of the journal *Music Critique* (*Ongaku hyōron*), and, in 1942, as a board member of the JAPRC, representing the Japan Musical Culture Association. While his attitude toward popular songs during the early years of his career was predictably critical and dismissive, much of his postwar career was dedicated to examining the history and nature of popular songs, leading him to produce a slew of monographs in the immediate aftermath of Japan's surrender in 1945, including volumes like *On Popular Music* (1948), *Class Hierarchy in Music* (*Ongaku no kaikyūsei*, 1950), and *Japanese History from Enka to Jazz* (*Enka kara jazu eno nihonshi*, 1954).[35] However, as we saw in his analysis of Kasagi Shizuko's boogie-woogie and Koga Masao's music in Chapter 4, Sonobe remained fundamentally skeptical of the value of popular songs as they existed, seeing them as, at best, reflections of a degenerate society under capitalist oppression and the shadow of Cold War.

Nevertheless, Sonobe's persistence in analyzing popular songs in subsequent decades betrayed a deep interest in the musical lives of ordinary people and a sense of mission in his desire to enrich the musical culture of Japan's masses. While enrichment had clearly been a sentiment expressed by members of Japan's musical establishment since the Meiji period, Sonobe stood out in the persistence with which he pursued this in the postwar period. As he wrote in the postscript to *On Popular Music*, Sonobe believed that what he saw as the "democratic revolution" taking place in Japan in the wake of World War II presented an opportunity for "the vast majority of [Japan's] citizens to rediscover culture, from which they have been hitherto alienated, within their everyday lives," which would, in turn, lead to the creation of a "truly Japanese music."[36] Along with producing books that explored such themes, this conviction led him to pay particular attention to music education for children.

The trajectory of the shift in Sonobe's attitude toward popular songs can be most clearly traced in these postwar writings. In the introduction to *Japanese History from Enka to Jazz,* Sonobe began with a notable confession: "Until a few years ago, I had an extremely moralistic, narrow, and therefore overly critical attitude toward popular songs. One cannot hope for progress in popular songs by simply decrying their vulgarity and decadence. In fact, such an attitude may well lead to Nazi-style calls for regulation, ban, and eradication."[37] As if to further atone for his previous mistakes, Sonobe dedicated the book to the lyricist Nakayama Shimpei, who, according to Sonobe, "loved children, loved the people, and left many songs that came from his warm love for humanity." The book itself is an attempt to emphasize the importance of popular songs by writing a survey of Japanese history through a chronological discussion of major hit songs and their historical contexts—a work that is, in many ways, similar to that of Ogawa Chikagorō in style and even in its conclusions. Throughout the book, Sonobe, like Ogawa, emphasized the origins of the popularity of various songs in the specific political and social contexts of particular historical moments. As such, popular songs were ultimately the products of social realities, for better or worse.

Sonobe's praise of Nakayama in this book was, however, also indicative of his still strongly critical attitudes toward many of the songs that were produced after Nakayama's heyday in the late 1920s. In particular, Sonobe remained as deeply critical of Koga Masao's music as he had been in his analysis of Koga melodies, pointing to what he saw as a significant difference between the two composers: "It is important to note that Nakayama's folk-song inspired ballad and dance tunes, while containing vulgar elements, nonetheless possessed a liberatory aspect and even some cheerfulness at times. In contrast, Koga's [tunes'] character only deepened in their plaintiveness as well as vulgar degeneracy . . . ultimately, such sentimentality reverted to the self-absorbed plaintiveness of the *shamisen* [three-stringed lute] music of the Edo period."[38] From Sonobe's perspective, such a predicament was not entirely the fault of musicians like Koga, in that the popularity of their music clearly reflected broader social and historical realities that made people desire vulgar music. Nevertheless, Sonobe did fault Koga and other creators of popular songs for failing to go beyond simply pandering to the musically conservative popular taste and indulging in what he decried as the shallow sentimentality that pervaded most of their songs.

In 1962 Sonobe expanded his arguments with another book, *On the History of Japanese Popular Songs,* which sought to deepen his earlier analysis of the historical significance of popular songs by tracing the same historical trajectory from the beginning of Meiji period through the postwar period. While the book is notable in that Sonobe's critique of songs by Koga and others is significantly toned down, its most important observations emerge in its last chapter of the book, in which Sonobe pointed to steps he believed were necessary for the popular song genre, especially the "Japanese-sounding songs," to reform itself and overcome its stagnation: "First, I would like to imagine that lyricists and composers of popular songs would be able to gain a place where they could freely exercise their creativity. An example of this can be seen in how film makers created independent production companies and produced many excellent films. Without this, producers of popular songs would continue to be subordinated to specific companies and their creativity would be constantly restrained by the conventionality of commercialism."[39]

In addition, Sonobe argued that songwriters should also overcome their fixation with the "Edo-style pentatonic scale" and the "unchanging plaintiveness" of their music. Without such reforms, Sonobe suggested, the taste of the audience would likely come to favor more and more Western-style music, resulting in the marginalization of *enka* and other Japanese-style tunes. As we have seen already, both Sonobe's suggestions for reform and his predictions about the fate of pop music in Japan were, in fact, quite prescient. It is unclear if or when Sonobe realized this himself. In 1980 he sought to republish a revised edition of his 1962 book but this endeavor was cut short by the rapid deterioration of his health and ultimately death in May of that year. The second edition was, in fact, published three months after his death but the book remained largely unchanged from the earlier edition, except for a short foreword that was written for the new edition. In it, Sonobe poignantly notes that, in hindsight, "I still did not sufficiently understand the nature of popular songs when this book was first published."[40]

Sonobe's death leaves us in the dark as to precisely how his thinking might have changed in relation to his 1962 book, but an article he wrote in 1969 for the Science of Thought group's *The Secret of Popular Songs* reveals his understanding that there were dramatic shifts under way in Japan's popular music scene. Pointing to developments like the emergence of the electric guitar and the growing prominence of teenagers among the consumers of popular music, Sonobe suggested that the change was ultimately global in scale, as "masses throughout the world are seemingly refusing all music that has been created by past conventions and rules."[41] While still expressing caution about the liberatory potentials of popular music, Sonobe echoed Tada, Terayama, and Mori's sense that they were indeed living in "a time of change," going so far as to refer to a line from Bob Dylan's "The Times They Are A-Changin'" (1964) that specifically admonishes "writers and critics" to refrain from hasty judgments.[42] Sonobe's use of Dylan's words is significant not only because it echoes his belief that a fundamental transformation was under way but also because he is seemingly alluding to the changing position of critics like himself within broader popular culture. Amidst the dramatic changes that were taking place around them, longtime critics like Sonobe found themselves in increasingly unfamiliar and unpredictable cultural territory where they no longer seemed to possess the security and authority they did in the previous decades.

Conclusion

By the time Sonobe quoted Bob Dylan in 1969, there were already signs that the critics who had hoped for the revolutionary potential of newly valorized popular songs would be sourly disappointed. Rather than celebrating social marginality, *enka* was, in fact, increasingly co-opted by the more conservative forces within Japan's political landscape as a saccharine symbol of the traditional Japan. The New Left movement, which led the critique of the older progressives' prejudice against mass culture, was also showing signs of weakness by the late 1960s, as the authorities regained control of university campuses and the movement disintegrated into increasingly fractious factions. And yet this did not lead the critics to revert to their previous critiques of popular music. In fact, they had no means to do so. The world of popular music had changed so fundamentally that such a reversal was impossible. By 1970 "popular songs" had, in effect, ceased to be a useful category to capture a body of musical commodity, unable as it was to capture the realities of what was by then a staggeringly more musically diverse market. At the same time, the dominance of the recording industry in the production of songs, which had underpinned the popular song genre from its beginnings in the late 1920s, was now completely undermined by the growing prominence of television broadcasters in Japan's entertainment scene which, in turn, spurred the rise of production companies as well as freelance artists. In short, Japan's Popular Song Era had come to an end.

However, a broader societal shift underpinned this transformation in popular music and its place in Japanese media culture,

namely the perceived realization of a "mass middle-class society."
In 1970 Japan's Prime Minister's Office published the now famous "Opinion Survey about National Life" (Kokumin seikatsu
boron chōsa), in which roughly 90 percent of respondents indicated that they considered themselves to be in "the middle stratum"
of society. Conducted annually since 1959, the survey asked the
respondents to choose from "upper," "upper middle," "middle of
middle," "lower middle," and "lower" to indicate what they saw as
the level of their lifestyle relative to the larger society.[43] This is not to
say that, in terms of actual demographic and economic realities,
Japan was in fact a mass, middle-class society. Ironically, economic
inequity had actually increased since the immediate postwar period, when a combination of wartime destruction, the contrasting
conditions of urban and rural residents, and the effects of Allied
reforms led to a dramatic closing of the wealth gap across various
economic strata.[44] Nonetheless, the dramatic boom witnessed in
the vaunted high economic growth period from the late 1950s
through the 1960s and the success of the LDP government's "Income
Doubling Plan" had managed to convince the vast majority of
Japanese that they were living in an increasingly classless society.

The emergence of such a perception coincided with salient debates within both intellectual and political circles. Since the late
1950s, social scientists had debated the nature of the mass society
that was seen to be emerging in Japan, along with its implications
for the nation's historical and political trajectory. As early as 1957,
the intellectual historian Fujita Shōzō (1927–2003), a student of
Maruyama Masao, argued that a "new middle stratum" accounted
for "the vast majority" of Japanese, suggesting that the more dual-
istic notion of class structure that was based on the existence of the
capitalist and working classes was no longer adequate.[45] Two decades later, the economist Murakami Yasusuke (1931–1993) argued
that Japan was now dominated by "an enormous intermediate

stratum of society, neither upper nor lower class," which was "highly homogenous in style of life and attitudes."[46] Citing the 1970 survey by the Prime Minister's Office, Murakami argued that this view was "supported by substantial data" indicating developments such as increasing homogenization, and cited increasingly blurred boundaries between blue- and white-collar employees due to changes in workplace management, spread of mass consumption, and the urbanization of agricultural communities. Attitudes were, in turn, increasingly standardized by the proliferation of both mass media and mass university education. Therefore, Murakami concluded, "There are no longer any fundamental differences in ways of talking, dressing or living among office supervisor, office worker, plant foremen, factory worker, store-owner, clerk or farmer."[47]

Both Fujita's and Murakami's arguments were greeted with deep skepticism and hostility from a range of critics, especially Marxist scholars who remained committed to the notion of proletarian masses as well as others who cast doubt on the alleged uniformity of the middle stratum. Similar debates emerged in the Diet after the publication of the 1970 survey, in which members of the JSP questioned the extent to which an opinion survey could grasp objective, social reality.[48] Nevertheless, the notion that Japan had become a uniform, middling society quickly gained currency, and "middlingness" was increasingly seen as a matter of subjective consciousness rather than a category based on objective socioeconomic status—a development that was not coincidental with the growing dominance of the conservative LDP government, whose hold on power was in no small part due to its successful outmaneuvering of the leftist opposition in the 1970s and 1980s.

What ultimately resulted was the gradual disappearance of the very notion of class from Japan's public discourse, and with it a regime of cultural hierarchy that was dependent on the implied superiority of "middle-class" culture. Conversely, in a society that

increasingly saw itself to be classless, it became increasingly difficult to make a credible case against mass culture from the basis of its
assumed, inherent vulgarity. This, perhaps more than anything
else, explains the marked shift in the tone of the critics of popular
songs and their ultimate disappearance in the last decades of the
twentieth century. This was not, after all, the same world as the
one in which in which "Tokyo March" was born. In 1929 and the
decades that followed, popular songs drew critical attention precisely because they emerged in the crux of two major historical
realities. On the one hand, the songs produced by the then nascent recording industry constituted what was the most credible
solution to what was by then a decades-old conundrum of realizing
a truly *popular* music that possessed mass appeal. On the other
hand, members of Japan's musical, intellectual, and political establishments lived in a society that was, both in reality and perception, so deeply divided by socioeconomic status and cultural hierarchy that, for most of them, their reflexive reaction was to quickly
judge that these songs, far from being the ideal middle-class music
that was neither too vulgar nor the exclusive domain of the educated
elite, were in fact irredeemably lowbrow.

When these two contradictory impulses collided, they sparked
a debate not only on popular songs but on mass culture in general
that survived what were arguably the most tumultuous decades of
modern Japanese history. Despite the hopes of various critics who
participated in this debate along the way, neither war nor changes
in political regimes managed to quell this discussion. It was only
when most Japanese began to believe that their society was not so
riven by class that the concern for "vulgar" culture receded. When
it did, it did so as quickly as the Popular Song Era came to an end,
ushering in what was aptly described by contemporary observers
as Japan's "Television Age."[49]

Conclusion: The Television Age and Beyond

By the 1970s the Popular Song Era was over. Mass consumer culture had succeeded in becoming part of the everyday lives of the vast majority of Japanese, who increasingly began to imagine themselves as a nation made up almost entirely of middle-class inhabitants. In the decades that followed, mass culture flourished, as television sets proliferated in Japanese households and introduced a paradigm shift in the ways that existing entertainment media, including music, were consumed. More broadly, Japan's rise to become the second-largest economy in the world during the same period facilitated the emergence of a new wave of Japanese mass cultural products, from animated cartoons to computer games, that began to capture markets far beyond Japan.

Despite Japan's economic decline beginning in the early 1990s, this trend has seemingly only accelerated in the new millennium, leading to an almost triumphalist valorization of Japan's pop culture by policy makers who had hitherto viewed mass culture with, at the very least, suspicion. During the same decades, mass culture critique lost much of the explicitly classist edge it had previously possessed, as anxieties surrounding class-based conflicts dissipated and critics risked being perceived as reactionary elitists who were out of touch with the everyday realities of the consuming majority. Popular songs produced by the recording industry became uncontroversial and even came to be seen as part of Japan's cultural establishment by new generations of musicians.[1] To be sure, the critique of mass culture and in particular new media, from television to cell phones, continued to emerge in the national discourse, leading to occasional controversies and efforts at regulation. Yet much of the mass culture critique that emerged in Japan during the second half of the twentieth century has served less as a sign of an ongoing assault on mass culture than as a sign of its seemingly inexorable ubiquity.

The Television Regime

Of particular note in this regard is the establishment of television's hegemony, not only in terms of the ways in which it forced the transformation of existing mass media, but also in the way that its emergence led to the fundamental restructuring of cultural politics and hierarchies in the last three decades of the twentieth century. Arguably for the first time in Japanese history, a single medium could rightfully boast of a truly national audience. While radio had succeeded in gaining similar ubiquity in the postwar era, it could not rival television's allure to the nation and was ultimately relegated to a secondary mass media that was more regional in its scope. It was left to Japan's television broadcasters, both public and private, to shape a viewership that was national not only in terms of its scope but also in the way that each viewer was implicated in Japan's postwar nation-state.

It was through television that the vast majority of Japanese experienced the mass projects of the postwar state, one of the most notable examples being the transformation of the imperial household into an emblem of the mass consumer society as demonstrated by the 1959 wedding of Crown Prince Akihito (b. 1933) and Shōda Michiko (b. 1934), which was televised and broadcast nationwide.[2] The second such event was the Tokyo Olympics of 1964, which not only showcased Japan's "economic miracle" and its newly achieved status in geopolitics but also reportedly prompted a surge in the purchase of color televisions. It was also through television that Japanese perceptions of some of the most tumultuous political struggles were shaped, including the Asama Sansō Incident of 1972, in which members of the New Red Army, a New Left group, took hostages in a resort villa in Nagano prefecture. Weeks of internal dissension eventually led to several members being lynched to death. The group's final stand-off with the police was broadcast live to a nation that was gripped with what many saw as the grisly conclusion and indictment of the New Left politics of the 1960s and 1970s. More subtly, however, television nationalized its audience by restructuring everyday life and the very "timetable" by which each viewer lived, syncing it with a nationally uniform one.[3] From the morning news shows to the evening prime time programs, known as "Golden Hour" in Japan, television standardized the flow of everyday life for the vast majority of Japanese to the extent that no other medium or institution had managed. Significantly, television broadcasting achieved this not in the guise of an external power intervening on the everyday life of individuals but, instead, by emerging as a force from *within,* as it transformed the most intimate social formations, including the postwar conceptions of "the family."[4]

At the same time, observant critics recognized from the outset the potential for television to upend the existing intellectual and cultural authorities that were, even into the 1950s, vested in the world of print media. It was primarily from this perch, after all, that the popular song critics waged their war on "vulgar" culture throughout the era discussed in this book. Television's ascendance was, in fact, initially greeted with serious, sustained, and occasionally searing critique from members of Japan's intellectual establishment, the most famous being the social critic Ōya Sōichi (1900–1970), who accused television of threatening to create "a nation of one hundred million idiots" in 1957.[5] While Oya was critical of what he saw as an abundance of superficial vulgarity in the new medium, he was ultimately more wary of the hegemony that he foresaw it would gain over the nation's intellectual and cultural life.

In fact, many of the early proponents of television were themselves quite sympathetic to such concerns. Many articulated a vision for the development of television primarily as an educational medium. This was not only the case for the Japan Broadcasting Corporation (Nihon Hōsō Kyōkai, NHK), which created an entire channel that was devoted to education in 1959, but also for the former police bureaucrat Shōriki Matsutarō's Nippon Television Network Corporation, which launched as the first private broadcaster in 1953. The demand for educational television found its most concrete legal backing in the revised Broadcasting Act of 1959, which mandated broadcasters to "achieve harmony" in their programming by including "educational" (*kyōiku bangumi*) as well as "cultural" (*kyōyō*) programs.[6] At the same time, many of the broadcasters that were subsequently licensed by the state were explicitly authorized as "educational" channels.

Within the first two decades of television broadcasting, however, it became clear that the vision for television as a medium that was primarily educational in purpose was not to be. From its early years, the most popular programs were those that occupied a category that could only be described as "entertainment," including the pro-wrestling matches featuring the notorious Rikidōzan, whose violent and even occasionally bloody escapades captured the audience of the late 1950s. As we have seen, popular music also became a major component of most broadcasters' programming, with the growing popularity of musical variety shows and singing contests. As each broadcaster sought to boost its ratings, the "harmony" mandated by the Broadcasting Act became a mere formality, as broadcasters designated a variety of programs, including high school baseball tournaments, as "cultural programs" to the incredulity of their critics.[7] The end of the education-focused vision for television ultimately became clear when most of the private broadcasters that were originally licensed as educational channels were relicensed as purely commercial entities that were less encumbered by the educational mandates of their initial arrangements. This development also signaled the ultimate failure of Japan's intellectual elites to keep television on a lower rung of nation's cultural hierarchy, leading to the rapid loss of the authority they had boasted until then.[8]

The new authority that television had gained as a predominantly entertainment-focused medium was most apparent in the way it not only rehabilitated previously maligned forms of mass culture like "Tonko Song," but also the way in which it elevated the social status of the leading popular song stars, the most notable example being that of Misora Hibari, who became the "ultimate icon of Japaneseness."[9] Such prominence would have been impossible without the increasingly close relationships singers like Hibari developed with key television broadcasters, including NHK. Similarly, the dominance of J-Pop as the mainstream pop genre emerged within the context of close relationships with television broadcasters. At the same time, television broadcasters did not shy away from their ability to enforce a more direct authority in the form self-censorship. A wide range of media outlets adopted standards as well as enforcement mechanisms for self-censorship in the course of the 1950s and early 1960s, including the recording industry. In the case of popular music, it ultimately became clear that the most effective form of regulation would come from the radio and television broadcasters themselves, in part because the diversification of the recording industry led to the recording of a growing amount of music by "underground" companies that were not regulated by the recording industry association. While the broadcasters have been generally silent about the process by which such censorship in conducted, it became widely accepted that each broadcaster produced internal lists of "banned songs" as well as "banned words" in the course of the 1960s and 1970s.

It is important to note that such practices of censorship continued long after popular songs ceased to be the favorite targets of mass culture critics in the way they were in the 1950s and the preceding decades. Quite apart from the issues and concerns that were particular to the political ferment out of which they emerged, self-censorship by postwar Japanese media and in particular television broadcasters appears to have increasingly operated via its own internal logic that was almost completely opaque to outsiders. This general lack of transparency has opened the broadcasters up to the critique that they were making their decisions based on political considerations, especially when canceled programs were considered to be seen as critical of government policies.[10] While there is a significant dearth of scholarly analysis of the inner workings of popular song censorship in the last decades of the twentieth century, existing accounts suggest that a combination of corporate self-preservation and a desire to avoid legal liability led broadcasters to reflexively ban songs in anticipation of complaints coming from a variety of imagined pressure groups, even when the possibility of such claims actually emerging was extremely low.[11] Regardless of the ways in which these practices came under critique from some segments of the viewing public, television broadcasters continue to exercise what is largely an internally driven form of self-censorship to this day.

Posttelevision Japan?

In the twenty-first-century, Japanese television has to a notable extent maintained its status as the hegemonic medium that occupies the heart of the nation's mediascape. The advent of new technologies as seen in the proliferation of personal computers, cell phones and increasingly ubiquitous access to the Internet has, of course, led scholars to suggest that another paradigm shift in media politics is well under way.[12] At the same time, many of the power dynamics that had underpinned media politics in Japan during the last decades of the twentieth century remain deeply entrenched despite the emergence of alternative visions. For example, in comparison to the United States, where first cable providers and subsequently online content providers have undermined the control of major television networks over the medium, Japanese viewing experiences remain far more centralized, organized as they primarily are around NHK, the public broadcaster, and the four private national networks, despite the growth in number of additional channels through satellite or cable services.

Perhaps more than anywhere else the continuing predominance of Japan's existing media companies, and especially that of television networks, is apparent in contemporary Japanese pop culture, which has gained global popularity over the last three decades. On the one hand, some of the most famous examples of these, including the Pokémon franchise and the pop music group AKB48, trace their roots to relatively newer media phenomena. Pokémon first emerged in 1996 as a popular video game by the industry giant Nintendo for its Game Boy platform, while AKB48 was formed in 2005 by the record producer Akimoto Yasushi as an "idol" group that performed live in the Akihabara district of Tokyo, which has come to be known as the center of the multimedia-infused, contemporary Japanese pop culture. Within just a few years, however, both gained prominence on television—developments that were in turn parlayed into the creation of a multimedia franchises that have come to boast global reach. As such, the so-called "Cool Japan" phenomenon of late is as indicative of the continuing power of existing media to

capitalize on the latest pop culture phenomena as it is of the emergence of potentially paradigm-shifting new media.

Nevertheless, it is also within the realm of Cool Japan that scholars
have identified the effects of broader social and political trends that
may well lead to yet more change in Japan's media politics. As the
anthropologist Anne Allison notes, during the same period in which
Cool Japan became a global phenomenon, "Japan has been beset
by a nagging recession, national malaise, and needling sense of fu-
turelessness," which have in turn prompted Japanese observers
and policy makers to take a critical view of the nation's youth,
whose lifestyle and culture have come under significant scrutiny.[13]
As journalists, academics, and politicians have identified new forms
of problematic youths in the new millennium, including "parasite
singles" and "NEETs" (Not in Education, Employment, or
Training), both the youth and the pop culture they consume have
been criticized for contributing to the perceived loss of the nation's
productivity, in both an economic and biological sense.

While this might suggest the emergence of a new riff on the time-
honored tendency for Japan's intellectual and political elite to con-
flate pop culture with a perceived crisis among the youth, a more
significant and potentially fundamental development may be seen
among the growing number of Japanese, both young and old, who
are finding themselves in an increasingly precarious position, both
economically and socially. The bursting of the "Bubble Economy"
in 1991 ultimately seems to have signaled the end of Japan as an
"enterprise society," in which citizens were disciplined as loyal
members of corporations and nuclear families in return for security
and prosperity within a nation that had come to boast the second-
largest economy in the world.[14] Instead, a growing sense of mis-
trust of the very institutions that formed the core of the enterprise
society, be it the central government or the major corporations,
accompanies an ongoing sense of national malaise and a seemingly

unsolvable set of challenges, from population decline to growing geopolitical competition with an ascendant China. Not insignificantly, this has also coincided with a growing discourse on the reemergence of an economically "stratified society" (*kakusa shakai*). In other words, even as television maintains its dominance in Japan's mediascape, many of the economic, social, and political underpinnings of the Television Age have, in fact, eroded in recent decades. Combined with ongoing technological changes in media, especially as they relate to the increasingly ubiquitous Internet, it seems more likely than not that Japan is facing yet another paradigm shift, not only in the ways in which people interact with media but also in how they are politicized.

Notes

Throughout the text and notes of this book, Japanese names are rendered following the Japanese convention, in which the surname precedes the given name, with the exception of authors whose works were originally published in English.

Introduction: The Popular Song Era

1. *Kayōkyoku* had actually already come into use during the second half of the 1930s and was used interchangeably with *ryūkōka* until it completely supplanted the latter term. As with *ryūkōka*, the term was a neologism that was derived from a previously used term, in this case *kayō* (songs and ballads), which had been used since the classical era to describe a wide variety of musical as well as literary arts, including traditional sung poetry.

2. For a comprehensive examination of the politics of *modan* culture and, in particular, the related phenomenon of *ero guro nansensu*, see Miriam Silverberg, *Erotic Grotesque Nonsense: The Mass Culture of Japanese Modern Times* (Berkeley: University of California Press, 2006); for an in-depth study of the intellectual history of modernity and everyday life in 1930s Japan, see Harry Harootunian, *Overcome by Modernity* (Princeton, NJ: Princeton University Press, 2000); in Japanese, Yoshimi Shunya, "Teito tokyo to modanitī no bunka seiji" [The imperial capital Tokyo and the politics of modernity], in Komori Yōichi et al., eds., *Iwanami kōza, kindai nihon no bunkashi* [The Iwanami cultural history of modern Japan], vol. 6, *Kakudaisuru modanitī* [Expanding modernity] (Tokyo: Iwanami shoten, 2002), 3–61, offers a

succinct summary of the cultural politics of modernity and urban life in Japan's capital.

3. This is especially apparent in standard surveys of popular song history that have been produced in Japan, such as Kurata Yoshihiro, *Nihon rekōdo bunkashi* [Cultural history of records in Japan] (Tokyo: Iwanami shoten, 2006); Komota Nobuo, *Shinpan nihon ryūkōkashi jō 1868–1937* [History of Japanese popular songs], revised edition, vol. 1 (Tokyo: Shakai shisōsha, 1994); Komota Nobuo, *Shinpan nihon ryūkōkashi chū 1838–1959* [History of Japanese popular songs], revised edition, vol. 2 (Tokyo: Shakai shisōsha, 1995).

4. For a succinct description of the place of "transwar" in Japanese historiography, see Andrew Gordon, "Consumption, Leisure and the Middle Class in Transwar Japan," Social Science Japan Journal 10, no. 1 (2007), 3.

5. For an example of a study on the issue of cultural authenticity, see E. Taylor Atkins on the ongoing efforts to "authenticate" jazz by its Japanese practitioners and aficionados in *Blue Nippon: Authenticating Jazz in Japan* (Durham, NC: Duke University Press, 2001). For an excellent example of a study on wartime cultural politics, see Louise Young's discussion of the prominence of Manchuria in domestic popular culture and mass media after the Japanese invasion of Manchuria in 1931 in *Japan's Total Empire: Manchuria and the Culture of Wartime Imperialism* (Berkeley: University of California Press, 1998). For the impact of the Allied occupation on Japanese politics and culture, there are few better introductions than John Dower's *Embracing Defeat: Japan in the Wake of World War II* (New York: W.W. Norton, 1999), while Yoshimi Shunya's *Shinbei to hanbei: Sengo nihon no seijiteki muishiki* [Pro-American and anti-American: The political unconscious of postwar Japan] (Tokyo: Iwanami shinsho, 2007) succinctly traces that changing presence of America within postwar Japanese imaginations as well as lived experiences.

6. Thomas C. Smith, "Japan's Aristocratic Revolution," in *Native Sources of Japanese Industrialization, 1750–1920* (Berkeley: University of California Press, 1989), 146–147; emphasis added.

7. For a detailed analysis of the Iwakura Embassy's encounter with Western music, see Okunaka Yasuto, *Kokka to ongaku* [The nation-state and music] (Tokyo: Shunjūsha, 2008), 41–87.

8. "The American Peace Festival," *Illustrated London News*, no. 1714 (Saturday, July 13, 1872), 47.

9. Kume Kunitake, comp., *The Iwakura Embassy, 1871–73: A True Account of the Ambassador Extraordinary and Plenipotentiary's Journeys of Observation through the United States and Europe,* vol. 6, ed. Graham Healey and Chushichi Tsuzuki, trans. Martin Collcutt (Princeton, NJ: Princeton University Press, 2002), 311.

10. Fukuzawa Yukichi, *Bunmeiron no gairyaku* [An outline of a theory of civilization], in William Theodore De Bary et al., eds., *Sources of Japanese Tradition,* vol. 2, *1600 to 2000,* part II, *1868 to 2000 (Abridged)* (New York: Columbia University Press, 2006), 35.

11. Izawa Shūji and Yamazumi Masami, eds., *Yōgaku kotohajime: Ongaku torishirabe seiseki shinpōsho* [The beginnings of Western music: Report on the investigation of music] (Tokyo: Heibonsha, 1994), 3.

12. Chōkichi Kikkawa, *Autobiography of Baron Chōkichi Kikkawa,* ed. by his sons (Tokyo: Public Domain, 1917), 30–31.

13. Nakamura Kōsuke, *Seiyō no oto, nihon no mimi: Kindai nihon bungaku to seiyō ongaku* [Western sound and Japanese ears: Modern Japanese literature and Western music] (Tokyo: Shunjūsha, 2002), 46.

14. Luciana Galliano, *Yōgaku: Japanese Music in the Twentieth Century* (Lanham, MD: Scarecrow Press, 2002), 16.

15. Tsukahara Yasuko, *Meiji kokka to gagaku* [The Meiji state and music] (Tokyo: Yūshisha, 2009) 6–7, 110.

16. Izawa Shūji, letter to Luther Whiting Mason, July 1, 1880, in Tokyo geijutsu daigaku hyakunenshi henshū iinkai, ed., *Tokyo geijutsu daigaku hyakunenshi: Tokyo ongakugakkō hen* [A hundred-year history of the Tokyo National University of Fine Arts and Music: Tokyo Music School] (Tokyo: Ongaku no tomosha, 1987), 93–94.

17. Izawa and Yamazumi, *Yōgaku kotohajime,* 288–289.

18. Megata Tanetarō, "Nihon ongaku ni kansuru megata no iken" [Megata's opinion on Japanese music], November 3, 1877, in Tokyo geijutsu daigaku huzoku toshokan, ed., *Ongaku torishirabe gakari jidai (Meiji 13 nen~20 nen) shozō mokuroku* [Collection index for the Music Investigation Committee era (1880–1887)], vol. 3 (Tokyo: Tokyo geijutsu daigaku fuzoku toshokan, 1971), 2.

19. Tsukahara, *Meiji kokka to gagaku,* 111; Carol Gluck, "The Invention of Edo," in Steven Vlastos, ed., *Mirror of Modernity: Invented Traditions of Modern Japan* (Berkeley: University of California Press, 1998), 265–266.

20. Satō Dōshin, *Meiji kokka to kindai bijutsu* [The Meiji state and modern art] (Tokyo: Yoshikawa kōbunkan, 1999), 22–42.

21. Ibid., 32–35.

22. Other opportunities to be trained as performers included military bands and Christian churches, as well as commercial bands that were initially created as a form of public advertisement.

23. In the prewar era, compulsory education ended at primary school; relatively few Japanese moved on to middle school and even fewer went to high school. High schools not only served as entryways to universities but were also conceived as institutions that would provide a broad-based liberal arts education for the nation's elite. Among them, the First High School (Tokyo) and the Third High School (Kyoto) were particularly renowned and associated with the elite imperial universities in their respective locale; in fact, both institutions were amalgamated into these universities as schools of liberal arts (*kyōyō gakubu*) in the postwar era.

24. Katō Yoshiko, "Kurashikku aikōka towa dareka" [Who were the classic fans?], in Watanabe Hiroshi et al., eds., *Kurashikku ongaku no seijigaku* [The politics of classical music] (Tokyo: Seikyūsha, 2005), 151–153. See also Katō Yoshiko, "Hyōronka to ensōka: Senzenki ninon ni okeru 'gakudan' no keisei" [Critics and performers: The formation of the "music establishment" in prewar Japan], *Osaka University Annals of Educational Studies 2* (1997), 33–45. Here the "old" middle class refers to what Ezra Vogel described as "the small independent businessman and landowner," including merchants, shopkeepers, and artisans, whereas the "new" middle class refers to university-educated, salaried, white-collar employees of larger corporations and bureaucracies. See Ezra Vogel, *Japan's New Middle Class* (Berkeley: University of California Press, 1963), 4.

25. Katō, "Kurashikku aikōka towa dareka," 153–158.

1. The Invention of Popular Song

1. Azami Toshio, *Popyurā ongaku wa darega tsukurunoka* [Who makes popular music?] (Tokyo: Keisō shobō, 2004), 112; Komota Nobuo, *Nihon ryūkōkashi* [History of Japanese popular songs] (Tokyo: Shakai shisōsha, 1970), 81; Kurata, *Nihon rekōdo bunkashi,* 177–178.

2. Ogawa Chikagorō, *Ryūkōka to sesō: Jihenka ni okeru kayō no shimei* [Popular songs and social currents: The mission of songs under the incident] (Tokyo: Nihon keisatsu shimbunsha, 1941), 148.

3. While the term *taishū* came into use in the late 1920s to describe an urban population that was made up of multiple social classes, a similar part of the population was identified in the preceding decades by the term *minshū* (people), which in many instances referred specifically to the working-class population. See Minami Hiroshi, ed., *Taishō bunka* [Mass culture] (Tokyo: Keisō shobō, 1977), 101–117; Harootunian, *Overcome by Modernity*, 106–107; Silverberg, *Erotic Grotesque Nonsense*, 44. In the eyes of these intellectuals, the *minshū* were often seen to possess positive political potential as subjects of political reform, but most did not see the possibility for such autonomy in the *taishū*, who were seen as increasingly at the mercy of the capitalist system.

4. Hosokawa Shūhei, "Ongaku, Onkyō / Music, Sound," *Working Words: New Approaches to Japanese Studies*, UC Berkeley Center for Japanese Studies, April 20, 2012, http://escholarship.org/uc/item/9451p047, p. 2.

5. Ibid., 3–5.

6. Gerald Groemer, "The Rise of Japanese Music," *World of Music* 46, no. 2 (2004): 32.

7. Nishiyama Matsunosuke, *Edo Culture: Daily Life and Diversions in Urban Japan, 1600–1868* (Honolulu: University of Hawai'i Press, 1997), 209.

8. Groemer, "Rise of Japanese Music," 33.

9. Ibid., 31, 34.

10. Hosokawa, "Ongaku, Onkyō / Music, Sound," 5–7.

11. *Shūgiin giji sokkiroku* (1890), in Tokyo geijutsu daigaku huzoku toshokan, ed., *Ongaku torishirabe gakari jidai (Meiji 13 nen~20 nen) shozō mokuroku* [Collection index for the Music Investigation Committee era (1880–1887)], vol. 3 (Tokyo: Tokyo geijutsu daigaku huzoku toshokan, 1971), 324.

12. Yatabe Ryōkichi, "Ongaku gakkōron" [On the music school], *Kokka kyōiku* 5 (February 1891), in Tokyo geijutsu daigaku hyakunenshi henshū iinkai, ed., *Tokyo geijutsu daigaku hyakunenshi: Tokyo ongakugakkō hen* [One-hundred-year history of the Tokyo University of the Arts: Tokyo Music School] (Tokyo: Ongaku no tomosha, 1987), 354–356.

13. Mariko Tamanoi, *Under the Shadow of Nationalism: Politics and Poetics of Rural Japanese Women* (Honolulu: University of Hawai'i Press, 1998), 55–84; E. Patricia Tsurumi, *Factory Girls: Women in the Thread Mills of Meiji Japan* (Princeton, NJ: Princeton University Press, 1990), is interspersed with evocative songs sung by young female textile workers.

14. Komota, *Nihon ryūkōkashi*, 15–27; for an overview of the transition of popular music from the late Edo to the early Meiji period, see Kurata Yoshihiro, *"Hayariuta" no kōkogaku* [Archaeology of *hayariuta*] (Tokyo: Bunshun shinsho, 2001).

15. Soeda Azembō, *A Life Adrift: Soeda Azembō, Popular Song, and Modern Mass Culture in Japan,* trans. Michael Lewis (London: Routledge, 2009), includes an overview of the history of *enkashi* along with the personal account of Soeda, the most famous of the prewar *enka* performers. As noted in Christine Yano, *Tears of Longing: Nostalgia and the Nation in Japanese Popular Song* (Cambridge, MA: Harvard University Asia Center, 2002), 28–41, the postwar *enka* derived its name from the prewar phenomenon. Nevertheless, as discussed in Chapter 5, the postwar *enka* was primarily the product of an invented connection to the past, including its supposed Meiji ancestor, and therefore should be considered to be a largely unrelated phenomenon.

16. On the creation of Japanese "suburbs" in the 1910s and 1920s, see Fujiya Yōetsu and Kadono Yukihiro, eds., *Kindai nihon no kōgai jutakuchi* [Suburbs of modern Japan] (Tokyo: Kajima shuppankai, 2000), and Higuchi Tadahiko, *Kōgai no fūkei: Edo kara tokyo e* [The view of the suburbs: From Edo to Tokyo] (Tokyo: Kyōiku shuppan, 2000). On the broader history of the transformation of the Japanese home in the context of the rise of consumer culture, see Jordan Sand, *House and Home in Modern Japan: Architecture, Domestic Space, and Bourgeois Culture, 1880–1930* (Cambridge, MA: Harvard University Asia Center, 2003).

17. Hatsuda Tōru, *Hyakkaten no tanjō* [The birth of the department store] (Tokyo: Sanseidō, 1993), 152–156.

18. For an in-depth discussion of the birth of the Takarazuka Revue, see Kawasaki Kenko, *Takarazuka* (Tokyo: Kōdansha, 1999), and Tsuganesawa Toshihiro, *Takarazuka senryaku* [Takarazuka strategy] (Tokyo: Kōdansha, 1991); for an ethnographic analysis of its more contemporary development, see Jennifer Robertson, *Takarazuka: Sexual Politics and Popular Culture in Modern Japan* (Berkeley: University of California Press, 1998).

19. Uchiyama Sōjūrō, *Asakusa opera no seikatsu* [Life in the Asakusa Opera] (Tokyo: Yūzankaku, 1967), 226–231; Uchiyama himself was involved with the Asakusa Opera as a director. See also Masui Keiji, *Asakusa opera monogatari* [The story of the Asakusa Opera] (Tokyo: Geijutsu gendaisha, 1990); Kamiyama Keisuke, *Asakusa no hyakunen: Kamiyabā no hitobito* [Asakusa's hundred years: The people at Kamiya bar] (Tokyo: Shinbisha, 1989).

20. Tsutsui Kiyotada, *Saijō Yaso* (Tokyo: Chūkō bunko, 2008), 58–69. For an in-depth introduction to the *dōyō* movement, see Shūtō Yoshiki, *Dōyō no kindai: Media no henyō to kodomo bunka* [Dōyō modernity: The transformation of media and children's culture] (Tokyo: Iwanami shoten, 2015).

21. Kurata, *Nihon rekōdo bunkashi*, 111.

22. Ishikawa Yoshikazu, "Taishū ongaku" [Mass music], *Ongaku to chikuonki* 13, no. 3 (March 1926); "Ongaku no taishūka" [Massification of music], *Ongaku to chikuonki* 13, no. 4 (April 1926); "Futatabi ongaku no taishūka ni tsuite" [Again on the massification of music], *Ongaku to chikuonki* 13, no. 5 (May 1926); "Gakkai no sōtō kara ongaku no taishūka e" [From conflicts within the music establishment to the massification of music], *Ongaku to chikuonki* 13, no. 6 (June 1926).

23. Ishikawa, "Taishū ongaku," 2.

24. Ishikawa, "Futatabi ongaku no taishūka ni tsuite," 7.

25. Ishikawa "Gakkai no sōtō kara ongaku no taishūka e," 2–4.

26. Part of Ishikawa's critique likely stemmed from his own marginal position within the music establishment, by which he was largely ignored. This was due in part to the fact that his overseas musical training had been in the United States rather than Europe, as well as to the eclecticism of his own musical endeavors that involved highly idiosyncratic and experimental compositional techniques. See Akiyama Kuniharu, *Shōwa no sakkyokuka tachi: Taiheiyō sensō to ongaku* [Shōwa-era composers: The Pacific War and music] (Tokyo: Misuzu shobō, 2014), 134–150.

27. On the introduction of the phonograph in early twentieth-century Japan, see Nihon rekōdo kyōkai, *Shadan hōjin nihon rekōdo kyōkai gojūnenshi* [Fifty-year history of the Recording Industry Association of Japan] (Tokyo: Nihon rekōdo kyōkai, 1993), 3–25; Kurata, *Nihon rekōdo bunkashi*, 1–78.

28. Nihon Chikuonki Shōkai, ed., *Nitchiku (Koromubia) sanjūnenshi* [Thirty-year history of Columbia Japan] (Nihon Chikuonki Shōkai, 1940), 19–22.

29. Kurata, *Nihon rekōdo bunkashi,* 76–84.

30. On the development of *shingeki,* see Matsumoto Kappei, *Nihon shingekishi: Shingeki binbō monogatari* [History of *shingeki* in Japan: The story of *shingeki* in poverty] (Tokyo: Chikuma shobō, 1967); Ōzasa Yoshio, *Nihon gendai engekishi: Taishō Shōwa-hen* [History of modern Japanese drama: Taishō and Shōwa periods] (Tokyo: Hakusuisha, 1986).

31. Nakayama Shimpei, "Hayariuta mondō" [Questions and answers on popular songs], *Minzoku geijutsu* 1, no. 6 (February 1929): 47.

32. Azami, *Popyurā ongaku wa darega tsukurunoka,* 65–79.

33. Nihon rekōdo kyōkai, *Shadan hōjin nihon rekōdo kyōkai gojūnenshi,* 36.

34. Ibid., 35.

35. Azami, *Popyurā ongaku wa darega tsukurunoka,* 93–94.

36. David Suisman, *Selling Sounds: The Commercial Revolution in American Music* (Cambridge, MA: Harvard University Press, 2009), 268–269; U.S. Columbia was eventually resold due to the antitrust concerns that were raised by the EMI merger.

37. Kikuchi Kan, *Tokyo kōshinkyoku* [Tokyo march], in *Kikuchi kan chōhen shōsetsushū* [Collection of Kikuchi Kan's novels], vol. 8 (Tokyo: Bungei shunjū, 1994), 296.

38. Zen ongakufu shuppansha shuppanbu, ed., *Fukkokuban zen'on kayōkyoku zenshū, 2* [Republished zen'on popular song collection, 2] (Tokyo: Zen ongakufu shuppansha, 1995), 229. Translation by the author.

39. Yano, *Tears of Longing,* 34–35. The term *yonanuki* literally refers to production of the five-note, pentatonic scale through the removal of the fourth and seventh notes found in the more typically Western heptatonic scale.

40. Saijō had already written a similar song in 1928 that was dedicated to Ginza, "Today's Ginza March" ("Tōsei ginza bushi"). See Yoshimi, "Teito tokyo to modanitī no bunka seiji," 18–19.

41. Azami, *Popyurā ongaku wa darega tsukurunoka,* 96–98.

42. In a postwar autobiography, Saijō recalls that the payment he received for "Tokyo March" was minimal because of this: Saijō Yaso, *Uta no jijoden* [Autobiography of songs] (1948), reprinted in *Saijō yaso zenshū, 17* [Saijō Yaso collection, 17] (Tokyo: Kukousho kankōkai, 2007), 50–51.

43. Saijō, *Uta no jijoden,* 47–48.

44. Azami, *Popyurā ongaku wa darega tsukurunoka*, 116–117.

45. Ibid., 112.

46. On the relationship among the original novel, film, popular song, and even stage adaptation of "Tokyo March" as media products, see Shimura Miyoko, "Fukusō sareru media—'Tokyo kōshinkyoku' no eigaka wo megutte" [Media convergence—on the film adaptation of "Tokyo March"], *Engeki kenkyū sentā kiyō: Waseda daigaku 21 seiki COE puroguramu* [The Institute for Theatre Research bulletin: The 21st century COE program, Waseda University], vol. 8 (2007), 253–259; and Nishii Yaeko, "Kikuchi kan kōsaku suru 'tokyo kōshinkyoku'—eiga kouta no ken'inryoku" [Kikuchi Kan and *Tokyo March*—the effect of a movie song on fiction].

47. Saijō, *Uta no jijoden*, 45.

48. Furukawa Takahisa, "Ryūkōka to eiga" [Popular songs and film], in Tonoshita Tatsuya and Chōki Seiji, eds., *Sōryokusen to ongaku bunka: Oto to koe no sensō* [Musical culture and total war: War of sounds and voices] (Tokyo: Seikyūsha: 2008), 55–77.

49. Satō Takumi, *Kingu no jidai* [The times of *Kingu*] (Tokyo: Iwanami shoten, 2002), 33.

50. Komota Nobuo, *Shinpan nihon ryūkōkashi jō 1868–1937* [History of Japanese popular songs], rev. ed., vol. 1, 171; Nihon rekōdo kyōkai, *Shadan hōjin nihon rekōdo kyōkai gojūnenshi*, 44; both sources base their numbers on the Commerce Ministry's Factory Statistics.

51. Naimushō keihokyoku, *Shuppan keisatsu gaikan* [Publication Police Summary] (hereafter "Publication Police Summary"), 1935 (repr., Tokyo: Ryūkei shosha, 1981), 559. Some 3,983 popular songs were submitted for censorship out of a total of 12,210; the second-largest category was "Western music" (2,467).

52. Naimushō keihokyoku, *Shuppan keisatsuhō* [Publication Police Report] (hereafter "Publication Police Report"), vol. 72, 1934 (repr., Tokyo: Ryūkei shosha, 1981), 289–290.

53. Kurata, *Nihon rekōdo bunkashi*, 184.

54. "Iyashii uta no ryūkō ni kokumin kyōiku wo yūryo" [Popularity of vulgar songs causes worry for national education], *Asahi shimbun*, November 13, 1929; Kamita Seiji, "Ongaku kyōshikara tekishisareta merodī no kyōikuka" ["Educationalization" of melodies antagonizes music educators], *Kyōikugaku kenkyū* 74, no. 1 (2007): 18.

55. Tanaka Sumiko, "Kōkaijō: josei no uta wo" [Open letter: Song for women], *Yomiuri shimbun*, August 3, 1929.

56. Kurata, *Nihon rekōdo bunkashi*, 180–181.

57. Andrew Gordon, *A Modern History of Japan: From Tokugawa Times to the Present* (Oxford: Oxford University Press, 2009), 99, 151.

58. Major works on this topic that emerged in this period include Gonda Yasunosuke, *Minshū goraku no kichō* [Foundations of popular leisure] (1921), reprinted in *Gonda yasunosuke chosakushū* [Collected works of Gonda Yasunosuke], vol. 1 (Tokyo: Bunwa shobō, 1974), 289–403; Ōbayashi Munetsugu, *Minshū goraku no jissai kenkyū* [Study on the realities of popular amusement] (1922), reprinted as *Yoka goraku kenkyū kiso bunkenshū* [Basic sources on the study of leisure and entertainment], vol. 3 (Tokyo: Ōzorasha, 1989); Nakata Toshizō, *Goraku no kenkyū* [Study of leisure] (1924), reprinted as *Yoka goraku kenkyū kiso bunkenshū*, vol. 6 (Tokyo: Ōzorasha, 1989); Kon Wajirō and Yoshida Kenkichi, eds., *Moderunorojio: Kōgengaku* [Modernology] (1930), reprinted (Tokyo: Gakuyō shobō, 1986). For a comparative study of Gonda and Kon, see Miriam Silverberg, "Constructing the Japanese Ethnography of Modernity," *Journal of Asian Studies* 51, no. 1 (February 1992): 30–54. For a study on Ōbayashi and his work in Osaka, see Jeffrey Hanes, "Media Culture in Taishō Osaka," in Sharon Minichiello, ed., *Japan's Competing Modernities: Issues in Culture and Democracy, 1900–1930* (Honolulu: University of Hawai'i Press, 1998), 267–285.

59. Andrew Gordon, *Labor and Imperial Democracy in Prewar Japan* (Berkeley: University of California Press, 1991), 26–62.

60. Sasō Tsutomu, *Mizoguchi kenji zen sakuhin kaisetsu 6* [Commentary on all of the works of Mizoguchi Kenji, 6] (Tokyo: Kindai bungeisha, 2009), 116–117, notes that unfortunately much of the original film of *Tokyo March* has been lost. In fact, the extant twenty-five-minute digest of the film excludes all the scenes that featured Sayuri. Consequently, the digest is largely devoid of the depiction of *modan* life that was centered on Sayuri, leaving only the scenes with Michiyo, which mostly take place in the geisha houses. As a result, the setting of the extant *Tokyo March* appears much more traditional than it was in the original film.

61. Kikuchi, *Tokyo kōshinkyoku*, 239.

62. "Eiga kyakuhon 3, Nikkatsu gendaigeki tokusaku, Tokyo kōshinkyoku" [Film scenario 3, Nikkatsu modern film, *Tokyo March*], *Eiga chishiki* 1, no. 3

(July 1929): 93, reproduced in Makino Mamoru, ed., *Senzen eizō riron zasshi shūsei* [Collection of prewar journals on film theory], vol. 8 (Tokyo: Yumani shobō, 1989).

63. Sasō, *Mizoguchi kenji zen sakuhin kaisetsu 6*, 111–114.

64. Kikuchi, *Tokyo kōshinkyoku*, 155.

65. Iba Takashi, "Kōkaijō: nanjaku, akushumi no gendai minyō" [Open letter: Weak and vulgar modern people's songs], *Yomiuri shimbun*, August 4, 1929.

66. Ibid.

67. Ibid.

68. The series included four articles by Iba as well as rebuttals from other musicians, including Tokuyama Tamaki, a popular song singer known for his comical songs: Iba Takashi, "Nihon gakudan no seisan jikō . . . sono 1: Gakudan no daraku wo ikagasen" [Settlement for the Japanese music establishment, 1: What to do with its degeneration], *Ongaku seikai* 4, no. 9 (September 1932): 10–14; "Gakudan no seisan jikō . . . 2: Gakkai wo kyō no suiun michibikitarumono" [Settlement for the Japanese music establishment, 2: What led the music establishment to its decline today], *Ongaku seikai* 4, no. 10 (October 1932): 18–23; "Gakudan no seisan jikō . . . 3: Sakkyokuka no mushiki to hōkanteki taido jō" [Settlement for the Japanese music establishment, 3: The ignorance of composers and their attitude of appeasement, 1], *Ongaku seikai* 4, no. 11 (November 1932): 14–17, 52; "Gakudan no seisan jikō . . . 4: Sakkyokuka no mushiki to hōkanteki taido ge" [Settlement for the Japanese music establishment, 4: The ignorance of composers and their attitude of appeasement 2], *Ongaku seikai* 4, no. 12 (December 1932): 14–21, 70–71; Tokuyama Tamaki, "Boku mo mata daraku wo ikaganisen: Iba sensei no ron ni kotaete" [I, too, will do something about the degeneration: In response to Mr. Iba's argument], *Ongaku seikai* 4 no. 10 (October 1932): 24–27.

69. Iba, "Nihon gakudan no seisan jikō . . . sono 1," 10.

70. Ibid., 12.

71. Iba, "Gakudan no seisan jikō . . . 2," 19.

72. Iba, Gakudan no seisan jikō . . . 3," 16.

73. Iba, "Gakudan no seisan jikō . . . 4," 15, 21.

74. Saijō Yaso, "Iba takashishi ni atau: 'Tokyo kōshinkyoku to boku" [Rebutting Mr. Iba Takashi: "Tokyo March" and I], *Yomiuri shimbun*,

August 4, 1929. Notably, Saijō uses the term *minyō* (people's song) rather than *ryūkōka* to refer to "Tokyo March." The song was one of the earliest hits of the industry, and this indicates that *ryūkōka* had not become the key term to identify such songs in 1929.

75. Ibid.

76. Ibid.

77. Iba, "Gakudan no seisan jikō . . . 4," 20.

78. Kawaji Ryūkō, "Ryūkō kakyoku no haitaisei ge" [The decadence of popular songs 2]," *Yomiuri shimbun*, August 13, 1929.

79. Kawaji Ryūkō, "Ryūkō kakyoku no haitaisei jō [The decadence of popular songs 1], *Yomiuri shimbun*, August 10, 1929.

80. Kawaji, "Ryūkō kakyoku no haitaisei ge."

81. Ibid.

82. Horiuchi Keizō, "Ryūkōka wa shinpo suru jō" [Popular songs are making progress, 1], *Yomiuri shimbun*, August 14, 1929.

83. Horiuchi Keizō, "Ryūkōka wa shinpo suru ge" [Popular songs are making progress, 2], *Yomiuri shimbun*, August 15, 1929.

84. Horiuchi Keizō, "Gendai bunka no kōsei wo kaibō suru, 8: Ryūkō kouta wa naze hayaru" [Analyzing the structure of contemporary culture, no. 8: Why are fashionable ditties popular?], *Yomiuri shimbun*, October 12, 1933.

85. Kanetsune Kiyosuke, "Nihon no ryūkōka wa kanari ni dōtokuteki" [Japanese popular songs are quite moral], *Yomiuri shimbun*, August 16, 1929.

86. Kanetsune Kiyosuke, "Kouta ni mo ideorogī wo" [Bring ideology into songs], *Yomiuri shimbun*, June 23, 1929.

87. Nakano Shigeharu, "Mō hitotsu no tokyo kōshinkyoku e" [Toward a different "Tokyo March"], *Yomiuri shimbun*, August 20, 1929; see also Miriam Silverberg, *Changing Song: The Marxist Manifestos of Nakano Shigeharu* (Princeton, NJ: Princeton University Press, 1990), 125–127.

88. Hara Tarō, "Iba sensei no kago" [Mistakes of Mr. Iba], *Ongaku seikai* 4, no. 11 (November 1932): 18–26.

89. Ibid., 20.

90. Ibid., 21.

91. Ibid., 23.

92. Gonda Yasunosuke, "Ryūkōka no shōhinsei to bunka no mondai" [The nature of popular songs as commodity and the problem of culture], *Hōchi shimbun*, October 4, 1936, reprinted in *Gonda yasunosuke chosakushū*

[Collected works of Gonda Yasunosuke], vol. 4 (Tokyo: Bunwa shobō, 1975), 317.

93. Horiuchi, "Gendai bunka no kōsei wo kaibō suru."

94. Iba Takashi, "Gakudan wo tsuku jō" [Piercing the music establishment, 1], *Yomiuri shimbun,* March 15, 1934.

95. Iba Takashi, "Gakudan wo tsuku ge" [Piercing the music establishment, 2], *Yomiuri shimbun,* March 16, 1934.

96. Nakai Masakazu, "Dan no kaitai" [The dissolution of establishments], *Osaka Asahi shimbun,* January 19, 1932.

97. Nakai Masakazu, "Bundan no seikaku: Dan no kaitai ni tuite (so no ni)" [The characteristics of the literary establishment: The dissolution of establishments, 2], *Osaka Asahi shimbun,* January 20, 1932.

98. Nakai Masakazu, "Geijutsu no shūdansei: Dan no kaitai ni tsuite (so no yon)" [The mass-ness of art: The dissolution of establishments, 4], *Osaka Asahi shimbun,* January 22, 1932.

99. Ōsawa Satoshi, *Hihyō mediaron: Senzen nihon no rondan to bundan* [On critical media: Critical and literary establishments in prewar Japan] (Tokyo: Iwanami shoten, 2015), 23–28.

100. Theodor Adorno, "On the Social Situation of Music," in *Essays on Music,* ed. Richard Leppert and trans. Susan Gillespie (Berkeley: University of California Press, 2002), 391.

101. Ibid., 393–395.

102. Theodor Adorno, "On Popular Music," in *Essays on Music,* 458–459.

103. Ibid., 464–465.

104. Theodor Adorno, "National Socialism and the Arts," in *Essays on Music,* 376–377.

105. Ibid., 377–378.

106. Michael Bourdaghs, *Sayonara Amerika, Sayonara Nippon: A Geopolitical Prehistory of J-Pop* (New York: Columbia University Press, 2012), 23.

107. Ibid., 47–48.

2. The State as Critic and Consumer

1. "Atara hōkoku kōshintai keikan ni kechirasaru: 'Uchiwa daiko wa fukei da!' to nijūbashi de kensokusawagi" [For shame, patriotic marchers

driven away by police: Commotion of arrest in front of the Double Bridge and fan drums accused of lèse-majesté], *Yomiuri shimbun*, March 7, 1934.

2. Takashi Fujitani, *Splendid Monarchy: Power and Pageantry in Modern Japan* (Berkeley: University of California Press, 1996), 79–81; Hara Takeshi, *Kōkyomae hiroba* [Imperial Palace Frontal Plaza] (Tokyo: Chikuma shobō, 2007), 84–95.

3. "Atara hōkoku kōshintai keikan ni kechirasaru."

4. William P. Malm, *Traditional Japanese Music and Musical Instruments*, rev. ed. (Tokyo: Kodansha International, 2000), 73.

5. Robert Kisala, *Prophets of Peace: Pacifism and Cultural Identity in Japan's New Religions* (University of Hawai'i Press, 1999), 45–46.

6. On the interactions between the state and "new religions," see Sheldon Garon, *Molding Japanese Minds: The State in Everyday Life* (Princeton, NJ: Princeton University Press, 1997), 60–87. On the origin of the Myōhōji group and its transformation from a fervent supporter of Japanese imperial ventures into one of the most famous pacifist religious movements in the postwar era, see Kisala, *Prophets of Peace*, 45–57.

7. "Shuppanhō chūkaisei hōritsuan iinkai giroku dai'ikkai" [Records of the proceedings of the Imperial Diet House of Representatives Committee on the Partial Revision of the Publication Law, 1], March 22, 1934, 11.

8. Ibid., 14, 17.

9. Ibid., 17.

10. Ibid., 18.

11. "Shuppanhō chūkaisei hōritsuan iinkai giroku daiyonkai" [Records of the proceedings of the Imperial Diet House of Representative Committee on the Partial Revision of the Publication Law, 4], March 25, 1934, 5.

12. Ibid., 8.

13. Ibid.

14. Since the Meiji period, there had been a long history of ongoing tension between the state's efforts to manage people's engagement with the newly Westernized, modern monarchy and the ways in which they actually behaved, which oftentimes reflected their attachment to traditional conceptions of rulers as well as outright ignorance of newly created civic rites. For example, Fujitani (*Splendid Monarchy*, 127) points out that in the late Meiji era "the authorities promoted singing in the practiced and reverent tones of what was be-

coming Japan's de facto national anthem, *kimi ga yo,* but the people often performed the spontaneous and frenetic music of revelry, the hayashi."

15. Gregory Kasza, *The State and Mass Media in Japan, 1918–1945* (Berkeley: University of California Press, 1993), 253.

16. Kasza, *The State and Mass Media in Japan,* 101.

17. Horiuchi Keizō, *Yume no kōkyōgaku: Waga zuisō kakunogotoshi* [Symphonic dreams: My thoughts] (Tokyo: Ongaku no tomosha, 1998; originally published by Tokyo: Kusama shobō, 1948), 128–129; Murai Sachiko, "Purodūsā toshiteno horiuchi keizō: Nihon kōsō kyōkai ni okeru yōgaku juyō kakudai wo mezashita kokoromi" [Horiuchi Keizō as producer: Attempts by NHK to increase the demand for Western music], *Tōkyō geijutsu daigaku ongakugakubu kiyō* 37 (2011): 158.

18. Horiuchi, *Yume no kōkyōgaku,* 183.

19. Ibid., 38; Murai, "Purodūsā toshiteno horiuchi keizō," 160.

20. Horiuchi, *Yume no kōkyōgaku,* 28–29.

21. Terada Hiroshi, *Jidai wo tsukutta henshūsha 101* [101 editors who defined their era] (Tokyo: Shinshokan, 203), 86–87.

22. Horiuchi Keizō, *Ongaku gojūnen shi ge* [Fifty-year history of music], vol. 2 (Tokyo: Kodansha, 1977), 190.

23. Ibid.

24. Horiuchi, *Yume no kōkyōgaku,* 9–23.

25. Historians of modern Japan have identified the broader contexts of censorship by exploring the various ways in which cultural endeavors had long been policed since the Meiji era. See, for example, Gregory Kasza, *The State and Mass Media in Japan, 1918–1945* (Berkeley: University of California Press, 1993); Richard Mitchell, *Censorship in Imperial Japan* (Princeton, NJ: Princeton University Press, 1983); Elise Tipton, "Cleansing the Nation: Urban Entertainments and Moral Reform in Interwar Japan," *Modern Asian Studies* 42. no. 4 (2008): 705–731. More recently, Jonathan Abel has produced an excellent study on the continuities of censorship up to 1945 in *Redacted: The Archives of Censorship in Transwar Japan* (Berkeley: University of California Press, 2012). Rachael Hutchinson, ed., *Negotiating Censorship in Modern Japan* (New York: Routledge, 2013), contains essays on a wide range of censorship in modern Japan.

26. Obinata Sumio, *Keisatsu no shakaishi* [A social history of police] (Tokyo: Iwanami shoten, 1993), 31.

27. Ibid., 36.

28. For an overview of leisure and entertainment in prewar Japan, see Ishikawa Hiroyoshi, *Goraku no senzenshi* [A prewar history of leisure] (Tokyo: Tōsho senshō, 1981).

29. David Ambaras, *Bad Youth: Juvenile Delinquency and the Politics of Everyday Life* (Berkeley: University of California Press, 2006), 162.

30. Kamita, "Ongaku kyōshikara tekishisareta merodī no kyōikuka," 18.

31. "Monbushō no ero torishimari" [Education Ministry to regulate eroticism], *Asahi shimbun,* February 8, 1931; the committee members included Gonda Yasunosuke and Takano Tatsunobu, a professor at Tokyo Music School.

32. Tanabe Hisao, *Chikuonki to rekōdo no erabikata kikikata* [How to choose and listen to phonographs and records] (Tokyo: Senshinsha, 1931), 138–139.

33. " 'Ero,' 'aka' bayarikara rekōdo nimo ken'etsusei" [Move to introduce record censorship due to the popularity of "erotic" and "red" songs], *Yomiuri shimbun,* April 5, 1931.

34. See Chapter 1, note 51.

35. Kasza, *State and Mass Media in Japan,* 126–128.

36. *Kanpō* (Official gazette of the Japanese government), no. 2934, April 14, 1893, 164; *Kanpō,* no. 2197, May 2, 1934, 33.

37. Kasza, *State and Mass Media in Japan,* 129–133.

38. Abel, *Redacted,* 3.

39. Ogawa, *Ryūkōka to sesō,* 71–73; Kasza, *State and Mass Media in Japan,* 9. As Kasza notes, this twin principle, which had been at the heart of media censorship since the time of its establishment in the Meiji period, left a vast space for the censor's personal discretion due to its vagueness.

40. Ogawa Chikagorō et al., "Ryūkōka to ken'etsu no mondai" [Tendencies of popular songs and the problem of censorship], *Ongaku sekai* 8, no. 8 (August 1936): 20; Hosokawa Shūhei, "Senzen rekōdo ken'etsu: 'Shuppan keisatsuhō' kara saguru" [Record censorship in prewar Japan: Examination through the Publication Police Report], reprinted in *Censure, Autocensure et Tabous* (Arles: Éditions Philippe Picquier, 2010), 256.

41. The former was a monthly report of censorship and the latter was an annual summary of the former.

42. Publication Police Report, vol. 94, 1936 (repr., Tokyo: Ryūkei shosha, 1981), 24–25.

43. Ibid.

44. Ogawa et al., "Ryūkōka no keikō to ken'etsu no mondai," 15.

45. Publication Police Report, vol. 109, 1937, 91–92; Publication Police Report, vol. 110, 1937, 205–206.

46. Publication Police Report, vol. 88, 1936, 162–163.

47. The Home Ministry records also indicate other types of records that were banned, including two Chinese popular songs that were imported into Japan and were seen to be anti-Japanese; see Publication Police Report, vol. 110, 1937, 146. A Korean *manzai* with an erotic undercurrent was also banned; see Publication Police Report, vol. 113, 1938, 48–49. These, however, were exceptional cases that were not repeated. Records produced for the Korean and Taiwanese markets were generally censored by the local governor general's office and the Home Ministry usually deferred to their judgment.

48. For historical overview of the "consultation" system in press censorship, see Kasza, *State and Mass Media in Japan*, 172–173.

49. Publication Police Summary, 1936, 561.

50. *Naietsu* was already well established in other forms of media censorship.

51. Publication Police Report, vol. 72, 1934, 294.

52. Ogawa, *Ryūkōka to sesō*, 111.

53. Ogawa et al., "Ryūkōka no keikō to ken'etsu no mondai," 19–20. Hosokawa Shūhei ("Senzen rekōdo ken'etsu," 259) surmises that the producers that most frequently produced records that risked an outright ban tended to be the smaller labels that based their profits on records that featured overtly erotic content or copycat songs of those produced by of major companies like Columbia and Victor, reproducing the relationship between major publishing companies and the small-scale publishers of erotic books.

54. Publication Police Report, vol. 108, 1937, 21–22.

55. Ogawa, *Ryūkōka to sesō*, 168.

56. Publication Police Report, vol. 108, 1937, 22.

57. Andō Minoru, "Rekōdo kyōkai 20 nen no ayumi 1" [Twenty years of the Record Industry Association of Japan, 1], *Record* (June 1963), 2. On

"war fever" in mass media prompted by Japan's military adventures in China, see Young, *Japan's Total Empire*, 55–114.

58. Ogawa, *Ryūkōka to sesō*, 192–193.

59. Maruya Yoshizō, "Kaisō zakki 4: Kigen 2600 nen zengo" [Notes on reminiscence, 4: Around the year 2600], *Record* (September 1961), 2–4.

60. Zen ongakufu shuppansha shuppanbu, ed., *Fukkokuban zen'on kayōkyoku zenshū, 1* [Republished zen'on popular song collection, 1] (Tokyo: Zen ongakufu shuppansha, 1995), 163. Translation by the author. In the narrow sense *kokyū* refers to a Japanese stringed instrument, but Saijō appears to be using the term here to refer to a Chinese instrument.

61. Abel, *Redacted*, 1.

62. Ibid., 13.

63. Ogawa's own words and an internal Home Ministry report both attest to this striking fact: see Ogawa et al., "Ryūkōka to ken'etsu no mondai," 26; "Rekōdo ken'etsujo wo ken'etsusuru" [Censoring the record censorship office], *Ongaku Sekai* 6, no. 9 (September 1934): 101–102; Publication Police Report, vol. 89, 1936, 221.

64. For example, "Rekōdo ken'etsujo wo ken'etsusuru"; "Ken'etsukyō ni utsuru rekōdo jō" [Record's reflection in the mirror of censorship, 1], *Asahi shimbun*, July 30, 1938; "Ken'etsukyō ni utsuru rekōdo ge" [Record's reflection in the mirror of censorship, 2], *Asahi shimbun*, July 31, 1938; "Jikyokuka no ken'etsugan 2" [Censor's eyes during the time of national emergency, 2], *Yomiuri shimbun*, August 24, 1938.

65. Ogawa Chikagorō et al., "Ryūkōkaron" [On popular songs], *Ongaku kōron* 2, no. 12 (December 1942): 41.

66. Hosokawa, "Senzen rekōdo ken'etsu," 256.

67. Ogawa Chikagorō et al., "Keiongaku zadankai" [Roundtable discussion on light music], *Gekkan gakufu* (July 1941), 25.

68. Publication Police Report, vol. 77, 1935, 274.

69. Hosokawa, "Senzen rekōdo ken'etsu," 271–272.

70. Ogawa et al., "Ryūkōka no keikō to ken'etsu no mondai," 11–34.

71. Ibid., 21.

72. Ibid., 11.

73. Ibid., 22.

74. Ogawa Chikagorō, "Hijō jikyoku to rekōdo no torishimari" [Time of national emergency and record regulation], *Ongaku sekai* 9, no 10 (October 1937): 15–16.

75. Ibid., 16.

76. Ogawa, *Ryūkōka to sesō*, 170.

77. Ogawa, "Hijō jikyoku to rekōdo no torishimari," 17.

78. Horiuchi Keizo's *Ongaku gojūnen shi jō* [Fifty-year history of music], vol. 1, was originally published in 1942 and was perhaps the most comprehensive survey of the history of modern Japanese musical culture up until that time. In it, Horiuchi mentions several sources that he drew on but none of them approaches the comprehensive chronological coverage of either Horiuchi's or Ogawa's work. See Horiuchi, *Ongaku gojūnen shi ge*, 225–226.

79. Ogawa, *Ryūkōka to sesō*, 138–139.

80. Ibid., 170.

81. Yamauchi Fumitaka, "Higashi ajia no bunsho kenryoku to onsei media no shokuminchi kindaiteki hensei" [East Asian literary authority and the organization of media under colonial modernity], *Tokyo daigaku tōyō bunka kenkūjo kiyō* (March 2014), 33; this article also includes an outline of the history of the recording industry as well as record censorship in colonial Korea on pp. 17–38.

82. E. Taylor Atkins, *Primitive Selves: Koreana in the Japanese Colonial Gaze, 1910–1945* (Berkeley: University of California Press, 2010), 167–168.

83. Yamauchi, "Higashi ajia no bunsho kenryoku to onsei media no shokuminchi kindaiteki hensei," 56–58. Yamauchi points out that much of the shared vocabulary used by Japanese and Korean intellectuals had a common heritage in Chinese, hinting at the work of tradition within what is typically discussed in the context of colonial modernity. The notion of a "nation-ruining" (in Japanese, *bōkoku*) song, for example, can be traced as far back as the Confucian classic, *Book of Rites* (*Liji*).

84. Ogawa, *Ryūkōka to sesō*, 116–117.

85. Ogawa et al., "Ryūkōka no keikō to ken'etsu no mondai"; Ogawa et al., "Ryūkōkaron."

86. Ogawa et al., "Ryūkōka no keikō to ken'etsu no mondai," 31.

87. Ogawa, *Ryūkōka to sesō*, 6.

88. Horiuchi, *Ongaku gojūnen shi ge*, 227.

89. Horiuchi, *Ongaku gojūnen shi jō*, 4.

90. Makino Mamoru, "Katsudō shashin kaidō wo kakenuketa nisoku no waraji no shōgensha" [A witness who ran through the highway of motion

pictures with two hats on], in Makino Mamoru, ed., *Saisentan minshū go-raku eiga bunken shiryō shū* [Source collection of ultramodern popular leisure and film], vol. 15 (Tokyo: Yumani shobō, 2006), 321.

91. Ibid., 323.

92. Tajima Tarō, *Ken'etsu shitsu no yami ni tsubuyaku* [Muttering in the darkness of the censor's office], in Makino Mamoru *Saisentan minshū goraku eiga bunken shiryō shūi*, vol. 18 (Tokyo: Yumani shobō, 2006), 182.

93. Nihon rekōdo kyōkai, *Shadan hōjin nihon rekōdo kyōkai gojūnenshi*, 40–42.

94. As early as 1940, the government attempted to create a single in-terdepartmental agency responsible for mass media censorship and propaganda by establishing the Cabinet Information Bureau. However, the participating ministries, including the Army, Navy, and Home Ministries, refused to let go of their jurisdictions, leaving the bureau ineffective in the end.

95. The Japan Musical Culture Association was represented by Sonobe Saburō, a prominent music critic.

96. Andō Minoru, "Rekōdo kyōkai 20 nen no ayumi 3" [Twenty years of the Record Industry Association of Japan, 3], *Record* (June 1963), 8.

97. By this time, Ogawa had received a dual appointment at both the Home Ministry and the Cabinet Information Bureau. Though it is tempting to speculate whether his move to Nara was a de facto demotion, there is no evidence to confirm this. More likely, it was due to both the staff shortage within the Home Ministry and the decreased need for record censorship, as record production plummeted in the years immediately preceding Japan's defeat.

98. Atkins, *Blue Nippon*, 147–148; Horiuchi Keizō, "Daitōa sensō ni shosuru ongaku bunka no shinro" [The direction of musical culture as it engages with the Greater East Asian War], *Ongaku no tomo* (January 1942): 10–13.

3. The Long War on Popular Song

1. For an ethnographic account of right-wing activism and sound trucks, see Nathaniel Smith, "Facing the Nation: Sound, Fury, and Public

Oratory among Japanese Right-Wing Groups," in Joseph Hankins and Carolyn Stevens, eds., *Sound, Space and Sociality in Modern Japan* (New York: Routledge, 2014), 37–56.

2. Junko Oba, "To Fight the Losing War, to Remember the Lost War: The Changing Role of *Gunka*, Japanese War Songs," in Timothy Craig and Richard King, eds., *Global Goes Local: Popular Culture in Asia* (Vancouver: University of British Columbia Press, 2002), 225–226.

3. Horiuchi, *Ongaku gojūnen shi ge,* 217.

4. Andrew Gordon points to Thomas Havens, *Valley of Darkness: The Japanese People and World War II* (New York: W. W. Norton, 1978), and Minami Hiroshi and Shakai Shinri Kenkūjo, eds., *Shōwa bunka 1925–1945* [Shōwa culture, 1925–1945] (Tokyo: Keisō shobō, 1987), as examples of this perspective. See Gordon, "Consumption, Leisure and the Middle Class in Transwar Japan," 4.

5. Ibid.

6. Young, *Japan's Total Empire,* 87–88.

7. In explaining the sudden rise in Manchuria-themed phonograph records, for example, Young (*Japan's Total Empire,* 72) suggests that "suddenly, the languorous jazz rhythms which had been the rage only weeks before were replaced by a boom in *gunka* (war songs)"—not only implying that the wartime climate was somehow inherently hostile to jazz and other Western frivolities but also that such hostility manifested itself overnight. Gordon ("Consumption, Leisure and the Middle Class in Transwar Japan," 13, 16) counters this by pointing out that theme songs from Hollywood films and jazz retained a significant following in Japan right up to and, in some cases, even after American music was deemed to be "enemy music," noting that "the Japanese people marched into the so-called 'dark valley' of war singing cheery movie theme songs as often as they hummed somber or strident military marches."

8. Oba, "To Fight the Losing War, to Remember the Lost War," 236.

9. Gordon, "Consumption, Leisure and the Middle Class in Transwar Japan," Abel, *Redacted,* and Atkins, *Blue Nippon,* are examples of the fruitful adoption of the transwar periodization.

10. By 1941 the Japanese branches of Columbia and Victor had severed their financial ties with their Western counterparts and instead came under the control of Japanese corporations such as Nissan and Tokyo Electric

(the future Toshiba); see Nihon rekōdo kyōkai, *Shadan hōjin nihon rekōdo kyōkai gojūnenshi,* 45–46.

11. Zen ongakufu shuppansha shuppanbu, ed., *Fukkokuban zen'on kayōkyoku zenshū, 6* [Republished zen'on popular song collection, 6] (Tokyo: Zen ongakufu shuppansha, 1995), 221. Translation by the author; lyrics by Itō Toyota.

12. Furukawa Takahisa, "Kyōgoku Takatoshi no shisō to kodō" [The ideology and activity of Kyōgoku Takatoshi], *Gunji shigaku* 44, no. 2 (September 2008): 8.

13. Takatoshi was also the blood brother of Kato Ikurō (1903–1961), better known as Furukawa Roppa, who was one of the most celebrated comedic actors of the prewar period. Roppa in fact starred in the film *The Grand March of Music (Ongaku daishingun)*, which was created shortly after the release of the "Patriotic March" to promote the song.

14. Furukawa, "Kyōgoku Takatoshi no shisō to kodō," 9–10.

15. Ibid., 8–9.

16. Furukawa Takahisa and Yoshihara Jun, eds., "Shōwa zenhanki no jōryūshakai to ongaku geinō" [The upper-class society and music and arts during the first half of the Shōwa period], *Yokohama shiritsu daigaku ronsō jinbun kagaku keiretsu* 54, nos. 1–3 (2003): 422–424.

17. Horiuchi Keizō, "Ongaku seisaku no jikkō e" [Toward the execution of music policy], *Ongaku seikai* 12 (February 1940): 7.

18. "Shintaisei wo shokunōbetsu ni kiku" [Hearing about the New Order in different fields], *Shukan Asahi,* September 25, 1940.

19. Sonobe Saburō, *Ongaku to seikatsu* [Music and everyday life] (Tokyo: Chūō kōronsha, 1942), 4–5.

20. Ibid., 9.

21. Ibid., 11–12.

22. Atkins, *Blue Nippon,* 147–148.

23. Horiuchi, "Daitōa sensō ni shosuru ongaku bunka no shinro."

24. Sonobe, *Ongaku to seikatsu,* 12.

25. Ibid.

26. Moroi Saburō, "From Our Standpoint: Reflections on Overcoming Modernity," in Richard F. Calichman, ed. and trans., *Overcoming Modernity: Cultural Identity in Wartime Japan* (New York: Columbia University Press, 2008), 73.

27. Ibid., 74.

28. Ibid.

29. Ibid.

30. Nihon sengo ongakushi kenkyūkai, *Nihon sengo ongakushi jō, sengo kara zen'ei no jidai e, 1945–1973* [Postwar history of music in Japan, vol. 1, From the postwar era to that of avant-garde, 1945–1973] (Tokyo: Heibonsha, 2007), 55–56 (hereafter *Nihon sengo ongakushi jō*).

31. Horiuchi, "Daitōa sensō ni shosuru ongaku bunka no shinro," 12.

32. Imagawa Kyōko et al., eds., *Senjika no kodomo, ongaku, gakkō: kokumin gakkō no ongaku kyōiku* [Children, music, and schools during wartime: Music education in the national schools] (Tokyo: Kaisei shuppan, 2015), 35–43.

33. Ibid., 216.

34. Ibid., 215–220.

35. *Nihon sengo ongakushi jō*, 54–55.

36. Horiuchi, "Ongaku seisaku no jikkō e," 7.

37. Tonoshita Tatsuya, *Ongaku wo dōinseyo: Tōsei to goraku no jūgonen sensō* [Mobilize music: A fifteen-year war of control and leisure] (Tokyo: Seikyūsha, 2008), 118–122.

38. Ibid., 258–259.

39. Yoshida Yutaka, *Asia taiheiyō sensō* [Asia-Pacific War] (Tokyo: Iwanami shoten, 2007), 128–129.

40. Katō Atsuko, *Sōdōintaisei to eiga* [Film and the total mobilization regime] (Tokyo: Shinyōsha, 2003), 268.

41. Ibid., 252–257.

42. Atkins, *Blue Nippon*, 151–152.

43. Aoki Seii, "Henshū kōki" [Editor's note], *Rekōdo bunka* (February 1943), 66.

44. *Nihon sengo ongakushi jō*, 55.

45. Translation taken from Dower, *Embracing Defeat*, 172.

46. Ibid., 173.

47. Nihon rekōdo kyōkai, *Shadan hōjin nihon rekōdo kyōkai gojūnenshi*, 85–87.

48. "Eigahyō: soyokaze (shōchiku)" [Film review: *Soyokaze* (Shōchiku)], *Asahi shimbun*, October 12, 1945.

49. Komota, *Nihon ryūkōkashi*, 128. Translation by the author.

50. Nihon rekōdo kyōkai, *Shadan hōjin nihon rekōdo kyōkai gojūnenshi,* 74–76, 83–85.

51. Ibid., 74.

52. Ibid., 85, 127. In a roundtable hosted by a local journal in Sapporo, Hokkaidō, record company officials stated that every company was operating in the red in 1948, for which they largely blamed the tax placed on records and phonographs; see "Rekōdogaisha uchiakebanashi" [Inside stories of records companies], *Sandē taimusu* (June 13, 1948): 3–4.

53. Saijō Yaso, *Waga ai no ki* [The record of my love] (1962), reprinted in *Saijō yaso zenshū, 17* [Saijō Yaso collection, 17] (Tokyo: Kukousho kankōkai, 2007), 178–179.

54. Komota, *Shinpan nihon ryūkōkashi chū 1838–1959* [History of Japanese popular songs], rev. ed., vol. 2, 38–39. Translation by the author.

55. Saijō, *Waga ai no ki,* 178.

56. Ibid., 179–180.

57. *Nihon sengo ongakushi jō,* 89–90.

58. Dower, *Embracing Defeat,* 405–440. See also Takemae Eiji, *Inside GHQ: The Allied Occupation of Japan and Its Legacy* (New York: Continuum, 2002); Yamamoto Taketoshi, *Senryōki media bunseki* [Analysis of occupation-period media] (Tokyo: Hōsei Daigaku Shuppankyoku, 1996).

59. W. F. Corkery, "Record Censorship Procedure" (December 31, 1946), in GHQ/SCAP Records, Civil Intelligence Section, "Music & Lyrics—Operations," Box no. 8656, National Diet Library, *Nihon senryō kankei shiryō* [Documents relating to the occupation of Japan] (hereafter GHQ, Box 8656). The original copies of all official SCAP documents cited in this chapter are housed at the U.S. National Archives and Records Administration, within Records of Allied Operational and Occupation Headquarters, World War II (Record Group 331).

60. "Distribution by JOAK of Lists of Approved Music Lyrics" (September 25, 1946), in GHQ/SCAP Records, Civil Intelligence Section, "Music & Recording Censorship," Box no. 8602, National Diet Library, *Nihon senryō kankei shiryō* [Documents relating to the occupation of Japan] (hereafter GHQ, Box 8602). For the actual list, see: "A List of Music & Lyrics, Approved by PPB District Station I, Tokyo, PPB District Station II, Osaka, Master List, August 1946 to May 1947," Box no. 8582, National

Diet Library, *Nihon senryō kankei shiryō* [Documents relating to the occupation of Japan].

61. Arisaka Yoshihiko, "Shinsei no rekōdokai" [The newly reborn record world], *Ongaku no tomo* 4 (January 1946): 41; "Rescission of Ban on Musical Recordings," (May 2, 1946), GHQ, Box 8656. The CCD officers identified "Hakone hachiri" as "Hakone no yama" ("The Mountain of Hakone") for reasons unknown.

62. "Japan: The Day Gone By," *Time* 46, no. 23 (December 3, 1945), 37.

63. "Recording of Shina no Yoru" (April 1, 1946), GHQ, Box 8656.

64. "Recording of Kojo no Tsuki" (April 11, 1946), GHQ, Box 8656.

65. John J. Costello, "Rescission of Ban on Musical Recordings" (May 2, 1946), GHQ, Box 8656.

66. In the case of literature, some Japanese observers have argued that the SCAP censorship was more thoroughgoing than what was achieved by the Home Ministry, especially in the way that it sought to make any trace of censorship itself invisible to the public. The conservative literary critic Etō Jun is especially famous for using this point to argue that the occupation censorship was fundamentally more oppressive than its prewar Japanese counterpart. Jonathan Abel (*Redacted*, 11) cautions us, however, that such an interpretation not only ignores the fact that the effacement of censorship was already practiced in wartime Japan, but also keeps us from recognizing "what the Japanese and US empires shared and how their power, so seemingly different in rhetoric, culture, and history, was similarly structured, organized, and practiced."

67. "Letter from Chinese Young Man's Confederation" (October 15, 1946), GHQ, Box 8602.

68. Ibid.

69. John J. Costello, "Memorandum for Record" (September 19, 1946), GHQ, Box 8602.

70. Katsuhiko Isohata, letter to Civil Information and Education Section, Motion Picture Section (August 21, 1947), GHQ, Box 8602.

71. John J. Costello, untitled memorandum (September 4, 1947), GHQ, Box 8602.

72. Saijō Yaso, *Watashi no keirekisho* [My resume] (1962), reprinted in *Saijō yaso zenshū, 17* [Saijō Yaso collection, 17] (Tokyo: Kokusho kankōkai, 2007), 368–369.

73. For an in-depth study of continuities and shifts in NHK's musical programming during the transitional year of 1945, see Takeda Yasutaka, "Showa 20 nen no ongaku hōsō kentō—'yōgaku hōsō kiroku' no dēta wo mochi'ite" [A review of music radio program of Japan in 1945—using the data of "western music broadcast record"], *Bunka shigengaku* 12 (2014): 61–75.

74. Dower, *Embracing Defeat*, 96.

75. Kasuga Yoshikazu et al., "Kirisute gomen ni mono mōsu: hōsō uchimaku banashi" [Rebutting unfair critique of radio: Inside stories from broadcasting], *Sandē mainichi* 28, no. 35 (August 28, 1949): 7. Here, the official uses the term *kayōkyoku* (literally "ballad song"), which had come to be used interchangeably with *ryūkōka* by this time to denote the English term "popular song."

76. Kasuga Yoshikazu et al., "Zadankai: Shūkan asahi 'NHK no ojikan ni kotaete'" [Roundtable: In response to *Weekly Asahi*'s "Time for NHK"], *NHK Hōsō bunka* 4, no. 7 (September 1949): 31–32.

77. Hosokawa Shūhei, "Utau minshushugi: 'Nodo jiman' to chinpusa no kōyō" [Singing democracy: "Nodo jiman" and the utility of a cliché], in Tōya Mamoru, ed., *Popyurā ongaku eno manazashi* [Perspectives on popular music] (Tokyo: Keisō shobō, 2003), 183–182.

78. Ibid., 195.

79. Ibid., 185.

80. Kubo Kinya, "WVTR hōsō no kikikata" [How to listen to the WVTR broadcast], *Jiyū fujin* 8, no. 7 (August 1948): 38.

81. Horiuchi Keizō, "Ryūkōkashu no miryoku" [The charm of the popular song singers], *Toppu raito* 2, no. 2 (February 1947): 37.

82. For an in-depth study on the experience of Japanese musicians inside the bases, see Tōya Mamoru, *Shinchūgun kurabu kara kayōkyoku e: Nihon popyurā ongaku no reimeiki* [From base clubs to *kayōkyoku*: The dawn of Japanese popular music] (Tokyo: Misuzu shobō, 2005). See also Atkins, *Blue Nippon*, for a transwar history of the Japanese jazz community. For a broader understanding of postwar Japanese "Jazz culture," including its intersection with literature, film, and the uniquely Japanese phenomenon that is "jazz café" (*jazu kissa*), there is no better introduction than Michael Molasky, *Sengo nihon no jazu bunka* [Postwar Japan's jazz culture] (Tokyo: Seidosha, 2005).

83. "Sugoi jazu no ninki: Ryūkōka rekōdo wo shinogu ureyuki" [Amazing jazz boom: Sales pass those of popular songs], *Yomiuri shimbun,* October 30, 1949; "Seibumono ryūkōka: Chikagoro no rekōdokai" [Western popular songs: Record world these days], *Yomiuri shimbun,* November 9, 1950.

84. "Jazuteki ryūkōka e: Tenkanki no rekōdokai" [Toward a more jazz-like popular song: Record world in transition], *Yomiuri shimbun,* May 16, 1952.

85. Maruyama Tetsuo, "Saikin no ryūkōka ni tsuite" [On recent popular songs], *Ongaku no tomo* 6 (July 1948): 44–45.

86. Maruyama Tetsuo, "Senji ongaku no hansei to korekara no ongaku" [Reflection on wartime music and the music of the future], *Chōryū* (May 1946), 69.

87. Ibid., 70.

88. Ibid., 71.

89. Sonobe Saburō, *Minshū ongakuron* [On people's music] (Tokyo: San-ichi shobō, 1948), 34.

90. Sonobe Tameyuki, "Uta wa yo ni tsure yo wa uta ni tsure: Ryūkōka to sesō" [Songs follow the world and the world follows the songs: Popular songs and social currents], *Gekkan shinmai* 2 (August 1949): 33.

91. Horiuchi Keizō, "Korekara no ryūkōka: Kurai uta kara akarui uta e" [Today's popular songs: From dark songs to bright songs], *Jiji shinpō* (January 1947), 53.

92. Sonobe Saburō, "Ongaku wo seikatsu no naka ni" [Bringing music into everyday life] (1947), in *Minshū ongakuron,* 26–27.

93. Sonobe Saburō, "Ongaku minshūka no michi" [The path to the popularization of music] (1947), in *Minshū ongakuron,* 7–9.

94. Emphasis added.

95. Sonobe, "Ongaku minshūka no michi," 11–12.

96. Sonobe, "Ongaku wo seikatsu no naka ni," 30–34.

97. Sonobe, "Ongaku minshūka no michi," 12–13.

98. Sonobe, *Minshū ongakuron,* 185–188.

99. Dower, *Embracing Defeat,* 176–180.

100. "Tensei jingo" [Voice of heaven, words of people], *Asahi shimbun,* February 19, 1948.

101. Akutagawa Ryūnosuke, "Kappa [Water imp]," in *Akutagawa Ryūnosuke zenshū, 14* [Collected works of Akutagawa Ryūnosuke, 14] (Tokyo: Iwanami shoten, 1995).

102. "Kayōkyoku wa hatashite mimi no nai kappa no kuni no sanbutsu ka" [Is *kayōkyoku* really the product of a nation of earless Kappa?], *Kayō stā* (May 1948), 26.

103. Ibid., 31.

104. Aragaki Hideo, "Kayōkyoku to kappa no kuni" [*Kayōkyoku* and the nation of Kappa], *Josei kaizō* 4 (July 1949): 74.

105. Ibid., 75.

106. Dower, *Embracing Defeat*, 180–187.

107. Sources discussed here come from the University of Maryland's Gordon W. Prange Collection, which is an archive made up of publications that were submitted to SCAP officials for censorship. While one should proceed with caution in drawing conclusions on the nature of the public opinion at that time on the basis of a single archive, let alone one with an especially politically charged origin, the publications contained in the Prange Collection suggest nonetheless that the elite critics' war on popular songs had in fact found some resonance beyond Tokyo.

108. "Ryūkōka shokan" [Impressions of popular songs], *Shindō*, no. 2 (Spring 1947): 23–24. Featuring lyrics written by a Japanese soldier interned in a Soviet prisoner of war camp in Siberia, "Hill in a Foreign Land" ("Ikoku no oka") became a hit popular song after another soldier who was also in Siberia sang it on NHK's *Amateur Singing Contest*.

109. "Bōkokuteki na ryūkōka" [Popular songs that will doom the nation], *Sanshū* 2 (January 1948), 10.

110. Yoshioka Shigeaki, "Ryūkōka ni tsuite" [On popular songs], *Bungaku nōto* (July 1949).

111. Kawanishi Akira, "Ryūkōka gūkan" [Thoughts on popular songs], *Kashi*, no. 1 (January 1949): 30–33.

112. "Warera no utade eroguro wo tuihō shiyō" [Banish the erotic-grotesque popular songs and replace them with our own songs], *Kōzan rōdōsha* (August 1948), 28. The songs that are mentioned here, including "The Song of the Red Flag" ("Akahata no uta"), "From the Town, from the Village, from the Factory" ("Machikara murakara kōjōkara"), and "Connect the World in a Ring of Flowers" ("Sekai wo tsunage hana no wa ni"), were part of the leftist Utagoe (Singing Voice) movement led by Seki Akiko.

113. Hashimoto Kenji, *Kakusa no sengoshi: Kaikyū shakai ninon no rirek-isho* [Postwar history of stratification: Japan's resume as hierarchical society] (Tokyo: Kawade shobō shinsha, 2009), 38–39.

4. Boogie-Woogie Democracy

1. Hosokawa Shūhei, "The Swinging Voice of Kasagi Shizuko: Japanese Jazz Culture in the 1930s," in Patricia Fister and Hosokawa Shūhei, eds., *Japanese Studies around the World*, vol. 13 (Kyoto: International Research Center for Japanese Studies, 2007), 159. The Hosokawa essay also emphasizes the importance of understanding Japan's "Swing Era" as a transwar phenomenon that started in the 1930s and continued into the early 1950s, interrupted only at the height of the war (160).

2. Bourdaghs, *Sayonara Amerika, Sayonara Nippon*, 32.

3. Ibid., 22; Hosokawa, "Swinging Voice of Kasagi Shizuko," 179.

4. Bourdaghs, *Sayonara Amerika, Sayonara Nippon*, 33–35.

5. Sonobe Saburō, "Gendai ryūkōka ni tsuite" [On contemporary popular songs], in Kata Kōji and Tsukuda Jitsuo, eds., *Ryūkōka no himitsu* [The secrets of popular songs] (Tokyo: Bunwa shobō, 1970), 265–269. The Sonobe article was originally published in Shisō no kagaku kenkyūkai, ed., *Yume to omokage: Taishū goraku no kenkyū* [Dreams and Resemblances: Research on mass leisure] (Tokyo: Chūō kōronsha, 1950).

6. Sonobe, "Gendai ryūkōka ni tsuite," 265–269; Bourdaghs, *Sayonara Amerika, Sayonara Nippon*, 21.

7. Oguma Eiji, *Minshu to aikoku: Sengo nihon no nashonarizumu to kōkyōsei* [Democracy and patriotism: Nationalism and public-ness in postwar Japan] (Tokyo: Shinyōsha, 2010), 255.

8. Ibid., 260.

9. Kanzaki Kiyoshi, "Furyō bunkazai to dō tatakauka: Tamaranbushi tsuihō no keiken kara" [How to fight against degenerate cultural products: On the experience of banishing "Yokosuka Dance"], *Kyōiku gijutsu* 9, no. 8 (September 1954): 85.

10. Ambaras, *Bad Youth*, 193.

11. Sumi Tomoyuki, "Jishu kisei wo umidasumono: Rekōdo gyōkai no jirei kenkyū" [What gives birth to self-regulation: Case study on the record industry]," *Shimbungaku hyōron* 31 (1982): 91–111.

12. Garon, *Molding Japanese Minds*, 18–21.

13. On the postwar conditions of *kyodatsu* (total exhaustion), see Dower, *Embracing Defeat*, 33–64.

14. Ibid., 62–63.

15. May 5 was the day in the traditional calendar known as Tango no Sekku, which was designated for celebrating the healthy growth of boys. Girls were celebrated on March 3 (Jōshi no Sekku), which is also known as the day of the Dolls' Festival (Hinamatsuri).

16. Chūō seishōnen mondai kyōgikai, *Seishōnen jidō hakusho* [Whitepaper on youth and children] (Tokyo: Seishōnen mondai kenkyūkai, 1956), 13–18.

17. Kōseishō jidōkyoku, *Jidō kenshō seiteiroku* [Records of the establishment of the Children's Charter] (Tokyo: Chuō shakai fukushi kyōgikai, 1951), in Jidō mondaishi kenkyūkai, ed., *Gendai nihon jidō mondai bunken senshū* [Sources on children's issues in contemporary Japan], vol. 36 (Tokyo: Nihon tosho sentā, 1988), 101.

18. Ibid., 1–2.

19. Zen'nihon sangyōbetsu rōdō kumiai kaigi, *Jidō no seikatsu wa mamorareteiruka: Jidō hakusho* [Are the everyday lives of children being protected? A white paper on children] (1949), in Jidō mondaishi kenkyūkai, ed., *Gendai nihon jidō mondai bunken senshū* [Selected sources on children's issues in contemporary Japan], vol. 41 (Tokyo: Nihon tosho sentā, 1988).

20. *Nihon kodomo wo mamorukai kaihō*, no. 1 (September 1952): 7.

21. Ibid., 2.

22. Ibid., 4–5.

23. Kanzaki, "Furyō bunkazai to dō tatakauka," 85. Emphasis added. The Kanzaki article is one of the few contemporary sources that has preserved the original lyrics, which were ultimately revised by Columbia.

24. On geisha singers, see David Hopkins, "Memoirs of (Renegotiating) Geisha: The Geisha as Pop Singer in the Early Shōwa Era," in Fister and Hosokawa, *Japanese Studies around the World*, 13:231–236.

25. Zen ongakufu shuppansha shuppanbu, ed., *Fukkokuban zen'on kayōkyoku zenshū, 1* [Republished zen'on popular song collection, 1] (Tokyo: Zen ongakufu shuppansha, 1995), 227. Translation by the author.

26. Kanzaki, "Furyō bunkazai to dō tatakauka," 86.

27. Ibid., 88.

28. Ibid.

29. Yamakawa Kikue, "Bōkokuchō senden: Hiratsuka ondo ga shimesu josei jinken no kiki" [An advertisement that will doom the nation: The crisis of women's human rights as seen in "Hiratsuka Dance"], *Yomiuri shimbun*, June 20, 1953.

30. Yamakawa Kikue, "Hazukashī nihon no sugao: Toshi no kenzen na hatten wo gaisuru bakuchi ya baishun gyōsha wo yurusuna" [Embarrassing realities of Japan: Do not forgive the organizers of gambling and prostitution who inhibit the wholesome growth of cities], *Yomiuri shimbun*, July 9, 1953.

31. Yoshimi, *Shinbei to hanbei*, 116–120.

32. These include *Baishō naki kunie* [Toward a country without prostitution] (Tokyo: Ittō shobō, 1949), *Musume wo uru machi: Kanzaki repōto* [The town that sells its daughters: Kanzaki report] (Tokyo: Shikō shuppansha, 1952), *Yoru no kichi* [The base at night] (Tokyo: Kawade shobō, 1953), *Sengo nihon no baishun mondai* [The prostitution problem in postwar Japan] (Tokyo: Shakai shobō, 1954), and *Baishun kono jittai wo dōshitara iika* [Prostitution: What should we do with this reality?] (Tokyo: Aoki shoten, 1955).

33. Kanzaki, "Furyō bunkazai to dō tatakauka," 86.

34. Dower, *Embracing Defeat*, 123–139; Oguma, *Minshu to aikoku*, 277–280.

35. Dower, *Embracing Defeat*, 127.

36. Emphasis added. Minami Hiroshi, "Ryūkōka no mondai" [The problems with popular songs], *Bungaku* (November 1953), 78.

37. Ibid.

38. Various artists, *Exotic Japan: Orientalism in Occupied Japan*, Audio-Book: ABI29, 1996.

39. Ibid.

40. "'Gomennasai' wa gomen" [No thank you to "Gomennasai"], *Yomiuri shimbun*, June 20, 1953.

41. Bourdaghs, *Sayonara Amerika, Sayonara Nippon*, 51. Hibari's prominence also explains why she is typically referred to by her first name in English or Japanese. See Yano, *Tears of Longing*, for an in-depth, ethnographic research on inner workings of the postwar *enka* industry and its place in Japanese identity politics.

42. Bourdaghs, *Sayonara Amerika, Sayonara Nippon*, 55.

43. Shisō no kagaku kenkyūkai, ed., *Yume to omokage: Taishū goraku no kenkyū* [Dreams and memories: Research on mass entertainment] (Tokyo: Chūō kōronsha, 1950).

44. On the development of Science of Thought and their subsequent transformation, see Adam Bronson, *One Hundred Philosophers: Science of Thought and the Culture of Democracy in Postwar Japan* (Honolulu: University of Hawai'i Press, 2016).

45. Ibid., 98–99.

46. Ibid., 91.

47. Minami Hiroshi, "Nihon no ryūkōka" [Japanese popular songs], reprinted in Kata and Tsukuda, *Ryūkōka no himitsu*, 138–139.

48. Ibid.

49. Sonobe, "Gendai ryūkōka ni tsuite," 253–254.

50. Ibid.

51. Oguma, *Minshu to aikoku*, 255–260.

52. Nihon rekōdo kyōkai, *Shadan hōjin nihon rekōdo kyōkai gojūnenshi*, 130.

53. Ibid., 146.

54. *Nihon kodomo wo mamorukai kaihō*, no. 1 (September 1952): 4–7.

55. On the history and politics of picture plays, see Kan Jun, *Kamishibai to "bukiminamono" tachi no kindai* [Modernity of picture plays and the "grotesque"] (Tokyo: Seikyūsha, 2007).

56. *Nihon kodomo wo mamorukai kaihō*, no. 1 (September 1952): 7.

57. "Dōsureba yokunaru? Kodomo no ongaku kankyō" [Children's musical environment: How will it improve?], *Yomiuri shimbun*, November 11, 1954.

58. Nihon kodomo wo mamorukai, *Kodomo wo mamoru*, no. 37 (April 1955): 4.

59. "Teizoku bunka eno jishuku wo nozomu" [Calling for the self-regulation of vulgar culture], *Yomiuri shimbun*, November 24, 1954.

60. Nihon kodomo wo mamorukai, *Kodomo wo mamoru*, no. 37 (April 1955): 1.

61. "Furyō zasshi wo yaku" [Burning degenerate magazines], *Asahi shimbun*, July 17, 1954.

62. For contemporary coverage of the movement, see "Kyōkara 'warui hon' tsuihō undō" [The movement to banish "evil books" begins today], *Yomiuri shimbun*, May 1, 1955.

63. Chūō seishōnen mondai kyōgikai, ed., *Seishōnen mondai zenkoku kyōgikairoku* [Records of the National Meeting for Youth Problem] (1951), 11–22.

64. Ibid., 23–37.

65. Takeuchi Osamu, "Akusho tsuihō undō no koro" [The days of the Evil Books Expulsion Movement], in Nakagawa Nobutoshi and Nagai Yoshikazu, eds., *Kodomo toiu retorikku: Muku no yūwaku* [The rhetoric of childhood: Temptations of innocence] (Tokyo: Seikyūsha, 1993), 54–58.

66. "Kodomono bunka wo taisetsu ni" [Valuing children's culture], *Nihon kodomo wo mamorukai kaihō* (October 1953): 1.

67. Nihon kodomo wo mamorukai, "Kodomoni akarui seikatsu wo" [Bright life for children], *Kodomo wo mamoru*, no. 33 (December 1954): 1.

68. Nihon kodomo wo mamorukai, "Furyō bunkazai torishimari ni hantai" [Against the regulation of degenerate cultural products], *Kodomo wo mamoru*, no. 39 (June 1955): 1.

69. Nihon kodomo wo mamorukai, *Kodomo tokushūgō: Kichi no kodomotachi* [Special edition of *Kodomo:* Children and military bases] (1953); Nihon kodomo wo mamorukai, "Dai ni kai kichi no kodomo wo mamoru zenkoku kaigi hōkoku tokushūgō" [Special report on the second National Conference on Protecting Children around Military Bases], *Kodomo wo mamoru*, no. 61 (May 1957): 1.

70. Nihon kodomo wo mamorukai, *Kodomo tokushūgō*, 19.

71. For example, Nihon kodomo wo mamoru kai, "Dai 19 kai tokyo chiiki renrakukai no hōkoku" [Report for the nineteenth Tokyo regional meeting], in Ohara shakai mondai kenkyūjo, *Sengo genshiryō: Fujin kodomo* [Postwar primary sources: Women, children], October 17, 1958.

5. The End of Popular Song and of Critique

1. Keizai kikakuchō, *Keizai hakusho* [Economic white paper] (1956), translated as "Declaration of the Director of the Economic Planning Agency on the Occasion of the Publication of the White Paper on the Economy," in De Bary et al., *Sources of Japanese Tradition*, 390–391.

2. Hashimoto, *Kakusa no sengoshi*, 97–105.

3. *Natsukashi no utagoe, toshiwasure daikōshin* [Songs of Nostalgia, New Year's Eve Grand March], Tokyo 12 Channel (Tokyo: JOTX-TV, December 31, 1969). On the early history of Tokyo Channel 12, see Tokyo 12 channel shasi hensan iinkai, *Tokyo 12 channel 15 nenshi* [Fifteen-year history of Tokyo 12 Channel] (Tokyo: Tokyo 12 Channel, 1979).

4. On the reassessment of popular songs as an object of nostalgia within the context of television shows, see Kondō Hiroyuki, "Sengo nihon no 'natsumero' no seiritsu to būmu no tokushitsu ni kansuru kenkyū" [Research on the development of the "nostalgic melody" boom in postwar Japan and its significance] (MA thesis, Nagoya University, 2006).

5. Ibid., 55–59.

6. Ibid., 48–53.

7. Ibid., 60–62.

8. Ibid., 71–76.

9. Azami, *Popyurā ongaku wa darega tsukurunoka*, 132–135; Ōta Shōichi, "Miru mono toshite no kayōkyoku: 70 nendai utabangumi toiu kūkan" [*Kayōkyoku* as something to be viewed: Television song shows in the 1970s], in Hase Masato and Ōta Shōichi, eds., *Terebidayo! Zen'in shūgō: Jisaku jitsuen no 70 nendai* [It's TV! Everyone gather around: The self-made, self-performed 1970s] (Tokyo: Seikyūsha, 2007), 58–64.

10. Ōta, "Miru mono toshite no kayōkyoku," 57.

11. Atkins, *Blue Nippon*, 185–192.

12. Azami, *Popyurā ongaku wa darega tsukurunoka*, 133–135.

13. Ibid., 133.

14. Aku Yū, *Yume wo kutta otokotachi: 'Sutā tanjō' to kayōkyoku ōgon no 70 nendai* [The men who ate dreams: *A Star Is Born* and the golden age of *kayōkyoku* in the 1970s] (Tokyo: Bunshun bunko, 2007), 23.

15. Ibid., 135–136.

16. Ibid., 137–146.

17. Ibid., 156–157.

18. For Aoshima's own account of his career, see Aoshima Yukio, *Chotto matta aoshima dā* [Wait a minute, it's Aoshima] (Tokyo: Iwanami shoten, 2006).

19. Ōta, "Miru mono toshite no kayōkyoku," 64–68.

20. Tōya, *Popyurā ongaku eno manazashi*, 41.

21. Maeda Kisa et al., "Puresurī wa kirisuto" [Presley is like Christ], *Chūō Kōron* 74, no. 14 (October 1959): 220–227.

22. On the development of the diverse strands of popular music in postwar Japan in the context of U.S.-Japan relations, there is no better introduction than Bourdaghs, *Sayonara Amerika, Sayonara Nippon*.

23. Azami, *Popyurā ongaku wa darega tsukurunoka*, 151–156.

24. Yano, *Tears of Longing*, 41–42; Wajima Yūsuke, " 'Enka' no tanjō: 'Shuryū' to 'taikō' bunka no kōsaten toshite" [The birth of *enka*: An intersection of the "mainstream" and "oppositional" culture], in Tōya Mamoru, ed., *Kakusansuru ongaku bunka wo dō toraeruka* [How to analyze the expanding musical culture] (Tokyo: Keisō shobō, 2008), 184–185.

25. Yano, *Tears of Longing*, 7.

26. Wajima, " 'Enka' no tanjō," 179–182.

27. Itsuki Hiroyuki, "Enka," in *Saraba mosukuwa gurentai* [Farewell, Moscow gangsters] (Tokyo: Kōdansha, 1967), 235.

28. Wajima Yūsuke, *Tsukurareta "nihon no kokoro" shinwa: "Enka" wo me guru sengo taishū ongakushi* [The invention of the "Japanese spirit" myth: The history of postwar mass music centered on *enka*] (Tokyo: Kōbunsha, 2010), 240.

29. Tsuda Rui, "Taishū, taishūsei: Ryūkōka wo meguru hyōka to sayoku erīto no ishiki" [Masses, massness: assessment of popular songs and the leftist elite consciousness], *Gekkan shakaitō*, no. 107 (1966): 155–161.

30. Minami, *Nihon no ryūkōka*, 139–152.

31. Tada Michitarō et al., "Ryūkōka ni miru taishū shisō" [Mass ideology as seen in popular songs], in Kata and Tsukuda, *Ryūkōka no himitsu*, 382–384.

32. Ibid., 393.

33. Wajima, *Tsukurareta "nihon no kokoro" shinwa*, 202–203.

34. Katō Yoshiko, "Hyōronka to ensōka: Senzenki ninon ni okeru 'gakudan' no keisei" [Critics and performers: The formation of the "music establishment" in prewar Japan], *Osaka University Annals of Educational Studies* 2 (1997): 40.

35. Sonobe, *Minshū ongakuron*; *Ongaku no kaikyūsei* [Class hierarchy in music] (Tokyo: Naukasha, 1950); *Enka kara jazu eno nihonshi* [Japanese history from *enka* to jazz] (Tokyo: Wakōsha, 1954).

36. Sonobe, *Minshū ongakuron*, 185–187.

37. Sonobe, *Enka kara jazu eno nihonshi*, 2–5.

38. Ibid., 183.

39. Sonobe Saburō, *Nihon minshū kayōshi kō* [On the history of Japanese popular songs] (Tokyo: Asahi shimbunsha, 1980, originally published 1962), 215–219. Notably, Sonobe precedes his prescriptions for popular songs by invoking the wartime call to "overcome modernity": "Many artists and scholars call for modernity to be overcome. I agree with that. But if popular songs continue to be controlled by mass media and if they continue to possess premodern characteristics as they do today, such reform would not be an easy task." In fact, Sonobe suggests, preference for such conventional music may well exist among the "intellectual stratum who call for the overcoming of modernity."

40. Sonobe, *Nihon minshū kayōshi kō*, ii.

41. Sonobe, "Gendai ryūkōka ni tsuite," 270.

42. Ibid., 286–287; Bob Dylan, *Lyrics: 1962–2001* (New York: Simon and Schuster, 2004), 81.

43. Jordan Sand, "中流 / *Chūryū* / Middling," *Working Words: New Approaches to Japanese Studies*, UC Berkeley Center for Japanese Studies, April 20, 2012, http://escholarship.org/uc/item/3rw380hc, p. 10; Hashimoto, *Kakusa no sengoshi*, 138–139.

44. Hashimoto, *Kakusa no sengoshi*, 67–95.

45. Hashimoto, *Kakusa no sengoshi*, 113–115.

46. Murakami Yasusuke, "The Reality of the New Middle Class," *Japan Interpreter* 12, no. 1 (1978): 1, originally published as "Shinchūkan kaisō no genjitsusei," *Asahi shimbun*, evening ed., May 20, 1977; *Hashimoto, Kakusa no sengoshi*, 139–141; Sand, "中流 / *Chūryū* / Middling," 9.

47. Murakami, "Reality of the New Middle Class," 2.

48. Sand, "中流 / *Chūryū* / Middling," 11.

49. Jayson Makoto Chun, *"A Nation of a Hundred Million Idiots"? A Social History of Japanese Television, 1953–1973* (New York: Routledge, 2007), 168.

Conclusion: The Television Age and Beyond

1. Ōta, "Miru mono toshite no kayōkyoku," 58–61.

2. To this day, the most illuminating analysis of this transformation, including the discussion of the media frenzy surrounding Shōda known as

"Michy Būmu," remains that of the political scientist Matsushita Keiichi, in "The Emperor System of the Masses" (1959), trans. Andrew Gordon, in De Bary et al., *Sources of Japanese Tradition*, 391–393.

3. Yoshimi Shunya, "Terebi wo dakishimeru sengo" [The postwar embrace of television], in Yoshimi Shunya and Tsuchiya Reiko, eds., *Taishū bunka to media* [Television culture and media] (Tokyo: Minerva shobō, 2010), 188.

4. Ibid., 190–191.

5. Chun, *"Nation of a Hundred Million Idiots,"* 3.

6. Sato Takumi, *Terebiteki kyōyō: Ichioku sōhakuchika e no keihu* [Television education: The path to the creation of the educated one hundred million] (Tokyo: NTT shuppan, 2008), 8.

7. Ibid., 10; Chun, *"Nation of a Hundred Million Idiots,"* 188–190.

8. Kitada Akihiro, "Overview: 60/70 no bunkaseijigaku—mitts nomondaikei" [Overview: The cultural politics of the 1960s/1970s—three sets of issues], in Kitada Akihiro et al., eds., *Karuchuraru poritikusu 1960/70* [Cultural politics 1960s/1970s] (Tokyo: Serika shobō, 2005), 244–245.

9. Bourdaghs, *Sayonara Amerika, Sayonara Nippon*, 84. On the role of television in postwar *enka*, see Yano, *Tears of Longing*, 84–89.

10. Chun, *"Nation of a Hundred Million Idiots,"* 196–197.

11. Mori Tatsuya, *Hōsō kinshika* [Songs banned from broadcasting] (Kōbunsha, 2003), 231–234. Other works on "banned songs" of this period include Mihashi Kazuo, *Kinka no seitaigaku: Nerikan burūsukō* [The anatomy of forbidden songs: Thoughts on *nerikan* blues] (Tokyo: Ongaku no tomosha, 1983), and Mori Tatsuya and Ishibashi Harumi, *Hūin kayō taizen* [Collection of banned songs] (Tokyo: Sansai bukkusu, 2007). All of these works, generally journalistic rather than scholarly in nature, discuss songs that have allegedly been banned from broadcasting from the 1960s onward. As fascinating as they are, the accuracy of these works is difficult to assess given the continuing secrecy surrounding the system of self-censorship by broadcasters.

12. Likely the most intriguing development in this regard was the proliferation of cell phones and their creative use, in which Japan emerged as a pioneering market. See Mizuko Ito et al., eds., *Personal, Portable, Pedestrian: Mobile Phones in Japanese Life* (Cambridge, MA: MIT Press, 2006).

13. Anne Allison, "The Cool Brand, Affective Activism, and Japanese Youth," *Theory, Culture & Society* 26, nos. 2–3 (2009): 97.

14. Tomiko Yoda, "A Roadmap to Millennial Japan," in Tomiko Yoda and Harry Harootunian, eds., *Japan after Japan: Social and Cultural Life after the Recessionary 1990s to the Present* (Durham, NC: Duke University Press, 2006), 30–33.

Acknowledgments

This book explores the historical dynamics behind the often harsh critiques that were leveled against popular music in twentieth-century Japan. The book and its author, however, have been the beneficiaries not only of critique in the most constructive, collegial, and nurturing sense of the word, but also of countless instances of encouragement and support from family, friends, mentors, and colleagues around the world.

Since the first time I was intrigued by the deep historical, political, and cultural resonances of music in Japan and other parts of the world, I have been fortunate to be mentored by many scholars whose exemplary work as researchers, teachers, and writers continues to inspire me, including Theodore Bestor, Harold Bolitho, Daniel Botsman, Andrew Gordon, Helen Hardacre, Jennifer Hevelone-Harper, Mary Lewis, Ian Miller, and Judith Surkis. I am especially grateful to Jennifer Hevelone-Harper, who introduced me to the work of the historian as my undergraduate adviser, and to Andrew Gordon, whose generous and incisive engagement with my work ever since I began my doctoral studies under him has shaped me indelibly as a historian of modern Japan.

This book ultimately emerged out of countless conversations in classrooms, conference halls, cafés, and beyond with talented scholars and generous friends whom I am honored to call my colleagues, many of whom have given me valuable feedback on various parts of the book. These include Marié Abe, Jonathan Abel, Raja Adal, Marjan Boogert, Michael Bourdaghs, Adam Bronson, Jamyung Choi, Craig Colbeck, Fabian Drixler, Sharon Domier, Denise Ho, Rachael Hutchinson, Mark Jones, Sarah Kashani, Nick Kapur, Loretta Kim, Konrad Lawson, Motokazu Matsutani, Elizabeth Singer More, Matthew Mosca, Andrea Murray, Izumi Nakayama, Abé Markus Nornes, Se-mi Oh, Sang Mi Park, Franziska Seraphim, Hiroe Saruya, Deborah Solomon, Amy Stanley, Jun Uchida, Fumitaka Wakamatsu, Timothy Yang, Christine Yano, Alexander Zahlten, and Lawrence Zhang. I am particularly thankful for feedback from E. Taylor Atkins, Jordan Sand, and Julia Adeney Thomas, who, along with Andrew Gordon, have read through the entire manuscript and provided me with invaluable comments and critiques.

During the course of my archival research in Japan, I was extremely fortunate to become acquainted with eminent pioneers as well as talented young scholars, all of whom not only set a remarkably high bar for me to emulate, but also continuously lent their generous assistance as I navigated numerous archives as well as the richness of historical scholarship in Japan. For this I am grateful to Igarashi Jin, Kaneko Ryūji, Matsuoka Masakazu, Nagao Yōko, Numano Yūji, Ogawara Masamichi, Edgar Pope, Sakai Kentarō, Saruya Hiroe, Shimizu Yuichirō, Shūtō Yoshiki, Suzuki Akira, Takeda Yasutaka, Wajima Yūsuke, and Yamauchi Fumitaka. I am especially indebted to Hosokawa Shūhei, Tōya Mamoru, and Yoshimi Shunya. All three of these preeminent scholars have not only laid the key foundations for this book through their groundbreaking research but also generously provided opportunities for me to discuss my work in front of a wide range of Japan-based scholars within the context of seminars, symposia, and other gatherings in their home institutions.

I could not have imagined a better, more collegial environment to complete this book than the History Faculty at the Massachusetts Institute of Technology, where I have been blessed with colleagues who have not only encouraged me as I endeavored to bring this project to fruition but have also lent critical assistance along the way. I am particularly grateful to the support from my chairs, Anne McCants, Jeffrey Ravel, and Craig Wilder, as well as to Sana Aiyar, Christopher Capozzola, Eric Goldberg, Christopher Leighton, and Emma Teng. At MIT I have also had the fortune of joining and being mentored by a stellar group of Japan studies scholars, including Ian Condry, John Dower, Shigeru Miyagawa, and Richard Samuels. John Dower in particular provided consistent encouragement to keep my nose to the grindstone, not only through the example he has set with his own monumental scholarship but also by asking a simple question every time I encountered him, namely, "Where's the book?"

This book could not have been completed without ongoing assistance from academic departments, research centers, archives, and libraries in Japan and the United States. I received generous funding from the Reischauer Institute of Japanese Studies and the Department of History at Harvard University, whose staff, both past and present, I am especially thankful to, including Mary Amstutz, Margot Chamberlain, Matthew Corcoran, Ted Gilman, Montana Higo, Stacie Matsumoto, Ruiko Connor, and Gail Rock. I have also benefited from the invaluable support of Kuniko McVey at Harvard-Yenching Library and Kazuko Sakaguchi at the Fung Library's Documentation Center on Contemporary Japan. In Japan, the Ōhara Institute for Social Research at Hōsei University and the University of Tokyo Graduate School of Interdisciplinary Information

Studies provided genuinely welcoming and intellectually stimulating settings for my research as well as access to their archival sources. This project also received generous support from the MIT History Faculty and the School of Humanities, Arts, and Social Sciences (SHASS), especially in the form of the sponsorship of an author's workshop, in which I was given the opportunity to invite leading scholars to review the book manuscript, and the Cecil and Ida Green Career Development Professorship. In particular, I would like to thank the deans of SHASS, Deborah Fitzgerald and Melissa Nobles, as well as Mabel Chin Sorett and Margo Collett at the History Faculty. Andrew Kinney, my editor at the Harvard University Press, has been a patient guide and an invaluable ally in the publication process of my very first book. I would like to thank Andrew and his team at HUP; Pamela Nelson, who guided the final production phase; as well as Junichi Tsuneoka, who created the wonderful cover illustration.

Part of Chapter 2 has been previously published as "The Censor as Critic: Ogawa Chikagorō and Popular Music Censorship in Imperial Japan," in Rachael Hutchinson, ed., *Negotiating Censorship in Modern Japan* (Routledge, 2013), 58–73, and is reproduced in this book with permission from Taylor & Francis.

Perhaps my greatest debt of gratitude is owed to my family and friends beyond the academy, who have shown me incredible patience, kindness, and care as I have gone through the joys and challenges of researching and writing this book during a period that has lasted more than ten years. For their nearly two-decades-long friendship, special thanks go to Daniel Cloutier, Matthew Gagne, Douglas Priore, and Joshua Tilton, as well as to those in the Reservoir community in Cambridge, MA. My parents, Hajime and Mari Nagahara, and my sister, Minori, have not only been the most reliable source of encouragement over these years but have also continued to ground me in my sense of connection to Japan—a place where I have not lived on a permanent basis since I left to go to college in the United States but a place which has, if anything, now come to occupy more of my thinking than it did in the past. The greatest thanks go to my wife, Elizabeth Boschee, whose love and partnership I cannot now imagine living without. She has had the dubious pleasure of reading and editing more of my writing than anyone else but has somehow continued to be by my side. Our marriage has given me an entirely new set of extended family in the United States, to whom I am also deeply grateful. More recently, the Boschee Nagaharas have been expanded by the birth of our daughter, Izumi, whose happiness has been infectious enough to get this book across the finish line. It is to each of these beloved people that this book is dedicated.

Index

Numbers in italics refer to figures.